Braddock at the Monongahela

GEN. BRADDOCK.

PAUL E. KOPPERMAN

Braddock at the Monongahela

UNIVERSITY OF PITTSBURGH PRESS

Library of Congress Cataloging in Publication Data

Kopperman, Paul E.
　Braddock at the Monongahela.

　Bibliography: p. 307
　Includes index.
　1.　Monongahela, Battle of the, 1755.　2.　Braddock,
Edward, 1695?–1755.　I.　Title.
√ E199.K77　　　973.2'6　　　　76-6662
　ISBN 0-8229-3326-8

The following organizations and individuals have graciously permitted reprinting of copyrighted material: The Historical Society of Western Pennsylvania, Maryland Historical Society, Mrs. Stanley Pargellis, and the University
of Oklahoma Press.

TO MY PARENTS

My smallest debt is existence,

My greatest sorrow, that they cannot read this together

Contents

Illustrations

Preface

ON JULY 9, 1755, even as the invading Anglo-American
army approached its destination, Fort Duquesne, it was attacked and thoroughly routed by a much smaller force of
French and Indians. One-third of the vanquished were mortally wounded, including their commander, Major General Edward Braddock. A young George Washington achieved lasting
fame for the valor he displayed in the heat of battle. Braddock,
on the other hand, was marked out for ignominy. So began the
French and Indian War. This, every schoolboy knows.

But . . . does any schoolboy *care*? Clearly. For better or worse,
Braddock's Defeat remains one of the most famous battles of
our colonial period. Tens of thousands of pages have poured
from the presses, detailing every aspect of the encounter, from
the number of horses Washington had shot out from under him
to the ultimate fate of Braddock's sash. Along the way, some of
the finest American historians have contributed work that ranks
with their best. Only the continuing interest of generations of
schoolboys, and former schoolboys, could justify such coverage.

Should any schoolboy care? I believe so. To begin with, interest is its own justification. The study of history for no higher
end than enjoyment is scarcely insidious. But the historian—or,
at least, *this* historian—has reason to hope that an examination
of Braddock's Defeat may do more than merely entertain. In
its own day, after all, the battle held great significance. As a
result of this one action, the British drive to break the power of
France in North America was stymied. Thousands of Indians
who had been straddling the fence to see which way the im-
pending war would turn now allied themselves with the
French. Recriminations rent the colonies.

xi

Moreover, the battle had implications that were to affect profoundly the last years of our pre-Revolutionary era. On the banks of the Monongahela were born myths that would mature with the idea of independence. As Braddock's forces prepared for the expedition, as they marched off toward the fort in impressive order, Americans by and large looked to them, to this British presence, as their first line of defense. As the shattered remnants of the army retreated, these same men and women began to see local forces as their strength. They saw too, or thought they saw, that the tactics which had evolved in the colonies were better suited to the American situation than were those of the British. After all, had not Braddock during the battle tried to force his troops to fight in the Continental manner, only to see them massacred by an enemy force using the irregular forest fighting tactics of the American backwoods? Indeed, as rumor—and soon legend—had it, the provincials in Braddock's force had distinguished themselves by bravery and effectiveness during the battle. If only he had let them fight in their own way, surely the enemy would have been routed! So thought the Americans. England, to which they had earlier looked for leadership, now seemed a burden. They would hereafter turn to themselves for salvation, and particularly to compatriots like the heroic Washington.

Certainly Braddock's Defeat had significance in its own time, and far beyond. But to note the importance of this event is not to justify another study of it. Almost forty years ago, Stanley Pargellis, in introducing his brief discussion of the battle, commented that "there would be no point in adding another article to the scores which have been written on Braddock's defeat if a recent discovery of new documents . . . had not made possible a revaluation of the traditional interpretation."[1] One who writes an entire monograph on the Battle of the Monongahela should, I believe, provide even greater justification than does Pargellis. Along the lines of his own rationale, I might mention that I shall introduce several previously unpublished accounts of the engagement and also make use of various eyewitness reports which, although in print, have apparently never been incorporated into an examination of it.

More important, at least to my mind, I shall attempt to apply the various accounts in a more critical way than have earlier writers. To date, the known testimony has been used primarily for stylistic impact, to provide the appropriate quotation. A few historians, notably Pargellis, have shown the way in their careful handling of the available material, but they have generally been hampered by a lack of sources. By comparing the various eyewitness reports of Braddock's Defeat—British, American, and French—I hope to produce a more accurate account of the battle than any currently in print. On that foundation, I plan to evaluate the tactics Braddock used, in an attempt to determine the extent to which he was responsible for the fiasco.

I aim at no "root-and-branch" revision of the traditional account of the affair, but at a more precise portrayal. Though our "facts" even at best lack chemical purity, by employing data with care we can approximate past events in such a way that our conclusions will bear the scrutiny of future generations. On the other hand, the insufficient accumulation of data, or the sloppy handling of it, will certainly lead to faulty conclusions. This, any schoolboy knows. But sometimes he tends to forget.

Acknowledgments

IT IS ONLY FITTING that before proceeding with this book I give thanks to those who played a part in its creation. Since the work that follows is heavily reliant on eyewitness accounts of Braddock's Defeat, published and unpublished, I first of all thank those who have granted permission to excerpt and append these invaluable sources: the British Library Board, the Historical Society of Pennsylvania, the Historical Society of Western Pennsylvania, the Maryland Historical Society, Mrs. Stanley Pargellis, the Public Record Office, London, the University of Oklahoma Press, and the U.S. Superintendent of Documents.

I wish to express my gratitude also to those who have generously granted me permission to reproduce portraits and maps: the Commonwealth of Massachusetts State Library, the Historical Society of Pennsylvania, the Library of Congress, the National Gallery, London, the Public Archives of Canada, the Royal Library at Windsor Castle, and Washington and Lee University.

Finally, there are those whose advice has helped to make this book better than it would otherwise have been. Two scholars, separated by thousands of miles but linked by their mutual interest in military history, have been particularly welcome readers and critics: Dr. George Raudzens, Macquarie University, Sydney, Australia, and Nancy Jo Padgett, University of Illinois, Urbana. I would also like to thank the following for their encouragement and advice: Dr. Henry Collins, of Macquarie University, Gary Steller, Robert Frye, Lt. Col. Franklin T. Nichols, Bernard P. Chamberlain, R. Bruce Wood, and Dennis Walle. The arduous task of proofreading was lightened greatly by the efforts of Endre Agócs and Larry Leveque. Finally—symbolically, since she had the last word on everything, and always used it well—I would like to express my deepest gratitude to Beth Luey, who edited my book for the University of Pittsburgh Press.

Introduction

EVERY PROJECT PRESENTS unique problems in methodology. In analyzing Braddock's Defeat, the historian is confronted with the basic question of what criteria to use in judging the validity of the numerous battle reports. Since there are many accounts, particularly on the British side, we can afford to be demanding.

To begin with, we are well advised to avoid wherever possible secondhand versions of the affair. I say this for several reasons. By sticking to eyewitnesses, we limit the likelihood of an individual's corroborating his own testimony. A secondhand reporter, relying on eyewitnesses, may use information supplied to him by one or many, and may or may not name his sources. An eyewitness may therefore present his account of what happened directly through his own report, and indirectly through the writings of those who have been impressed by his description. We can limit the likelihood of being misled by such self-corroboration if we rely as much as possible on firsthand reports. Of course, we can never eliminate the danger entirely. Even those who were present at the Battle of the Monongahela saw it from necessarily limited perspectives, and, in order to enhance their accounts, some of them may well have sought out the testimony of others. Fortunately, the reports are individualized enough to suggest that no single eyewitness had an undue influence on his fellows and that, in fact, most observers seem to have concentrated on action they themselves saw.

If we allow second- or thirdhand reports to affect our thinking, we also run the risk of not knowing how carefully our informant has recorded the testimony that others had given him. Unless he is obvious about it, we cannot be certain how much he is interpreting or interpolating, or generally how his biases may be coloring the account. In any case, we must try to minimize the number of memories at work and, thus, the refraction of actuality. Even the most careful eyewitness remembers primarily what seems important to him at the time he observes a given event, and he then tends to discard what does not fit into his overall conception of what occurred. Someone reporting his testimony may remember only what strikes *him* as probable and significant, and in this way may remove us still further from the truth.

Among secondhand versions of Braddock's Defeat, the most famous is the so-called Seaman's Journal. There are in addition four or five others particularly worthy of note. I shall discuss these accounts individually in Appendix E.

A second criterion for judging the accounts of the battle is their immediacy to the event. How soon after it were they written? As time passes, removing a reporter from the incident he has witnessed, his memory becomes at once more clouded and more selective. Some trivial but vivid events are remembered, while others of far greater significance are forgotten. Even more important, rumor and the reminiscences of others become entirely interwoven in what originally may have been an accurate and personalized account.

Fortunately, the wealth of material again allows us to be highly selective. Most extant eyewitness accounts by those who marched with Braddock were written within weeks of the battle. As a result, we can afford the luxury of restricting ourselves primarily to versions written before the close of 1756. This limits the importance of such reporters as Dr. Thomas Walker, Billy Brown, Tom Faucett, and William Butler. The autobiographical notes that George Washington prepared in 1783 are likewise deemphasized, though since we possess several accounts written by him at the time of the battle, we do not thereby lose him as an eyewitness. The four lesser figures mentioned here would be of limited value in any case, since their testimony was transmitted by others. Like the major sec-

ondhand reports, those whose value may be questioned because they were prepared long after the event will be discussed
at length in Appendix E.

When I note that I intend to deemphasize a given account,
this does not mean that it will be ignored entirely. Besides the
appended discussion, I plan to use such versions to corroborate
evidence found in reports that I consider more reliable. For the
most part, this corroboration will be pointed out in notes. In a
very few cases, references to these lesser accounts will appear in
the text itself, when one of them contains important information that is not found in a better source, but that seems accurate on the basis of circumstantial evidence.

Similar reservations apply to another version by a purported
eyewitness. The writer involved is Francis Peyton, and my fear
in this case is that the account ostensibly prepared by him is
partly or entirely fabricated. If so, the blame rests not with him,
but rather with his descendant, John Lewis Peyton, who published the alleged account. I dislike having to make such an
accusation and hope that my suspicions are unfounded, for the
manufacture of source material is the historian's equivalent of
high treason. However, for safety's sake I must treat Francis
Peyton as an unreliable source. I hope to justify this position in
Appendix D, where I reprint the pertinent section of his
lengthy account and comment further on it. In chapter 4, my
central discussion of the battle, his testimony is relegated to
notes.

Having stated my primary reservations, I shall mention one
account that stands in a category of its own. Among those
firsthand reports prepared within an acceptable period after
the battle, almost all are in the hand of the witness. The lone
exception is that of George Croghan. This famed Indian agent
was an important member of Braddock's army, and one whose
testimony is worth having. Unfortunately, his version is available only in paraphrase, in a letter written by his friend Charles
Swaine. Although technically Swaine's is a secondhand account,
it differs from others in this category in that it clearly involves

the testimony of one person, whose identity can be established, and who is not represented by any report in his own hand. Furthermore, Swaine recorded Croghan's comments within three days of having heard them. We would therefore do well to include Croghan among our eyewitness communicants.

Patrick Mackellar, like Croghan, is something of a special case. Although he left behind brief remarks on Braddock's Defeat, his chief service to the historian is that he prepared two detailed maps of the battlefield, showing the disposition of both forces before and during the engagement. I have reproduced his maps and comments, as well as the other eyewitness accounts, in Appendix D.

Counting Croghan and Peyton, but not Walker, Faucett, Brown, or Butler, we have twenty-two eyewitness reporters who fought under Braddock. Those who can be identified include, in alphabetical order, Duncan Cameron, John Campbell, Croghan, William Dunbar, James Furnis, Thomas Gage, Horatio Gates, Harry Gordon, Philip Hughes, Matthew Leslie, Mackellar, Robert Orme, Peyton, Sir John St. Clair, Adam Stephen, Robert Stewart, and Washington. The authors of five accounts are unknown. The first four will be referred to as "British A, B, C, and D," respectively, while the last, who served as Captain Robert Cholmley's batman, or servant, will be designated as "Cholmley's Batman."

With twenty-two firsthand reporters, we can still afford to be selective. How are we to judge the worth of their respective accounts? Obviously some are fuller than others. The reports by British A and Gordon are perhaps the most detailed, while Hughes and Campbell provide only brief glimpses of the action. But what can we say about the more important question of credibility? It may be established by corroboration, provided that we have no reason to suspect that one reporter is simply repeating what another has told him. It is indeed reassuring to note that most questions concerning the Battle of the Monongahela may be answered by the simple expedient of noting testimony and corroboration. But should a reporter stand alone, or should he be challenged by the account of another, it is necessary to know something of his physical and mental perspective before deciding whether to accept his testimony.

In attempting to pinpoint the biases of the various eye-witnesses, I have categorized them in various ways, some of which have proven useful, others not. At one point in my research, I hypothesized that perhaps those who were wounded in the battle might have borne a grudge against Braddock, which was reflected in their writing. This may have been true in individual cases, but cannot be proven in any; and indeed Orme, who was severely wounded, showed himself to be the staunchest of Braddock's defenders. A somewhat more promising criterion involves the various feuding parties into which the army was divided. Those close to Braddock centered around Orme, while the general's antagonists cleaved toward St. Clair. Unfortunately, although Washington and Peyton—assuming his account is at least substantially genuine—certainly fell in the former clique, and British B in the latter, it is impossible to be certain in most cases, and undoubtedly many of the eyewitnesses were members of no faction. Furthermore, the accounts of the five who may be categorized as belonging to one of the two groups vary considerably. It would therefore be unreasonable to suppose that because an individual was involved with a particular clique his report of a given aspect of the battle would be similar to that of Orme or St. Clair, as the case might be, or that the author of any such report was necessarily of the clique. Still, it is clear that in several cases reporters allowed a personal dislike of Braddock to color their description of the battle in general, or of his conduct in particular. The opposite may also be true, and probably is so in the case of Orme, but it is never so obvious.

As we shall see, much of the controversy surrounding Braddock's Defeat revolves around the behavior of the troops, particularly the British regulars. By and large, our eyewitnesses claim that the enemy carried the day because the men panicked and refused to follow orders. In view of this key criticism, it is obviously desirable to seek out the testimony of "common soldiers" and listen to their side of the story. Unfortunately, it appears that only two of them left accounts, and indeed most were probably illiterate. In this case, therefore, we must go further afield. We must backtrack, and use sources we would prefer not to. The most important of these is a report prepared by a commission that had been created in the wake of the battle to investigate the behavior of the troops. The report was framed by officers, particularly Gage, but it contains a purported paraphrase of the testimony of British privates, and the most thorough defense of their conduct extant. To include this account among our sources ushers in all the difficulties and drawbacks associated with secondhand material. We do not know how many privates testified, whether they did so as individuals or as members of a delegation, whether this testimony was oral or was presented in writing, or how accurately and fully the court of inquiry transmitted it. The document in question is not useless, but it must be handled with special care. More important than any account, however, is the simple recognition that the overall bias of our eyewitnesses is distinctly pro-officer, anti-private. We cannot always compensate for this slant, but we can bear it in mind.

Two lines of categorization prove especially useful in explaining the differences among the various accounts. One rests on nationality. Some may object to differentiating between "British" and "American" accounts of Braddock's Defeat, and certainly those Americans who have left us their testimony all considered themselves at the time to be loyal subjects of the Crown. But one has only to read the various accounts to see how important was national spirit. Those who were American by birth or adoption tend to speak glowingly of how their countrymen behaved during the battle, while the British eyewitnesses for the most part do not differentiate among the troops, or, if they do single out the provincials, it is to criticize them. Furthermore, the Americans generally analyze the battle in a considerably different way than do the

British, seeing in the debacle a vindication of their forest fighting tactics.

In their defense, most of the British eyewitnesses do not seem to have been malicious in ignoring the role of the American troops. Rather, they were looking to portray the overall scene, to note the rule rather than exceptions. And the rule, as they saw it, was cowardice. In a brief sketch of the battle, they were not likely to make note of the heroism of a few Americans, when the decisive element in defeat seemed to them to be the widespread panic of the regulars. Indeed, it is not at all unlikely that some of them, their attention drawn to attempting to rally the troops, failed to note what the provincials were doing, one way or the other. In any case, the cleavage between American and British eyewitness accounts is both real and important.

Of even greater moment is the line of categorization involving physical perspective. From which angle did each eyewitness view the battle? When judging the plausibility of an account, we must ask ourselves whether a given reporter was actually in a position to have seen the action he describes. Even if he was, is there a likelihood that he may have misinterpreted an event, owing to having been some distance from where it took place? Generally speaking, it can be said that our eyewitnesses are reasonably accurate in describing what happened near them, while in discussing action that they saw from a distance they are, as one might expect, prone to factual error and misinterpretation. Fortunately, with only a few exceptions, we can be fairly certain where the eyewitnesses were, at least during the crucial first moments of battle.

There are more questions, suggesting additional categories. Was a given eyewitness capable of interpreting the action he saw? On the whole, it is wise to take the opinion of an experienced military man rather than that of a novice. To whom did a particular reporter direct his account? If to a superior, he might have been prone to glorify his own activity during the battle, in hopes of winning a promotion. Indeed, several of those who addressed themselves to superiors claimed that Braddock had promised them favor, promises which, alas, he had not lived to keep. There is no case in which we may question the truthfulness of such a claim, but neither should we expect the man who makes it to be particularly hard on the general or his tactics. On the whole, we may look for a bit more candor in the remarks intended only for friends or relatives. But we should not expect any participant to put himself in a bad light, even implicitly. Furthermore, letters written to friends may have been intended for publication. Every writer knew that there were thousands anxious to hear his account of the action. Despite these reservations, we shall see that it is still worth remembering for whom the various reporters intended their comments, at least in first instance. I believe, however, that our flexibility in interpreting evidence in this area should be particularly great.

All of the preceding suggests the importance of knowing our eyewitnesses. A few, notably Gage, Gates, Croghan, Stephen, and, of course, Washington, are well known to historians. On the other hand, several of the reporters are entirely strangers to us, except for what little we can infer from their accounts. But in almost every case we have some ground on which to judge the bias of the individual, and in general those of whom we know little or nothing have left only brief and somewhat trivial testimony. In order to provide a basis for analyzing the various accounts, I present a sketch of each reporter in chapter 3.

Generally speaking, on Braddock's side of the action we have ample source material. As I have suggested, there is enough to allow us the luxury of deemphasizing secondhand versions, and those written long after the event. When we survey French accounts of the battle, however, we cannot afford to be so choosy. We must accept second- and even thirdhand reports, in full knowledge of the risks involved. Even when we make such concessions to the paucity of material, we find that we must rely on fewer than half the accounts that the members of Braddock's army have left us. Furthermore, most of the French reports are brief and contain surprisingly little information on the battle itself.

Disappointingly, only one French account would merit our attention if we were to apply the same criteria here that we have in the case of the English. This is the one by Captain Jean Daniel Dumas. We are in one sense fortunate, since Dumas emerged from the affair a hero, and was probably in the best position to relate the action from his side. But as we might expect, his report is extremely self-interested, and although most English accounts are as well, in their case we have enough material that we can generally cross-check for accuracy. With Dumas, we return to the problem of self-corroboration. His is the only French account definitely written by an eyewitness. One or two others may be firsthand, but we cannot know. It is, however, certain that most are secondhand at best, and that some of those who prepared them relied heavily on Dumas's testimony.

A survey of the French accounts, other than that of Dumas, reveals that five of the reporters are known. These are Claude-Pierre Pécaudy, sieur de Contrecoeur, Michel Alain de Lotbiniere, François Pouchot, and one whom we know only as M. de Godefroy. In addition, we have a fine account passed on to us by a M. Roucher, and although he may not actually have written it, for the sake of convenience I shall hereafter refer to it by his name. None of these five was present at the battle. This we know through their own testimony. For that matter, Lotbinière and Pouchot were both many miles from the scene. We would expect Contrecoeur to be of particular importance, since he was commandant of Fort Duquesne when the action took place. Unfortunately, it appears that he generally took Dumas's word for what happened and passed it along to his superiors. On the other hand, Pouchot in particular is free of Dumas's influence, having derived his account from the testimony of several Canadians who had fought Braddock.

The remaining French accounts are anonymous, and in the text will be designated "French A, B, and C," respectively.

They are apparently the work of officers who gathered testimony from associates, and who may not have participated in the battle themselves. Again, they show the influence of Dumas. This seems to be less true of French B, but the author of this document was definitely not an eyewitness.

Owing primarily to Dumas's pervasive influence, the French accounts are much more uniform than are those prepared by men who marched with Braddock. But if we must not be misled by such uniformity, neither must we ignore the whole. The French side is worth telling, and it can be told. Although most are similar, the French reports do not agree on all points, and where there are differences, we can be critical. Even when they do not disagree among themselves, we can check them against English accounts, always bearing in mind the question of perspective. In the end, I hope to prove that the "French side" of the affair was considerably different from that suggested by Dumas.

In the final analysis, however, the study which follows gives greater weight to the "English side" of the story. The difference in the availability of source material certainly encourages this, but my main reason for focusing on Braddock's forces is that I feel, as have many during the past two centuries, that this was a battle lost, rather than won. How could the invaders have thrown away the great advantages they held in manpower and weaponry? This is the basic question I hope to answer. The sources are many and, in sum, detailed and persuasive.

Braddock at the Monongahela

ONE

March to the Monongahela

JULY 6, 1755 An impressive array, this army in the forest. Perhaps the once resplendent uniforms were soiled and tattered after a month on the march, but still they bore a proud message to the murky green that echoed out in all directions. For here came the British, strong in number and weaponry, their red coats calling up a proud tradition. Among them, particularly to the head and rear of the column, marched several hundred Americans, distinct in blue uniforms, but revealing in red trim their loyalty to a distant sovereign.[1] Should their mission succeed, the troops would bring joy to both shores of the Atlantic, and glory to themselves. For they aimed to take Fort Duquesne, that citadel overlooking the nexus of three great rivers, that lynchpin of a network of outposts which the French had constructed to tighten their hold over the Ohio Valley.

And how could this army fail? The men were weary, and perhaps hungry as well. But they must have known that they were less than three days' march from their objective. Then a brief siege, and the prize for which they had sweated and suffered these long months would be theirs. Or possibly they would arrive to find the fort abandoned. They had the numbers. They had the artillery. They had every reason to hope for an easy triumph. Perhaps, for all their privations, optimism lightened their steps.[2]

But, deep down, were they uncertain of victory? The forest had been their enemy these long weeks, yet they knew that there were those who called it friend. The backwoodsmen who accompanied the troops had filled them with tales of Indian horrors, of scalping, torture, ambush. And they knew that the

3

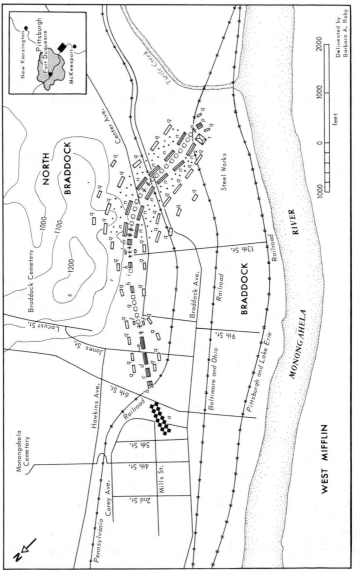

Map 1

French had "their" Indians out observing the march, skulking in the foliage, flitting from tree to tree, but invisible except for the briefest of glimpses. All-seeing, but themselves unseen, they sometimes reached out, snatching up an unwary straggler. The claws of the forest.[3] True, one of their own Indians had claimed that five of his French counterparts had been terrified at the mere sight of the approaching army, with its wealth of artillery.[4] The officers knew this, and possibly the men did as well. But still there were daily signs of the Indian menace. The forest was all around, shielding its Indians, imprisoning the marchers. Far ahead, and out of sight, a working party hacked away at the stubborn green foe, allowing the column to inch ahead.[5] And yet all knew that the enemy whose branches clutched at them would fight to the last. Perhaps, too, its claws would strike out once again, this time intent on a larger prey.

Suddenly, the sound of gunfire froze the men in their tracks. A small band of Indians had ambushed the rear, killing three. Without hesitation, a company of grenadiers marched to the scene and fired a volley, even as the attackers were melting into the woods. The moments passed, the march continued. But soon another round of gunfire crackled from the forest, this time along the right flank. Now confusion and panic spread among the troops. Some out-rangers fired at the enemy, but again it had disappeared. A few warriors who had accompanied the march set out in pursuit, but their maneuver merely confused the out-rangers, who were, as experience dictated, wary of all Indians. They fired into the forest, to be answered only by the shouts of the Indian allies, who were returning after an unsuccessful search. On orders, the warriors performed a ritualized countersign, holding up a bough and grounding their arms, thereby signaling that they were of the British party. But the rangers were edgy, perhaps did not see, certainly did not understand. They fired again, killing one brave—a son of Monakatooka, the Oneida sachem whose small company represented the only Indian aid the British had.

That night, the warrior was buried. All officers were ordered to attend, and a volley was sounded over the grave by way of special tribute. Gifts were distributed among the remaining Indians. It was the least the British could do, but, under the circumstances, the most as well.[6]

By the graveside stood a graying, heavyset man. At sixty, Edward Braddock was facing the greatest challenge of his long career. As a major general, as commander-in-chief, he was responsible for coordinating the entire North American campaign. He himself had been charged with driving the French from the Ohio Valley. The capture of Fort Duquesne would be much more than a promising start to his expedition. It would virtually clinch success, for the other French forts in the area were smaller and less well manned. He would sweep them away and soon rendezvous with the forces under William Shirley, the governor of Massachusetts and a major general in his own right. Together they would take Fort Niagara and, if the weather held, move against Fort Frontenac, at the head of Lake Ontario.[7] With luck, by the close of the year the French threat to the area south of the Great Lakes would be ended.

Fate owed him some luck. Ever since receiving his assignment the year before, Braddock had met with nothing but delay and recrimination. He had arrived in America on February 20, considerably later than he had planned, though eighteen days in advance of his men, who were being shipped in from Ireland.[8] The delayed start had proven ominous. Despite his desperate attempts to get on with the campaign, he had been stymied.

First, there had been differences over strategy. Shirley had wanted the basic plan of operation scrapped. Ignore Fort Duquesne for the moment, he had argued, and move a combined force against Fort Niagara. Even if the commander-in-chief had wanted to follow this advice, he in turn had his orders from the Duke of Cumberland himself. They dictated the approximate plan of march and specified not only that Fort Duquesne must be taken, but that it must come first. To revise the overall design, Braddock would have needed the permission of his superior, and, even if he had been of a mind to petition for it, the reality of communications meant that approval would be at least two months in coming.

But it is doubtful that he would have considered such a petition even if time had not been a factor. Braddock had spent more than forty years working his way up in the Coldstream Guards. He knew how to take orders. But during 1753 and 1754 he had served as acting governor of Gibraltar, and the administrative ability he had displayed there had shown that he knew how to give them as well.[9] Perhaps it was his unswerving loyalty to discipline that had commended him to the martinetish Cumberland when he was looking for someone to command the campaign in North America.[10] If so, the duke's nominee had not failed him. Almost as soon as Shirley had proposed his scheme, Braddock had thrust it aside, choosing instead to stand by his original orders.[11]

The question of strategy had proven simple compared with that of supplies. Braddock had probably not expected the Americans to treat him as a savior, but he had been astonished, as well as angered, by their lack of interest in his expedition. They had seemed confident that he would succeed, but unwilling to help. Those colonies far removed from the scene of conflict had felt no need to aid their neighbors against the French. Even Pennsylvania, Maryland, and New York, which were directly involved, had given aid grudgingly, while Virginia had been only slightly more forthcoming. Worse yet, the provincial contractors had repeatedly failed to live up to their agreements. And when they had delivered, their goods had often been substandard and sometimes entirely worthless.[12]

Originally, Braddock had hoped to begin his march to Fort Duquesne by the end of April,[13] but June had arrived with the general and his forces still at Fort Cumberland, on Wills Creek in Maryland, more than one hundred miles from their destination. The necessary supplies had not yet been delivered, and the contractors, far from sympathizing with his situation, had sought to extort vastly inflated sums for goods that would yet be months in coming. Braddock had become a desperate commander seeking out supplies, cajoling, threatening, pleading, all the while building up a contempt for the provincials that bordered on hatred.[14]

Then, when all the blustering and begging had failed, when the expedition itself had seemed jeopardized, help had arrived from an unexpected quarter. In early May, a middle-aged, bespectacled gentleman, entirely unheroic in appearance, had arrived in camp. This was Benjamin Franklin, on that occasion wearing the hat of deputy postmaster general. His original mission had been to aid Braddock in improving postal communication within the military, but in view of the desperate situation he had turned his attention to the problem of supplies. Braddock, in no position to be distrustful, had provided him with eight hundred pounds, and begged him to concentrate on the procurement of wagons, without which the expedition could not proceed. Miraculously, within a fortnight the wagons had come, loaded with provisions. Franklin had not only used the general's allotment wisely, but had contributed two hundred pounds of his own. The provisions, and twenty extra pack horses, had been the gift of the Pennsylvania Assembly. From that moment, Braddock had made Pennsylvanians an exception to his generally low opinion of colonials. With gratitude overflowing, he had written to Franklin that while Pennsylvania "had promised nothing and performed everything," Virginia and Maryland "had promised everything and performed nothing."[15] Thanks to Franklin, and the foraging missions of some of his own subordinates, Braddock had finally been able to lead his army from Fort Cumberland on June 10.[16]

JULY 7, 1755   A day of frustation. In order to avoid swampy ground, the army was forced temporarily to leave the old Indian road it had been following, and as a result the guides lost their way, delaying the march for "at least four hours," according to one source.[17] In the history of the campaign, this delay was probably insignificant, but it symbolized the bad luck which had from the beginning hindered the march.

The troops' departure from Wills Creek had not signaled a rapid advance on Fort Duquesne. Far from it. The problems of road-building, accidents, illness, the traditional "halting days" that allowed the men to rest, and above all the large and cumbersome wagon train had impeded the march. On June 16, the seventh day on the trail, the men had camped at the Little Meadows, a mere twenty-two miles from Fort Cumberland. This was impossibly slow progress, and, to make matters worse, a report had reached Braddock that a large body of reinforcements was heading for Fort Duquesne.[18] That night, he had reached a decision. In order to speed up the march and reach the fort before the reinforcements arrived, it would be necessary to divide the army and press forward in a flying column. The next day, he had marched on with a force of about thirteen hundred picked men and most of the artillery, but only about one-quarter of the cumbersome wagons, leaving the remainder with a detachment commanded by Colonel Thomas Dunbar.[19] This had been the true beginning of the march. Within twenty days, Braddock's force was at the Monongahela, only ten miles from its objective.

After their long day of skirting the swamps, the troops made camp and rested. Alone in the darkness, Sir John St. Clair pondered the state of the campaign and his own situation. Like most of his fellow officers, he saw the two entwined. To say that he was pompous in no way singles out the little lieutenant colonel. It would indeed be surprising if, in view of his experience, he had not been confident enough of his judgment to believe that he was qualified to advise his commander.

And advise he had, from the beginning. Even before Braddock had arrived in America, St. Clair had been there, acting in the role of deputy quartermaster general. It had been he who

Sir John St. Clair

had overseen the planning of the road along which the army now marched. It had been he who had rooted out misfits from the American auxiliaries which were to join the army. It had been he who had been most responsible for recruiting more Americans for the forces.[20]

Along the way, he had made many enemies. Quick-tempered, haughty, he was not the sort to hide his feelings. His most memorable outburst had been reserved for five agents of Governor Robert Morris of Pennsylvania. Morris had commissioned them to survey and lay out the road to Fort Duquesne. A shortage of funds had delayed them, as had other factors, and indeed they had made surprising progress under the circumstances. However, when they had attended St. Clair on April 12, he had complained that their commission should have been issued earlier, and had insisted

that the troops must march on the first of May; that the want of this road and the provisions promised by Pennsylvania, has retarded the expedition. . . . That instead of marching to the Ohio, he would in nine days march his army into Cumberland county to cut the roads, press horses, &c. That he would not suffer a soldier to handle an axe, but by fire and sword oblige the inhabitants to do it. . . . That he would kill all kind of cattle, and carry away the horses, burn houses, &c.; and that if the French defeated them by the delays of this province, that he would with his sword drawn pass through the province, and treat the inhabitants as a parcel of traitors to his master.[21]

Certainly Sir John was somewhat wanting in the art of diplomacy. Of course, his commander was known to make a scene now and then, so it is doubtful that Braddock would have held St. Clair's temper against him.[22] In the beginning, the two appear to have been close. Indeed, as late as June 13 Sir John had lauded the general as one who carried out his plans "with a great deal of vigour and Vivacity." But his attitude had changed rapidly after that. The decision to divide the army had certainly taken him by surprise, and he had always had reservations regarding it. Finally, on July 3 he had advised Braddock to bring up Dunbar's detachment. The general had called a council of war, and Sir John's proposal had been rejected.[23] But still he had worried about the weakness of Braddock's force, and about his own position.

For as his influence had waned, so had that of others risen. Braddock had from the beginning been close to a small group of favorites, and they had finally come to replace Sir John in his counsels. Most important among them was Captain Robert Orme, a handsome young Coldstream Guardsman who apparently had first attracted Braddock's attention when he had entered the regiment a decade before. Second only to Orme in the commander's circle was Lieutenant Colonel Ralph Burton. Just slightly less influential with Braddock was the young Virginian, George Washington, like his good friend Orme an aide-de-camp.[24]

And so, on the evening of July 7, St. Clair was worried, and not least of all for himself. He was not the type to worry alone. Instead, he again approached his fellow officers, and perhaps the general as well. Possibly he petitioned once more that the march be halted so that the convoy might be brought up. Certainly he suggested that a small detachment be sent ahead to invest the fort. Also certain is that he got nowhere. According to the fullest report of what transpired, the other officers told St. Clair that there would be no way to reinforce the detachment were it attacked, at which point "Sr. John immediately acquiesced." The reporter—Robert Orme.[25]

JULY 8, 1755   The army passed through a narrow valley, some three miles in length, commanded throughout by steep hills. There could be no more natural place for an ambush. Braddock answered by the book:

In this March Every proper precaution was taken to secure us. By Detaching all the men that cou'd be Spar'd from the Advancd party, that day Commanded By C: Burton on our flank the General Likewise orderd 350 men to take possession of the heights on Each Side; & the

Grenadier Company of Sir P: H[alket's]Regt, the Advance of the Ad vanc'd party, to Gain the Rising Ground, which Shut up the Valley in our front.[26]

The precautions proved unnecessary. Not so much as a sniper appeared to harass the troops.

As he passed the far end of the valley and rode on, men surrounding, Braddock must have been relieved. Certainly he would have been pleased that the enemy had not opposed his passage. Quite possibly this meant that they had already conceded Duquesne, or else were preparing for the siege. If they had planned to attack the approaching army, why not here?

But perhaps another thought cheered him. Two days before, a small party of Indians had spread confusion among his troops. Today, however, under pressure, they had followed orders with precision. Indeed, this was an army. The disciplinarian in Braddock must have smiled.

The troops that had followed him across the Atlantic had scarcely been the cream of the British army. Two regiments had been assigned to the American venture—the Forty-Fourth Foot, Colonel Sir Peter Halket, and the Forty-Eighth Foot, Colonel Thomas Dunbar. Both regiments had been comparatively new, and far undermanned. Braddock's superiors had directed that they sail at the strength of five hundred men apiece and that in Virginia their numbers be enhanced to seven hundred. But even to reach the first figure, it had been necessary to draft men out of other regiments, and naturally the officers who received orders for this levy had sent their misfits. Once across the ocean, Braddock and his subordinates had sought out recruits, at the same time despairing of their quality. Men had also been drafted into the regiments from the independent companies sent by Virginia, while three of these companies, intact, had accompanied the march. In the end, only about two-fifths of the troops that had assembled at Fort Cumberland had been original members of the two regiments, while one-quarter had been British draftees, and one-third Americans.[27]

Who were these Americans? Were they the backwoodsmen of legend, who blazed trails through the forest, could shoot the eye out of a squirrel at fifty paces, and knew as they did their own the mind of the Indian? A few of them were. But for the most part, they were the dregs of colonial society—seaboard society, at that. With few exceptions, they were Virginians, Pennsylvanians, and Marylanders, none of the three provinces owning a majority. Not only those who joined the two regiments, but the men of the independent companies as well, were generally recent recruits who had never known discipline or been under fire.[28]

Braddock himself had yet to serve in battle, but during his forty-five years in service he had come to accept the dictum that in an engagement the more disciplined force would usually emerge victorious. His years of garrison duty had enabled him to hone his abilities in drill.[29] He had become a devotee of precision. This devotion he would now attempt to instill in his motley troops.

It had been hard. The provincials in particular had resisted his attempts to forge them into a unit of his military machine. But in fact he had concentrated on them, for they had known nothing of Continental modes of warfare.

To Braddock's mind, they had proven to be poor students. Just before departing from Fort Cumberland, he had written the duke's secretary that "the whole of the Forces are now assembled, making about two thousand Effectives, the greatest part Virginians, very indifferent Men, this Country affording no better; it has cost infinite pains and labour to bring them to any sort of Regularity and Discipline: Their Officers very little better." At the same time, he had been pleased with the troops who had followed him across the Atlantic. As early as April 19, he had noted that "the officers and Men of these two regiments behave well and shew great Spirit and Zeal for the Service, which will be a good Example to the rest." He was to remain of this opinion. A British private, Duncan Cameron, would later recall fondly that the general's "Dependence was chiefly upon us Regulars." When issuing the orders of June 17, dividing his army, Braddock had directed that "the Men of the two Regts that Are to March [are] to be taken out of those Landed from Ireland."[30]

On July 8, the army camped near the east bank of the Monongahela. Fort Duquesne stood about eight miles northwest. But in order to march directly toward it, the men would have to pass through The Narrows, a strip of land lying between their camp and Turtle Creek, and then ford the creek itself. Throughout, this route would be time-consuming and dangerous. A path of sorts ran through The Narrows, but it was rough even by wilderness standards, and to make it passable would require many hours of labor, hours of delay. Not only was the path entirely inadequate, but for most of its length it paralleled the east bank of the river and was dominated by high ground to the right. Even after negotiating The Narrows, there would be hazards to face. The banks of Turtle Creek were steep on both sides. Much work would be necessary before the army could move across with its wagon train. In the meantime, it would be very vulnerable to attack.[31]

Perplexed, Braddock called on his guides. They suggested that the army could avoid both The Narrows and Turtle Creek by fording the Monongahela, marching north on its western bank, and recrossing it opposite Frazer's Cabin, a point above the creek. The river was low, they pointed out, and its banks easily ascended. The general accepted their proposal. He prepared his orders accordingly.[32]

Braddock had seldom been too proud to heed advice. In fact, he had often sought it, not only in frequent councils of war, but in private consultation. St. Clair, for one, had valued highly his influence over the general. Orme had always been something of a gray eminence, and his power had grown in recent weeks. Washington proudly claimed that when his commander had determined to divide the army and push on in a flying column, he had done so on his advice, advice that Braddock himself had solicited. Of course, as some officers had achieved greater influence, others had been pushed to the side. These included Halket, Dunbar, and, as we have seen, St. Clair himself.[33]

However, Braddock had continued to seek out the advice of those who were not his favorites. In particular, he had looked to his Indian guides. They must reconnoiter. They must be his eyes in the forest. To his chagrin, their aid had been minimal.

He had from the beginning had poor relations with the Indians. At the time of his arrival in Virginia, there had seemed every likelihood that a considerable number of warriors would accompany the march. Braddock can only have been happy at the prospect. Certainly he would need them to scout and, if need be, to fight. Besides, he knew that even traditional Indian allies were deserting the British. Every Indian he could win over would be one lost to the French.[34]

Throughout his stay in America, the general had been fortunate in his advisors on Indian affairs. When he had in mid-April held a conference in Alexandria to coordinate strategy for the coming year, he had met not only with a delegation of governors, but also with Colonel William Johnson. Johnson was already famed for his expertise in Indian affairs; one day, he would be a legend. The colonel had not accompanied Braddock on his march, for he had been assigned his own mission. However, two who had joined were Christopher Gist and George Croghan, both of whom had long since shown themselves to be capable in their dealings with the Indians.[35] Of the two, Croghan had probably played a greater role in Braddock's counsels. But both had advised their commander on matters relating to the Indians, and both had sought to win him more Indian allies. In the end, both had shared his failure. Not only they, but others, responsible men like Governor Robert Dinwiddie of Virginia, had assured Braddock that Indian allies were on their way to join the march. Indeed, they had for the most part spoken fairly. From all directions, warriors had moved toward Fort

Cumberland, anxious to swear allegiance to the English and to join in their campaign. But for a multiplicity of reasons, few had made it to camp. In the end, just eight had joined Braddock. His scouting could only suffer in consequence.

JULY 9, 1755   The men marched long before daybreak, the advance party, led by Lieutenant Colonel Thomas Gage, departing at three o'clock.[36] By noon, the army was at its second ford. More than one eyewitness would recall the beauty of the crossing. All was brilliant in the sunlight—the troops in their dazzling livery, the river afire with reflected radiance: "A finer sight could not have been beheld, the shining barrels of the muskets, the excellent order of the men, the cleanliness of their appearance, the joy depicted on every face at being so near Fort Du Quesne, the highest object of their wishes—the music re-echoed through the mountains."[37]

Still, the British were wary. Before their second crossing, some believed they saw Indians on the opposite bank. Braddock's guides had misled him. Far from being easily ascended, the east bank at the ford was steep and forbidding. It would take time to slope it so that the march might proceed. Worse still, the high ground offered a perfect opportunity for ambush.

But the crossing was completed without incident and the officers and men relaxed. As one of them later told a correspondent: "Every one who saw those Banks, Being Above 12 feet perpendicularly high Above the Shore, & the Course of the River 300 yards Broad, hugg'd themselves with joy at our Good Luck in having surmounted our greatest Difficultys, & too hastily Concluded the Enemy never wou'd dare to Oppose us."[38]

✍ TWO ✍

The French Prepare

EVEN AS BRADDOCK'S ARMY waded across the Monongahela, even as apprehension eased and gave way to euphoria, Fort Duquesne was alive with activity. There would be no retreat or abject surrender. Perhaps the siege would come. Perhaps the citadel would fall. But the general would pay for his victory.

When he had marched from Wills Creek on June 10, Braddock had expressed the hope that he would arrive at the fort within three weeks.[1] Of course, he had often rewritten his schedule in the face of delay, and would do so again. But even disregarding all of his earlier frustration, had he managed to reach the Ohio by the end of June, or the first days of July, the French defenders could have made no more than a token stand. As it turned out, his intelligence had been only too accurate. All of his reports, including those he had received just three days before, had indicated that the garrison was poorly manned, but that large bodies of reinforcements, French and Indian, were on their way. Such had indeed been the case; however, the fresh troops had arrived. And among the arrivals was a dynamic Canadian officer who had brought with him dreams of glory. There would be a stand at the forks.

The French knew they were playing for high stakes. Fort Duquesne was not merely another outpost. From the moment of inception, it had been singled out as a focal point of empire. Even its name symbolized this key role, for it honored Ange de Menneville, Marquis Duquesne, the governor general of New France. Its size contributed mightily to an impression of predominance. The great bastions jutting from its four corners made the whole more than one hundred fifty feet sqare, easily the largest of any of the four French forts in the area. It was the central garrison, the most heavily manned. Above all, it served as headquarters for the commander on the Ohio.[2]

The key importance of Fort Duquesne was no coincidence. Its location, overlooking the confluence of three broad rivers, placed it at the very heart of the Ohio Valley. And this valley was in turn the focal point of a spiraling struggle between England and France. In 1755, John Mitchell, who knew the area well, wrote:

Nature itself has conspired to render the river *Ohio* hereabouts a place of consequence of all the people in North America that are within reach of it, far and nigh. . . . To these ponds and other salt springs hereabouts, great flocks and herds of deer and wild oxen constantly resort. . . . This draws numbers of huntsmen here to pursue their game, the chief employment of these parts. The traders again follow the huntsmen for their skins and furs. These are the chief causes of war. . . . Fort *du Quesne* then is the very center of all the French force in N. America put together, and will unite their many settlements in it, and all the natives of that whole continent, in one body; if it has not done so already.[3]

French officials would by and large have agreed with Mitchell's assessment of why Fort Duquesne was important, but they would have suggested different priorities. Certainly the fur trade was important, and the fort was a major trading post. But the contest with Britain was for territory and strategic advantage. Whichever nation could make good its claim to the Ohio Valley would limit the other's ability to expand its North American empire, and enhance its own. Trade would be the mere concomitant of expansion.

Fort Duquesne therefore stood as both a symbolic and a real citadel of dominion. Even at that, it was more. It gave the French a major advantage in their struggle for men's minds. There were Indian allies to be won in the valley, allies who might easily tip the scales against Britain. As long as the fort stood unchallenged, it would bear witness to French predominance on the Ohio, to their power to protect the tribes which went to war on their behalf—and to punish those which sided with the enemy. Trade itself might go on at a loss. Within the walls of the fort, Indians were treated royally. Gifts were distributed among them, and items of all kinds were sold cut-rate. This was one means of forging an Indian alliance. As a noted French officer, Louis-Antoine de Bougainville, argued, "One cannot give too much care that goods be low priced, so that the Indians, finding the trade favorable there, may not go among the English, an objective important for trade and even more for policy."[4]

Time pressed the French as they sought to secure the valley. They had been at peace with England only since 1748, and even then both sides knew that the respite would be brief, for the last war had decided nothing. On both shores of the Atlantic, the ancient enemies jockeyed for position. Still, they lauded peace. All problems, including boundary disputes in the New World, might be settled amicably, claimed the two courts. However, this diplomatic ruse was an old one that never worked, and preparations for war continued. In Braddock's expedition, the British sought a preemptive strike, but the French were on guard.

From the beginning, Fort Duquesne had been an extension of its commander, Captain Claude Pierre Pécaudy, sieur de Contrecoeur. In January 1754, he had been charged with securing French authority in the Ohio Valley. Three months later, he had evicted Ensign Edward Ward, who with a handful of men had sought to entrench the British at those same forks where Fort Duquesne now stood. In an ironic twist, the victors had dismantled the facility that Ward had hurriedly constructed, and had used the timber in building their own fort. Later that same year, Contrecoeur had sent out two parties successively to drive Washington from the valley. Certainly he was most responsible for the military presence that had made formidable the French claim to the Ohio.[5]

When he had challenged Ward, Contrecoeur had addressed the local Indians with a bravado aimed at putting them in awe of French arms, while at the same time encouraging them to deride the British: "I warn you, my children, that I am calling upon the English to withdraw, and that if they do not I am quite able to force them to go."[6] But then he had faced only token opposition. Now, as Braddock approached the fort, the commander knew that this time he would be outnumbered.

The previous autumn, a chronic illness had caused Contrecoeur to ask Duquesne to relieve him of his command.[7] However, this wish could not be fulfilled immediately, and it was the old commander who had prepared the fort to face Braddock. By May 24, 1755, he was able to report to the marquis that "the works at Fort Duquesne are completed. It is at present mounted with six pieces of cannon of six, and nine of two [or] three pound ball [and is] in want of neither arms nor ammunition."[8] But where were the men?

Reinforcements had been slow to arrive. The year before, Fort Duquesne had been heavily manned in anticipation of an English attack, but none had come, and the bulk of the troops eventually departed. By winter there had remained only one hundred French and Canadian soldiers, and a like number of Indians. With spring had come an unexpected drought, which had caused the rivers to run shallow, slowing the movement of men down from Fort Presqu'isle. But help had come. Several detachments had arrived at the fort in early July, bringing the total of French or Canadian men and officers to something in excess of six hundred.[9]

Among those officers arriving with the reinforcements was Captain Daniel-Hyacinthe-Marie Liénard de Beaujeu, a strikingly handsome Canadian, in early middle age. He would succeed Contrecoeur as commander—if Braddock were somehow repulsed. There was a cruel irony in the fact that the most important command he had ever been assigned would likely be snatched away from him before he could assume it. But Beaujeu was not the sort to give up easily. Descended from a long and illustrious line of military men, he was very much the hero.

We shall never know whether it was Beaujeu himself who first formulated the plan to ambush Braddock's army. One

Captain Daniel-Hyacinthe-Marie Liénard de Beaujeu

anonymous reporter—hereafter known as "French B"—claims that Beaujeu did indeed originate the scheme, but the fact that this writer refers to the captain as commander of the fort, and also that he is relying on second- or thirdhand reports, limits his credibility. A letter written in mid-July strongly suggests that it was Contrecoeur who created the design; however, he also created the letter. Captain Jean-Daniel Dumas, in a lengthy panegyric dedicated to himself, claims that it was he who first suggested an ambush. Legend brings forth the name of Charles de Langlade, the great Indian agent, who had only recently arrived at the fort with more than six hundred of his followers.[10]

Any one of the four might merit the honor. All of them had considerable battle experience and knew well the tactics of forest fighting. Ambush was the obvious strategy, considering the circumstances. It would, of course, take advantage of the forest cover. It might provide an equalizer for the outmanned defenders of the fort. Finally, it was well suited to the Indians. And should it fail, the casualties would probably be few.

To plan was one thing. Of far greater importance was persuading the Indians to join in an attack. Undoubtedly, those who had accompanied Langlade to the fort had done so partly out of loyalty to him and to the French, but they had no desire to tie themselves to a lost cause. They had probably known that a battle was imminent, and had seen in it a chance for glory and plunder. However, they apparently had believed that the English force was small. Now, to their chagrin, they learned that the opposite was true.

Historians have tended to believe that long before Braddock arrived at the Monongahela, the French at Fort Duquesne were well aware of the strength at his command. This assumption is inaccurate. Our sources uniformly suggest that it was only on or about July 6 that Contrecoeur even learned that the British were at hand. He had, of course, known that they were on their way, but he had been able to learn little of their movements. What information he had received tended to convince him that

Braddock's army was small. Now, with a confrontation approaching, reconnaissance reports were swinging in the opposite direction, toward panic. French and Indian scouts alike
were bringing in alarming accounts of the enemy. They were
awed by the display of British artillery. And the numbers!
Some said there were three thousand men marching under
Braddock. Four thousand, claimed others.[11]

The Indians were in no mood to face such odds. Yet the
French would have to fight for them, as well as for the fort. To
surrender meekly, to abandon their stronghold, would be tacitly
to acknowledge their hated enemy the stronger. They had
worked too hard to lose now by default. For years they had
battled for control of the Indian. They had boasted that they
could, and would, drive the British from tribal lands. They had
bestowed countless gifts on the natives. And when persuasion
had failed, they and their Indian allies had wreaked vengeance
on those tribes which had yet cleaved toward Britain.[12] Should
they now give up, the Indians would see their boasts as empty.
The tribes that were wavering would join their enemy. Even
their traditional allies would decline to fight for them. But these
last must fight Braddock; otherwise, the cause was hopeless. The
French themselves knew their weakness. Only stout Indian support might win for their bravado a tenuous credibility.

There were Indians enough at the fort to provide at least a
hope of success. In all, there were about eight hundred warriors, a total perhaps exceeding the number normally to be
found in the entire Ohio Valley.[13] Where had they come from?
Historians have generally had little to say about the make-up of
this Indian force. Their unwillingness to speculate is under-
standable in view of the fact that there is only a small body of
evidence on the question. Basically, we have two major documents and some random testimony, all tending toward the
conclusion that the majority of these Indians, perhaps more
than 90 percent, had come from the area of the Great Lakes.
The first source is clearly not one that we would choose
willingly. In 1857, Captain Augustin Grignon gave a lengthy

account of the career of his grandfather, Langlade. At the time, Grignon was well into his seventies, and although he apparently was recalling stories he had heard from Langlade himself, time had probably clouded his memory. Some of the material he provides is plainly inaccurate, although of course it is possible that it had been so when passed on to him. With these reservations, we may note his statement that he "thought" the Indians whom his grandfather had led to Fort Duquesne in 1755 had been "the Ottawas, Chippewas, Menomonees, Winnebagoes, Pottawotomies, Hurons or Wyandotts, and perhaps others." A legend had persisted that the great Pontiac was of their number. Grignon thought this possible but was uncertain, and we should be as well.[14]

Our other source is in every way more dependable; indeed, it is the best we have on the French preparations to meet Braddock. This is the journal of a garrison officer, possibly M. Roucher, to whom I shall in any case ascribe it, for the sake of simplicity. Perhaps surprisingly, Roucher not only does not contradict Grignon's description of the Indian forces, but tends to corroborate it. Roucher, who was very much on the scene, does not list tribes, as does Grignon, but rather notes them in passing. His testimony confirms that there were Hurons, Pottawotomies, and Ottawas at the fort on that July day in 1755. In addition, he refers to the Shawnees, Missisaugas, and Iroquois. That the Shawnees were there is confirmed by other sources, and it also seems certain that Delaware and Mingo warriors were present, though few in number.[15] On the whole, the list is not surprising, for it shows the preponderant influence of the traditional "French Indians," the Algonquin tribes and western Iroquois. The other Iroquois noted by Roucher may have been renegades, although in fact the French had more impact within the Six Nations than they have generally been given credit for, and were particularly influential with the Senecas.[16] It appears, however, that the Ohio Indians, whom they were particularly anxious to impress, were little in evidence at Fort Duquesne in July 1755. On the whole, the local tribes were straddling the fence, waiting to see which way the nascent war would turn.

On the evening of July 8, Beaujeu approached the Indians. Having spent his life in New France, he was wise in their customs. He knew that he could not take their aid for granted. Moreover, he knew that he must not *seem* to do so. He must play on their anti-British feeling and on their pride. Certainly he was aware of the rumors sweeping the Indian camp to the effect that Braddock's army was unbeatable. He must persuade them that they could and would carry the day.

That night he failed. This much we know. Little else is certain. According to Roucher, Beaujeu called on the assembled warriors to aid him in driving out the enemy who had seized their lands. He then began the war song, and they joined in—all except the Pottawotomies. The Indians refused to go while some of their number held back, and the conference dissolved. During the night, some Shawnees and Iroquois of the Valley attended Contrecoeur and told him that they would try to persuade their fellows to join in an attack on the approaching army. By inference, their assistance was conditional, since Roucher asserts that they "were genteelly entertained in order to engage the other Nations, and not to spin out time, all their demands were granted."

A second account, by M. de Godefroy, is less specific. He says only that the Indians wished to delay their decision, but were persuaded on the spot to join in the attack. Godefroy credits their change of heart not to any verbal heroics on the part of Beaujeu, but rather to the persuasiveness of the brothers Normanville, two officers of whom little is known.

Both accounts are plausible, if prosaic. But so is a third, which has been repeated in countless versions, and has in the process become one of the great legends in the history of New France. Was it Beaujeu himself who, with a desperate eloquence, rallied the Indians to his cause? The anonymous reporter who tells us he did was not at the scene; in fact, he was many miles distant. Still, circumstantial evidence supports his version, without necessarily challenging either of the others. Beaujeu was a master of Indian diplomacy, fully capable of stirring up his followers.[17] More important, since it deals specifically with the case at hand, is the question of what delayed the captain's party on the morning of July 9. That there was delay is beyond question. Both Godefroy and Roucher claim that the men under Beaujeu marched at eight. Yet, within the next five hours, they were able to advance only about six miles. It appears that they had planned to ambush Braddock's army as it forded the Monongahela above Turtle Creek. In any case, they were never to arrive at their intended destination. How could such a force, lightly armed and led by scouts who knew the area well, make so little progress? There are various possibilities, but the most likely is that the detachment actually left considerably after eight, and not that it was delayed after it started. The French reporters have little to say about the march, but this in itself may indicate that no major obstacles arose to hinder it.[18]

Who, then, delayed the departure? Roucher claims that Beaujeu actually intended to march at daybreak, but that the Indians were not ready. Although he hurried them along, the detachment did not depart until eight. But this is too early to account for the facts. Did the Indians perhaps reconsider their decision to fight? As we have seen, rumor had made the enemy awesome. Did they, on this July morning, see discretion as the better part of valor? Our third reporter believes so, and his version best accounts for the lateness of departure. Perhaps Roucher and Godefroy are also correct, as far as they go, in their reports of what took place on the night of July 8 and the morning of July 9. Possibly the Indians wavered, one moment allowing themselves to be persuaded to join the French, the next moment reconsidering. There is enough glory to parcel out. Let legend have its way:

M. de Beaujeu . . . determined to attack the enemy. This he proposed to the Indians who were with him, but they at first rejected his opinion,

and said to him: "Father, you want to die and sacrifice us. The English
are more than four thousand, and we are only eight hundred, yet you
wish to attack them. Certainly you must see that you are making no
sense. We ask of you until tomorrow to make up our minds." They then
consulted among themselves, as they always do before marching. The
next morning M. de Beaujeu left his fort with the few troops he had,
and asked the Indians for the result of their deliberations. They
answered that they could not march. M. de Beaujeu, who was kind,
affable, and sensible, said to them: "I am determined to confront the
enemy. What—would you let your father go alone? I am certain to
defeat them!" With this, they decided to follow him.[19]

Certainly it would not have been that simple. So few words,
even emphatically spoken, could not have swayed the Indians.
Over an hour or more, Beaujeu must have played on their
emotions. He must have spoken glowingly of their loyalty to
the French, and of the need to stand together against a common foe. He must have insinuated that the world could only
despise those who would desert their father in his hour of
need. But most of all, he must have sought to convince them
that victory was theirs for the taking. Voice rising, eyes alive
with ardor, he must have hammered away at their doubt. The
long minutes passed, until it was almost too late. And then,
finally, his arguments carried the day! The Indians joined him!

Was Beaujeu actually so certain of defeating the British? He
had taken communion that morning, in anticipation of the
worst. But naturally one could die in a battle that proved
victorious for his cause. In point of fact, later testimony indicates that the French were indeed confident of victory, and
their leader in the field likely shared this optimism.[20]

Even if the ambush were to fail, the cause would not be
entirely lost. Contrecoeur had detached only one-third of his
men. Some four hundred of them remained behind to guard
the fort. Braddock's army might overcome the ambush, but was
unlikely to inflict very heavy casualties. The remaining men,
French and Indian, could continue to harass the march, or
they, particularly the former, could retire to the fort, there to

await investment. Considering the strength of Braddock's artillery and the size of his force, it was unlikely that they and their comrades could long withstand a siege. But they would not surrender without a fight.[21]

Although Beaujeu had persuaded the Indians to join him, he still faced delay. First, having driven them into a frenzy, he had to wait for them to calm down. Then they had to arm themselves. It appears that barrels of gunpowder and bullets had been left outside the gates of Fort Duquesne, on the assumption that the Indians would join Beaujeu. Now the warriors grouped together in front of the fort, sharing out the ammunition.[22]

It must have been at least nine before the detachment was ready to move out. According to the most detailed account, there were 36 officers, 72 French regulars, 146 Canadians, and 637 Indians.[23] Clearly, without Indian help Beaujeu's mission would have been not only hopeless, but pointless. As it was, his forces would be facing an enemy more than half again their size, and better armed as well.

Finally, hours behind schedule, the motley aggregation advanced into the forest. Now those defending the fort could only wait, and stare expectantly into the warmth of a July morning.

The Pen and the Sword

BY STAGES Braddock's army reassembled on the east bank of the Monongahela. It took St. Clair's working party a full hour to slope the banks sufficiently for the wagons and artillery to get over. All during this time, the troops were exposed, and Braddock had them drawn into a battle line. The work completed, however, he ordered them back into a line of march.[1]

Gage had led his advance party to Frazer's Cabin, a point perhaps one hundred yards east of the river. Here stood the charred reminders of French enmity. John Frazer, a Scottish merchant, had achieved ties with the Indians sufficiently close to have prompted the French to drive him from the valley. His cabin, which now served as a rendezvous point, had long since been put to the torch.[2]

With the crossing complete, Braddock ordered Gage to march on until three o'clock.[3] His apparent plan was that the army would then make camp, only three or four miles from Fort Duquesne. The next day they would reach it and occupy it quietly or commence a siege, as the case might be.

The troops marched off, slowly winding northward from Frazer's Cabin. This was not, by Continental standards, an exceptionally large force, but here in the wilderness it may well have seemed awesome. Included in it were some thirteen hundred men and officers, perhaps two-fifths of whom were Americans. There were in addition between forty and fifty women, most of them wives of soldiers on the march. A small but unknown number of volunteers accompanied the troops. Finally, there were the batmen, sutlers, and wagoners, totaling somewhat less than two hundred.[4] We should not be too quick to disregard the fighting capabilities of these "extras." The

31

volunteers were armed. More important, so were the batmen, on the strength of recent orders.[5]

The vanguard was that day divided into two main detachments, the advance party, headed by Gage, and the working party, St. Clair in command. Braddock himself commanded the main body, seconded by Burton. The rear guard, smallest by far of the three units noted, marched under the direction of Halket. Although we cannot be too precise on formations, enough evidence exists to fix the order of march, the numbers in each detachment, and the position of most key figures. Of particular importance to us are the twenty-two who would leave accounts of the day's action. Who were they? Where did they stand in the line of march? For which audience did they write and why? Did they have a particular ax to grind?

At the head of the troops marched the guides and light horse. They were few in number, certainly no more than twenty. Most of the Indians were in this small party. So was George Croghan, their commander and the first in our list of eyewitnesses.

Then about thirty, Croghan had been born in Dublin, but had emigrated to North America in 1741. Capable and intelligent, he had quickly established himself as one of the foremost traders and Indian agents in Pennsylvania, and had achieved fluency in several tribal tongues. He had constructed a series of trading posts in the Ohio Valley during the early 1750s and had been so successful in winning over the Indians that the French, fearing his competition, had raided the outposts and driven him from the area. When Braddock had appointed him as his Indian manager, with the rank of captain, Croghan must have looked on this as a chance to exact some share of vengeance. Certainly, too, if the operation were a success, he could again move into the valley. He always had been, and would remain, an avid speculator, and Washington among others had come to consider him unscrupulous. Croghan's experience during the expedition had not been altogether happy. Despite his promises to Braddock that considerable Indian aid was on the way, and his own efforts at recruitment, he had in the end managed to engage only Monakatooka and his small band. Still, Braddock seems not to have lost faith in him. For his own part, Croghan appears to have admired the general, and was never to speak of him except in fond terms. On the other hand, we may be certain that he was never close to St. Clair, for he had been one of the five whom Sir John had excoriated in his memorable eruption of April 12.[6]

Just behind Croghan and the guides came the van of the advance party, apparently consisting of a subaltern and twenty men. To either side of the van marched the headmost of a series of small flanking parties, each containing a sergeant and ten privates. There were perhaps twenty-five of these units covering the entire line of march, at a distance of one to two hundred yards from the column.[7] It does not appear that any of our eyewitnesses was a member either of such a group, or of the van.

Following its van, at a distance of perhaps fifty yards, came the advance party itself, consisting of about three hundred men led by Gage. Several members of this detachment would later recall the events of that day. Unfortunatley, it is often impossible to tell precisely where they marched or rode. The advance party may well have stretched back for two hundred yards.

Gage himself is, of course, well known to any student of American colonial history. As commander-in-chief of the British forces in North America, and as governor of Massachusetts, he would have a fateful role in the events of April 1775. By the time of Braddock's expedition he was already rising quickly in the officer caste, boosted by the fact that he was the son of an Irish peer. In early 1741, at the age of twenty, he had been commissioned a lieutenant in a new regiment that was soon to be designated the Forty-Eighth Foot. He would have advanced with even greater speed had the wars of the 1740s dragged on, or had he possessed a still more exalted social position than the one his father had provided for him. As it was, in 1751, he had been gazetted a lieutenant colonel in his regiment, and it was in

Thomas Gage

this capacity that he now accompanied Braddock. He appears to have gotten on well with the general. At least, if there was any ill will between the two, he, unlike St. Clair, did not choose to publicize the fact. In doing his part to further the expedition, Gage had won some admirers, including the young pamphleteer from Maryland, Daniel Dulany. He had also struck up a friendship with Washington. Needless to say, it would not stand the test of time.[8]

It appears that the troops directly behind Gage were grenadiers from the Forty-Fourth Foot, the elite of that regiment. Among them was Lieutenant William Dunbar. Little is known about him. Since he was still in active service when he died in 1788, he was probably no more than thirty at the time he joined Braddock. It appears that he possessed the stuff of heroism. During the French and Indian War, he would on several occasions distinguish himself by his bravery. But on this July day of 1755 his career was young, and he had yet to prove himself.[9]

Of much lower status than Dunbar, but wearing his private's rank with dignity, was Duncan Cameron, who also appears to have marched near the head of the advance party. Nothing is known of Cameron except what he himself reveals in a brief memoir that he wrote in 1756. According to him, he had been born in the highlands in 1722. He had entered the army at seventeen, had seen considerable action, narrowly escaping death on several occasions, and had been badly wounded at Culloden. If we take his word for it, he had spied on Bonnie Prince Charlie during the Forty-Five, and his report had contributed to Cumberland's greatest victory. After a few years away from the army, he had grown restless, and had in 1754 enlisted in the Forty-Fourth Foot. Cameron was always truthful enough to admit that his rank prevented him from writing the "inside" story of any campaign or battle. He notes in his memoir that privates of the day were "generally kept very ignorant of every Thing"—no great revelation, but a tribute to his honesty. Still, he was not in all ways a typical private. This he proved by the mere fact that he was literate. Through the medium of the written word, he indulged in the private's pastime of criticizing superiors. In some cases, while not naming names, he would describe officers in enough detail that their identities could be established. Then again, he might offer blanket condemnations. But there were two officers whom he would recall with particular fondness: one was Braddock, the other Halket. He does not appear to have known of the rift between them.[10]

Perhaps one hundred yards to the rear of the grenadiers marched an independent company, normally commanded by Captain Horatio Gates, but this day under the leadership of his superior in the field, Captain Robert Cholmley. Cholmley himself holds little interest for the historian. Of much greater importance is his batman, whose account of that day's action is one of the four or five most significant. Unfortunately, we know almost nothing about him. He was British or possibly Irish, since he had accompanied his master across the Atlantic. One can infer from his journal of the expedition that he was amiable, and not so critical of his superiors as was Cameron. On the other hand, he almost certainly lacked Cameron's experience and, therefore, his perspective on the behavior of those in command. The batman was young, perhaps still in his teens. He was, in his own small way, also heroic, with a strong sense of duty.[11]

In all probability, Gates rode next to Cholmley. It was only fitting that he should be a part of this expedition, since he had in a sense been involved with it even before Braddock. Like Gage, Gates was fortunate in his connections, knowing Horace Walpole as godfather and patron. He had early been connected with North America. As a teen-age lieutenant, he had served in Nova Scotia under General Edward Cornwallis. Perhaps it had been a combination of this limited acquaintance with the colonial scene and his tie to Walpole which in 1754 had brought about an extraordinary development. The Duke of Newcastle, whose ignorance of American affairs was already legendary,

had sent for Gates and had asked his advice on how to conduct
the projected campaign. Pleading youth and inexperience, the
twenty-six-year-old officer had declined to offer an opinion.
His disclaimer had done nothing to harm a budding military
career, for in September of that year he had been commissioned a captain in the New York Independent Company, and
it was in this capacity that he marched with Braddock. Despite
his experience in America and a friendship with Washington
that appears to have originated during this campaign, he, unlike Croghan, in 1755 still considered Britain his home, and he
would indeed spend most of the next decade there. Of course,
he would one day again cross the Atlantic, and finally emerge
as a major figure in the American Revolution. His behavior
toward Newcastle should not be taken as an indication of
diffidence. In fact, throughout his career he would show himself to be hot-tempered and quick to state a view.[12]

Hard on the heels of Gage's detachment came the working
party, St. Clair in command. Sir John was probably the oldest
member of Braddock's army to leave an account of that day.
He was in all likelihood well into middle age, having succeeded
his father as third baronet in 1726. Age and social status naturally made him anxious for advancement, but he appears not to
have made dramatic progress in the military prior to 1754, a
year whose entrance had found him lieutenant colonel of the
Twenty-Second Foot. Although the rank may appear impressive, Sir John himself would not have thought so. Gage, perhaps fifteen years younger than he, was his senior as lieutenant
colonel. Braddock's expedition had come as his great opportunity. In October 1754, he had been appointed deputy quarter-
master general in North America, a post he would hold until
his death in late 1767. As we have seen, he had from the
beginning been active in this role, if not always successful or
tactful. It must have galled him to see Orme, much his junior
in age, rank, and service, hurtle by him in Braddock's counsels.
St. Clair undoubtedly believed that he had done more than any
other officer aside from Braddock to insure the success of the

expedition. And certainly he had worked at a fever pitch, no
only in the early months of 1755, but during the march itself
when as commander of the working party he had been particu
larly responsible for building the road to Fort Duquesne. Fo
his efforts, he had expected the general's gratitude and favor
Instead, he had been shunted aside. It was an embittered and
frustrated man who now led the working party these last mile
to the fort. By his own testimony, he had decided to petition
for his recall, feeling that he "could be of little use being neve
listen'd to."[13]

With St. Clair rode the engineers, among them Harry Gor
don and Patrick Mackellar. It is not known exactly where Gor
don was situated. Mackellar was toward the rear of the working
party, which contained some two hundred and fifty men and
extended back for more than one hundred yards.

Gordon's specialty was road-building. It was on this basis tha
Cumberland had recommended him to Braddock. He had
joined the Royal Engineers in 1742, which would suggest tha
he was now in his early thirties. From the start, his career had
been active. He had served in Flanders in 1745, and had joined
Cumberland in the field in 1747–1748. Presumably, during thi
time he had become acquainted with battle condition
firsthand. Gordon, like St. Clair and others, seems to hav
hoped for great things from Braddock's campaign. As an engi
neer he held no commission, and this seems to have bothere
him. His obsession with status was never to disappear, and fo
that matter it was by no means unusual. In 1776, a dispute ove
rank would lead him to resign his place as chief engineer i
Canada. But in 1755, all he hoped for was a commission. A
matters stood, even among the four engineers who accompa
nied Braddock, he was outranked by Mackellar and by th
chief engineer, James Montresor.

Mackellar was several years older than Gordon, having bee
born in 1717. During the latter half of the 1730s he had spen
four years as a clerk in the Ordnance Department at Woolwich
but he had made his reputation as an engineer at Minorca

where he had served from 1739 until his appointment as Braddock's engineer *en second* in 1754. He was in particular an expert on military architecture and fortifications, and may have been looked to as a potential advisor should it be necessary to besiege Fort Duquesne, or, having taken it, to make extensive repairs. But his talents and powers of observation were far-ranging, as he was to show during a long and illustrious career.[14]

To the rear of the working party, a line of wagons loaded with ammunition and tools stretched back for almost two hundred yards. Quite possibly present in this procession was James Furnis, commissary of stores for the Ordnance Board. Furnis is for the most part a shadow figure, but it can be said with certainty that he, like Gordon, resented his inferior status. Commissaries held a peculiar position in the army, and indeed many of them were civilians in military service. Furnis himself may well have remained a civilian during Braddock's campaign. At least he appears not to have been an officer, although he was to win a commission later in the war. From offhand remarks in two of his letters that have come down to us, it is clear that he found his place under Braddock a source of humiliation.[15]

Immediately behind the wagons was the rear guard of the advance party. This completed the vanguard, which accounted for perhaps half of Braddock's men and was drawn out over a distance of about one-third of a mile.

Another hundred yards back, a detachment of twenty-nine light horse headed the main body. This unit was under the command of Captain Robert Stewart, a Scot by birth, a Virginian by adoption. Stewart was one of many who could call Washington friend, although he was almost a full generation senior to the squire of Mount Vernon. He had accompanied the young colonel on his abortive expedition the year before, and had been wounded in a skirmish with the French—on July 9. This failed to deter him, for he appears to have felt that he had a military vocation. He was anxious for advancement, and the passage of time made him impatient. As late as 1763, he was in London, petitioning Lord Bute to help him gain a command. But even in 1755, he may have felt that his years were against him. Although his character appears to have been very different from St. Clair's, and much more geared to the acceptance of frustration, he would probably have understood Sir John's fear that time was passing him by.[16]

The light horse was followed closely by a larger body of "sailors and pioneers." As one might guess, the pioneers were Americans, specifically those who had been recruited to assist in building the road. The sailors were British seamen whom Commodore Augustus Keppel had detached for Braddock's use. The general apparently intended to employ them in building bridges or floats, should there be any major rivers to cross. Later in the campaign, they might construct a makeshift navy to ferry the troops to Niagara. In the meantime, their skill with tools would be useful. It appears, finally, that Braddock expected them to help man the artillery in the event of a siege or battle.[17]

One hundred yards to their rear was the general's guard, some mounted, others on foot. Next we come to the main body proper. Perhaps five hundred strong, and composed almost entirely of regulars, it covered about one-third of a mile. The men were divided into twelve companies, six on either side of a long string of wagons that contained provisions and baggage. Complicating their march still further were herds of cattle and horses that on both sides separated them from their flank-guards. At the head of this conglomerate rode Braddock himself, surrounded by a personal staff that included two key aides-de-camp, Orme and Washington.

The accounts of Orme contrast so sharply that they seem to refer to two different men. This apparently stems from a tendency on his part to treat his inferiors with contempt, while turning on the charm for the benefit of those whom he wished to impress. During his career he had impressed many, and probably as a consequence had won promotions at a rate which

Robert Orme

should be considered imposing, in view of the fact that he does not appear to have had strong family connections. After serving briefly as an ensign in the Thirty-Fifth Foot, he had in 1745 entered the Coldstreams. Presumably it had been between that year and 1753, when Braddock himself had left the regiment, that the two had become close. Perhaps it was the older man who had in 1751 been responsible for Orme's promotion to the rank of lieutenant in the Coldstreams, equivalent to captain of the line. In any case, Braddock had looked to his protégé from the very beginning of the American campaign. In 1755, Orme would have been in his early thirties, old enough to impress Washington as one possessed of great experience and wisdom, yet young enough that their relationship might be one of brotherly affection. Nor was Washington alone in his closeness to the captain. During the campaign in America, Orme's combination of youth and experience, enhanced by charm, attracted many young officers to his circle. But what they admired, their aging superiors envied. Braddock himself seems to have preferred the company of younger officers to that of men his own age. This helps to explain not only Orme's great influence over him, but the fact that the captain was openly disrespectful in his attitude toward certain of his superiors, notably Colonel Dunbar. He knew that there was little they could do to him, or that the general *would* do. These men who despised him, who did their best to keep him down—was it not exhilarating to attack them with impunity?[18]

At Orme's side rode young Washington. It had taken considerable coaxing on Braddock's part to bring him here. An order issued by the general early in 1755, limiting the authority of colonial officers, had upset the proud Virginian to the extent that he had resigned his own commission. However, Braddock himself, far from wishing to see Washington shun the military, had early on singled him out as one who would profit from the experience of participating in a full-scale campaign. On March 2, he had ordered Orme to send a note to Mount Vernon, inviting Washington to join his "Family." Such flattery had had

George Washington

the desired effect, and on March 15 Washington had written back to Orme to say that although he had earlier wished to retire to a less active life, he was now anxious to learn the martial arts under Edward Braddock, their distinguished practitioner. In May, the general had appointed him an aide-de-camp, causing him to boast that "I am therefore freed from all commands but his, and give Orders to all, which must be implicitly obey'd." This assessment of his authority was vastly exaggerated, but he, like Orme, does appear to have had a more subtle influence, owing to his personal relationship with Braddock. We have seen that Washington himself claimed that the suggestion to divide the army had come from him, and that the general had actually sought his advice on this matter. However, their association was often stormy. Although Washington had in the beginning freely criticized the Pennsylvanians for what he saw as an uncooperative attitude toward the expedition, he had later condemned the general for his anti-American tirades. Perhaps what upset him most was that after a time Braddock had begun to mellow in his attitude toward Pennsylvania, while at the same time becoming ever more critical of Washington's own fair province. In any case, at the age of twenty-three Washington was himself headstrong and quick to judge. He had not yet decided on a military career. Yet he was already possessed of that blend of courage and compassion which was to be his key to greatness. The hero in him loved the crash of battle, even while his humane self recoiled from its carnage. In the wake of his Fort Necessity campaign, he had commented to his brother that "I heard the bullets whistle, and, believe me, there is something charming in the sound." It is a part of the Washington legend that, after a dangerous illness had forced him to remain behind with Colonel Dunbar, the young Virginian had left his sickbed and ridden hard to catch up with the main army. He had arrived in Braddock's camp on the evening of July 8, weak, but anxious to take part in any possible action. Perhaps, in those last long miles to the fort, the bullets would again whistle.[19]

In command of one of the companies in the main body was Captain Francis Peyton, like his friend Washington a young Virginian volunteer. On that day, he was acting as adjutant to Burton, whom he admired intensely. Peyton was more reserved in his attitude toward the general himself. Like many provincials, he admired him for his courage, yet feared that he was dangerously ignorant of the problems involved in forest fighting. He could only hope that this ignorance would not prove costly.[20]

Yet another member of the main body would one day recount the events of July 9, 1755. This was Philip Hughes, chaplain of the Forty-Fourth Foot. He was probably a rather young man, having secured his commission only in early 1752. Aside from this, we know nothing about him, which is of no great concern, since his account is a very minor one.[21]

Slightly less than one hundred yards behind the main body marched the rear guard, Halket in command. This was a small detachment, five- or six-score men, almost all Americans. Among those who marched here were an unknown number of Virginians from the First Company of Rangers, captained by Adam Stephen.

Today Stephen is remembered, if at all, as a friend of Washington's and as a fiery American general during the Revolution. Indeed, his military career would come to a somewhat ignominious end as the result of a court-martial's finding him guilty of being drunk during a 1777 battle—between his troops and another American regiment. But perhaps his finest hour would come in 1788 when, at about seventy, he used his oratory to persuade the Virginia Assembly to ratify the Constitution. Stephen was always a man of strong principles coupled with a combative and restless nature. Already in 1755 he could look back on a checkered career. Born in Scotland, he had at first seen medicine as his proper vocation, and had acquired a degree in this field at the University of Edinburgh. During the early 1740s he had served as surgeon on a British hospital ship, learning in the process at least the more gruesome aspects of war. Later in the decade he had begun to travel, a journey in keeping with his own belief that the desire to view foreign shores was "Natural to the Young & Curious." He had finally settled in Virgina, where he had "made himself known by making an incision into the Liver of Mrs. Mercer of Stafford County, [and] cleansing, & healing the Ulcers there." But the threat of a new war, and his own turbulent nature, had caused him to give up medicine in the early 1750s in order to devote himself to the military. He had accompanied Washington on his Fort Necessity campaign, in the process establishing a sound friendship. Now they were together again under Braddock. Stephen, like many and perhaps most of the officers and men on this expedition, had probably been involved in only a few battles. But during his brief military career he had evolved a fixed belief that the proper means of handling an Indian ambush was to fight the enemy in its own way.[22]

Behind the rear guard, there was only the charred remnant of Frazer's Cabin. Ahead of it, the column stretched on for about a mile, almost all of it invisible in the forest.

Such was the disposition of Braddock's troops as they marched off toward Fort Duquesne. In viewing them, we have so far encountered sixteen of the men who would in the near future record their recollections of that day. But there were another six—what of them? They cannot be placed in the line of march with any degree of certainty. For that matter, little is known about any of them.

Of the six, the only one whom we may know at all, beyond what we can infer from his testimony, is Lieutenant Matthew Leslie, who served St. Clair as assistant deputy quartermaster general. He appears to have been efficient in his post and was largely responsible for the success of the foraging expeditions that had at last allowed Braddock to march. Leslie was on good terms with St. Clair, and had apparently won his respect. But from the little we know of him, he seems to have lacked those negative qualities which Sir John possessed in such abundance. Leslie does not appear to have despised Americans. Indeed, he seems to have been an amiable sort, diplomatic in his relationships with civilians and brother officers alike. Perhaps, in view of his key role in dispensing supplies, he rode with the wagon train as it creaked its way toward the fort. The wagons also carried those who would have no place in any fighting, including women, sutlers, and possibly John Campbell, one of Braddock's messengers. That we know virtually nothing about Campbell should not upset us. Of the twenty-two eyewitnesses whose reports we shall examine, he is for our purposes the least important.[23]

The four remaining reporters cannot be identified at all, and can be discussed only in terms of what their testimony reveals about them. To differentiate them, I will refer to them as "British A, B, C, and D," respectively. I am using "British" here to reflect the fact that they were members of a British army. In point of fact, British B and, probably, British C were colonials. British A, on the other hand, was certainly one of those who had crossed the Atlantic, while British D excelled even St. Clair in despising things American. All four were almost undoubtedly officers, though probably none held a lofty rank. It is impossible to do more than guess where they stood in the line of march on July 9, and in fact even such conjecture is totally undesirable in the cases of British B and D, who provide no clues whatever. On the basis of inferences from their testimony, it is quite likely that British A served toward the rear of the advance party or perhaps in St. Clair's detachment, while British C was probably a member of the main body.[24]

Here we have our twenty-two British and American correspondents from the past. That afternoon, they would live through three hours of a horror which, even with their testimony, is difficult for us to envision. They would face not merely death, but the terrifying prospect of slow and searing torture at the hands of an enemy they considered demonic. They would see their comrades fall, and know the helplessness of challenging an unseen foe. The ranks would break, a proud army would dissolve into chaos. Valor would avail nothing. The forest would protect its own.

But they would survive, these twenty-two, wounded though most would be.[25] Their accounts of the action would convey to an anxious audience a message both pathetic and irate. For they would be the first to seek to answer the question, "How could it have happened?" Some would lay the chief blame on the troops, others on the general. Most would seek out scapegoats of some sort. All would rationalize in such a way that they themselves, and those whom they saw as comrades, might bear no part of the blame.

With such a chance to dip their pens in bile, some would not be able to resist the temptation to settle old scores. British B's account shows him to have been extreme in this regard. His dynamic was hatred, in this case directed primarily toward Braddock and Orme. Ranking just behind in vindictiveness was St. Clair, whose biases we know. Yet a third who bore ill will toward the general and his chief favorite was Furnis, who felt that Orme had treated him contemptuously and that, worse yet, Braddock had been slow to pay debts owed to him. But to Furnis's credit, his report bears no obvious marks of bias. On the other hand, there is the case of those favorably inclined toward the general, or, by the time they wrote, to his memory. Chief among them were Washington and, of course, Orme himself. Peyton was another who admired Braddock, making up in fervor what he lacked in importance. Cameron, British D, and Croghan likewise would continue to think fondly of their commander. Then there were those—Gage, Gordon, Stephen—who would remember him for a more practical reason, though perhaps sentimental ones as well. They would recall, for the benefit of their superiors, that the general had promised them favor but—bad luck!—had not lived to keep his word, leaving this task to others.[26]

The last point raises another question. To whom did our reporters write? Orme wrote numerous accounts, some intended for public consumption, others for colonial governors or for chiefs of the military. Washington was only slightly less prolific, but most of his testimony was directed toward relatives, although one report was addressed to Robert Dinwiddie, governor of Virginia. Otherwise our informants are known to us through only one account apiece, and that generally intended for a superior. Cameron wrote for a mass audience, while there is no way of knowing at whom Cholmley's Batman aimed his comments. British B, Croghan, Leslie, and Peyton directed their remarks to friends or relatives. Ostensibly, so did British C and D, Hughes, and Stewart, but we should be wary of private correspondence that "just happens" to find its way into print almost immediately, as did theirs.[27]

And what may be said of our French reporters? First and foremost, that in all probability only one of them was actually present at the battle. This was Dumas. His extant account is contained in a letter to Jean-Baptiste Machault d'Arnouville, the minister of the marine, written in late July 1756. The intervening year was not altogether a happy one to the mind of the French captain. He saw those junior to him in rank receive promotions and honors he felt should be his. Such real or imagined slights he complained of to Machault. At the same time he sought to correct any misimpressions the minister might have gotten as a result of having been "badly informed of the circumstances" of the battle—presumably, by those Dumas considered enemies.[28]

Taking into account such differences in background, motivation, and character, it is scarcely surprising that the accounts of our twenty-three eyewitnesses vary widely. Often apparent errors may be accounted for in terms of perspective. If not, there is the more difficult question of bias. No one remembers every detail of an incident. Instead he recalls a general impression, and some elements that fit into it. Such a conception is, in turn, almost certain to be shaped by partiality. To that degree, in most cases a large one, the process is involuntary. The most honest and perceptive of eyewitnesses may therefore fail us. But by taking into account what we know of each informant, we can minimize the impact of any such failure.

FOUR

"The Indiens Was Upon Us!"

THE BRITISH MARCH toward Fort Duquesne took them up a gentle but steady slope. Dunbar recalls the favorable scouting reports he had heard before leaving Frazer's Cabin: "The Ground . . . we were told was pretty good, & the woods open, but all upon the ascent."

Were the woods "open"? "Yes," answers St. Clair emphatically—so much so "that Carridges Could have been drove in any part." But British A and Orme suggest the opposite.[1] Obviously, not all of us would agree on what constitutes "open" woods, so we cannot expect that our eyewitnesses will. Still, the overall evidence suggests that St. Clair is exaggerating. Quite possibly the woods did thin out—a bit. But they remained dense enough to hide an enemy.

While the British marched deliberately, the French and Indians were racing toward the river. Here came the heroic Beaujeu, fresh from one victory, in search of one far greater. Like the warriors who followed him, he was stripped to the waist, his gorget alone marking him as a French officer.[2] Matching his quick stride was Dumas, his second-in-command.

About a mile from the river, a hillock rose to the right of the line of march.[3] The experienced Gage, heading his detachment, cannot have failed to notice it. Perhaps he thought for a moment of ordering a detachment to occupy this rising ground, potentially so strategic; certainly standard procedure suggested such a step. But the enemy was nowhere in sight, and Gage appears to have felt that this precaution would only slow the march unnecessarily. Just an hour before, at the river, St. Clair had asked him whether the advance party would continue to drag along the two six-pounders that had been in its keeping earlier in the day. Gage had answered, "No Sir I think not, for I do not think we Shall have much Occation for them and they being troubolsome to get forwards before the Roads are Cut." This was the voice of confidence. The enemy could have attacked the day before, with great advantage. The river, too, had been a perfect site for ambush. There had been no attack. Now, with those opportunities past, there would be none. The French and their Indian allies were clearly planning to make their stand at the fort, if at all. So thought Gage. He led his troops past the hill.[4]

The remaining units of the vanguard followed him, so that in a few minutes the rising ground on the right was bisecting the line of march. Still no enemy appeared, and the troops pushed on with confidence. It was one o'clock on a lazy July afternoon.[5] The warmth of the day, the sweet sounds of the forest, and most of all the anticipation of victory lulled the men into a soft contentment. They had worked hard and suffered much these long months. Now at last they could relax.

Suddenly, a cacophony of shouting rooted them in place. It was the guides, racing toward them through the forest. "The enemy!" they shouted. The enemy was but two hundred yards ahead!

Gordon, who had ridden toward the front in hope of finding the guides, perhaps to discuss with them the nature of the terrain that lay ahead, now found himself confirming their terrified reports. The enemy force was not large, he observed, only about three hundred. But its sudden appearance shocked him, as it had the scouts. As it had the troops.

The French, too, were surprised. They and their Indian allies halted, confused. Their scheme to ambush Braddock's army at the river had failed. Suddenly, they had no plan.

Perhaps Beaujeu, thinking quickly, recovered from his initial shock and hat in hand motioned his followers down the British flanks. If so, he had but little time to direct or to see to the execution of his orders. For now Gage's detachment poured forth a volley, or possibly several. Since the fire came from two hundred yards, and only from muskets, it caused few casualties. But among these few was Beaujeu, who fell dead at the roadside.

How badly shaken were the French forces? Certainly there must have been some confusion in their ranks, not only because of the surprise confrontation and the opening British volley, but most of all as a result of Beaujeu's death. It is the extent of disorder that is in question here. If we take the testimony of Dumas at face value, as have many historians in the past, we must conclude that the British firing caused the French and Indian force virtually to disintegrate, only to be rallied by the erstwhile second-in-command, now rising to glory. Dumas leaves us in no doubt of his own greatness, taking it upon himself to play both Horatius and Macaulay:

In the first moment of combat, one hundred militiamen—one-half of our French forces—shamefully turned tail, shouting "Every man for himself!" . . . This retreat encouraged the enemy to resound with cries of "Long live the King!," and they advanced quickly toward us. Their artillery, having been prepared during this time, commenced firing. This terrified the Indians, who fled. On the enemy's third discharge of musketry, M. de Beaujeu was killed. . . . It was then, Monseigneur, that by word and gesture I sought to rally the few soldiers who remained. I advanced, with an assurance born of despair. My platoon gave forth with a withering fire which astonished the enemy. It grew imperceptibly, and the Indians, seeing that my attack had caused the enemy to stop shouting, returned to me. Now I sent M. le Chevalier le Borone and M. de Rocheblave to tell the officers in charge of the Indians to seize the enemy's flanks.

Self-serving? Undoubtedly, and we must expect as much, in view of the fact that Dumas was directing his account to a superior, and was anxious to impress. But this does not disqualify the report, and in fact much of it is plausible. Furthermore, French A, French C, and Contrecoeur support his claim that at the first firing the troops fell back. Still, taking into account all of the evidence, it appears that at the very least he let his dramatic flair get the better of him. First, two French reporters,

Captain Jean-Daniel Dumas

Pouchot and Roucher, make no mention of a retreat, no matter how brief, and in fact both imply that their forces from the first stood up to the British. Pouchot is most emphatic here. According to him, the troops, including the Indians, were already in position and attacking the British flanks at the time of Beaujeu's death. On the fall of their commander, "M. Dumas took command of the French, or rather, they continued each one to do his best in the place they were in."

We must treat all of these accounts with care, however. Dumas is the only confirmed eyewitness on the French side to have left an account of the battle. Some of the other French reporters may have been present at the engagement, but this is unlikely. Therefore, we run into the problem of self-corroboration. Dumas, who returned to Fort Duquesne as commander of a victorious army, would certainly have been in a position to give the "official" account of what had occurred. It is not surprising, therefore, that several French reports besides his own bear his imprint. Among these are the three I have noted as supporting his account of the initial moments of battle. On the other hand, the fact that some (like Pouchot, who was definitely not an eyewitness) chose to relate the testimony of others does not suggest that their accounts are necessarily more correct; nor does it eliminate the possibility of self-corroboration. Pouchot, for that matter, seems to have disliked Dumas, so the fact that he disparages his contributions to victory should not surprise us. On the key question of how the French and Indians behaved during the first moments of battle, those who report from their side are not very helpful, except for Dumas, who is almost *too* helpful—to himself.

The British accounts, however, are enlightening and tend toward a strong consensus. In judging them, we may set aside those prepared by men who were not in the advance party or among the scouts when the firing began. These communicants cannot have known what was going on up front, and in fact most of them discuss only what happened in their little corner of the field when gunfire was first heard. We may also temporarily shelve the testimony of Gage, since that will be used momentarily in discussing a different point. Eliminating these and also, of course, the accounts that are vague even though the eyewitnesses who prepared them may have been close to the action, we are left with four reporters—Dunbar, Cameron, Cholmley's Batman, and Gordon.

Dunbar's testimony is brief, but worthy of interpretation: "We were allarmed by the Indian Hollow, & in an instant, found ourselves attacked on all sides." He may be telescoping events here, since the first fire likely came from the front, but it is nonetheless noteworthy that he conveys the impression of an immediate French attack. The suggestion is supported by Cameron: "The Firing as a Signal began in the Front, and immediately was follow'd from behind the Hills and Trees all-along each Flank." Cholmley's Batman writes in somewhat greater detail, noting that a guide, on first sighting the enemy, "immediately discharged his piece, turned Round his horse [and] Cried, the Indiens was upon us. My Master Called me to give me his horse which I tooke from him and the Ingagement began. Immediately they began to Ingage us in a half Moon and still Continued Surrounding us more and more." As usual, Gordon gives a particularly full and plausible account:

As soon as the Enemys Indians perceived our Grenadiers, they Divided themselves & Run along our right and Left flanks. The Advanc'd party Coll: Gage order'd to form, which Most of them Did with the front Rank upon the Ground & Begun firing, which they continued for several minutes, Altho' the Indians very soon Dispers'd Before their front & fell upon the flank partys.

In these four versions, we have a perfect cross-section of eyewitnesses. Those who wrote them were, respectively, an officer, a private, a servant, and an engineer, equally varied in their experience under fire. We may note that at least three of them were writing for an audience, and that Gordon and Dunbar may have been desirous of impressing superiors, but their motive for distortion on this point is not nearly as great as

Dumas's, and Cholmley's Batman in particular does not appear to have had anything to gain through his testimony. Their consensus that the French attacked immediately is therefore both plausible and impressive.

Gordon brings in another point worthy of note. He claims that the enemy began to run down the British flanks before Gage's troops opened fire, that is, *before* Beaujeu was killed. The implication is that Beaujeu himself ordered the move, assuming that it was in fact coordinated. Even if he did not, Gordon seems to challenge Dumas's assertion that it was *he* who gave the fateful order. In this, Gordon is far the more disinterested of the two, and is also supported by Pouchot, whose testimony in this regard has already been noted.[6] But we can still allow Dumas the benefit of the doubt here. He by no means claims that Beaujeu did not order his men to seize the enemy flanks, only that he himself *did*. In all probability, Beaujeu gave such an order but was killed before it could be satisfactorily carried out. His death caused confusion in the ranks, somewhat negating the command, but Dumas repeated it and saw to its execution.

Dumas's testimony is more directly challenged on a somewhat broader point. The French captain, perhaps unintentionally, gives the impression that his force almost disintegrated under the opening barrage. Clearly, it would have taken time to rally such a confused and panic-stricken army, and Dumas likewise suggests that it did. Let us recall his implied sequence: opening barrage, panic, flight, Beaujeu killed on the third British volley, further chaos, Dumas struggles to rally the men, a few of his own troops respond, their gunfire stops a British advance, Indians slowly return, he orders the French officers in charge of them to lead them down the enemy flanks, they carry out the order. It is inconceivable that this could have taken place in less than ten minutes. Even granted that during a battle one's sense of time may become distorted, it is unlikely that four British eyewitnesses would all have seen the attack starting immediately if it really took ten minutes to evolve. On the strength of their testimony, it seems clear that although the French forces may have given way at the first firing, they quickly regained the initiative and retaliated. This is not to deny Dumas his moment in the sun. He may well have been the individual most responsible for the flank attack. But the prism of his memory appears to have distorted the actual flow of events.

On still another important point Dumas differs from the British eyewitnesses. He claims that during the first volley the British made use of their cannon. As we might expect, French reporters under his influence make similar statements, but in fact so do those who, like Pouchot, work from other sources. On the other hand, no British eyewitness mentions that the advance party used artillery during the first moments of battle, and in fact we may recall that Gage had left his two six-pounders behind. It could be that the French reporters are simply confused in the sequence they suggest. Undoubtedly, the British did use their artillery later in the battle, but almost certainly not during these first crucial moments, when indeed it was probably not even at hand.

So much for the onset of battle—from the French point of view. The attackers, who had briefly become the attacked, had recovered from their initial confusion. Now most of them were racing down the enemy flanks. As they moved into their new positions, they disappeared from view. The consensus among reporters who fought for Braddock is that the enemy was virtually invisible. Cholmley's Batman recalls in his account that "if we saw five or six at one time [it] was a great sight," while Hughes tells us that "the French and Indians crept about in small Parties so that the Fire was quite round us, and in all the Time I never saw one, nor could I on Enquiry find any one who saw ten together."

How had they vanished, these enemy warriors who could see Braddock's forces and yet not be seen? The British eye-witnesses are, as we might imagine, not very helpful. Dunbar's assessment of enemy tactics is typical: "their methods, they immediately seise a Tree, & are certain of their Aim." But of course, to expect a more precise statement is to imagine that the eyewitnesses might describe what they could not see.

During the nineteenth century and well into the twentieth, historians regularly contended that the French and Indians had fired at Braddock's army from the sanctity of defiles. To my knowledge, their assertion has never been challenged, although it has been heard less lately. Like most historical legends, it originated at the time of the event. Within a fortnight of the battle, John Potter, sheriff of Carlisle, reported "that the French & Indians had cast an Intrenchment across the road before our Army, which they Discover'd not Untill they Came Close up to it, from thence and both sides of the road the Enemy kept a Constant fireing on them." Potter's account was quickly embroidered, and soon the belief spread that the enemy had fired not only from a defile to the head of the line of march, but from others lining the road.[7]

The trouble with this legend is that the French themselves appear to refute it. Unfortunately, Dumas throws no light on the issue. Having carefully described his own acts of heroism, he has little to say about the remainder of the battle. However, three other reporters, none an eyewitness but all privy to accounts besides his, state specifically that the Indians fought from behind trees. Roucher gives a rather confused version, stating that after Braddock's army had given forth with its initial volley, it had been "answer'd with the same Vivacity by our detachment who having advanced under cover of the Woods and the Indians being posted behind the Trees, attack'd the column of English in front." French B's account meshes better with those of the British: "The enemy . . . made a front, which allowed those behind the trees to knock over one or two with each shot." Pouchot is the most precise of all: "The French, on their part, upon seeing the English, threw themselves behind trees and began to fire, while the Indians [after momentary panic assumed] each a place behind every tree." On the strength of these three accounts, it seems that, legend or no, the bulk of the French and Indian forces were stationed behind trees on both sides of the road. However, it is quite possible that a large proportion of the French and a few Indians stationed themselves in a trench at the head of the British column. If so, they could not only have killed a number of Braddock's men but, more important, could have made it impossible for the British to advance.

The French and Indians had passed their moment of danger. They had recovered from their brief panic and were now concealed behind trees, with a clear sight of the enemy. Meanwhile, what of the British? To understand where they stood and why, it is necessary to backtrack slightly, to the first seconds of battle.

If we take Gage at his word, Braddock's army started to disintegrate even before firing began. According to him, on first hearing of the enemy's approach,

the guard in our van came to the right-about, but, by the activity of the officer who commanded them, were stopped from running in, and prevailed on to face again. The detachment was ordered to fix their bayonets, and form in order of battle, with intention of gaining a hill upon our right, which was partly already possessed by an officer's party that was scouring out right flank. The first was obeyed in a good deal of hurry, but none of them would stir to the posts assigned them. Though I had all the assistance that could be expected from the officers, not one platoon could be prevailed upon to stir from its line of march, and a visible terror and confusion appeared amongst the men. By this time, some few shots were fired on the parties who were on the right and left flanks, on which the whole detachment made ready, and notwithstanding all the opposition made by the officers, they threw away their fire, when, I am certain, scarcely two of the men could be seen by them.

Like Dumas, Gage clearly had something to gain by writing as he did. One was attempting to glorify his role in a victory, the other to minimize his responsibility for a defeat. In the end, neither reporter's effort is entirely persuasive. But if we restrict ourselves to their respective accounts of the opening moments of battle, we find that Gage holds up as a source slightly better than does Dumas. One key question here involves the sequence of events. According to Gordon and Croghan, the British made the opening volley, but Dunbar, Cholmley's Batman, and Cameron, as well as most French sources, support Gage in his claim that Beaujeu's men fired first. On this question of sequence, the evidence against him is not strong enough for us to reject his testimony. The same can be said on the question of whether the advance party panicked from the start. Gordon says no, but this in itself is not enough to discredit Gage. However, it does appear that he, like Dumas, though not to the same extent, exaggerates the amount of time involved.

Even if we treat with skepticism Gage's assertion that panic spread within the advance party before the enemy opened fire, we may conclude that soon after the battle began this key detachment started to disintegrate. During the first moments of action, at least, the enemy fire was deadly, a fact revealed in the testimony of almost everyone who was in the advance party or in a position to observe it. Gates claimed that during the first ten minutes of battle the enemy made such good use of its time "that fifteen out of eighteen Officers [in the advance party] were kill'd and wounded and half the 300 men that composed it." Dunbar supports him with his claim that before help arrived "most of our advanced Party were laid sprawling on the ground."

Gage's detachment writhed under the withering enemy fire. For a few minutes the men held their ground, then fell back— those who could. Perhaps, as Gage says, the retreat was disorderly, the first step in a process that would culminate with almost the entire army crushed together like an accordion:

This fire [the wild barrage by Gage's troops] killed several of our men on the flanking parties, who came running in on the detachment, as did also the vanguard, which completed our confusion. The enemy took advantage of it by coming round us covered by trees, behind which they fired with such success that most of us [officers] were in a short time killed or wounded, as also many of the men, and the rest gave way.

Gordon gives the impression of a more disciplined retreat, carried out under orders, presumably those of Gage himself. But
the difference between the two accounts is basically on the degree of disorder, for neither implies neatness:

The Indians Making their Appearance upon the Rising Ground on
our Right, occasion'd an Order for Retiring the Advanc'd Body 50 or
60 paces, there they confusedly form'd again, & a Good many of their
Officers were kill'd & wounded by the Indians, who had got possession
of the Rising Ground on the Right. There was an Alarum at this time
that the Enemy were attacking the Baggage in the Rear, which Occasion'd a second Retreat of the Advanc'd party.

We have noted references by both Gordon and Gage to "the
rising ground on the right." This was the hillock that Gage had
neglected to secure when he passed it earlier that afternoon.
Now it served the French and Indians as a vantage point from
which to pour fire down on the British.

Thus, within perhaps fifteen minutes of the first fire, we find
the enemy in a half-moon, almost entirely concealed behind
trees and perhaps in a trench to the fore, and in possession of a
strategic knoll. We also find the advance party in retreat, bearing with it the remnants of its vanguard and outscouts.

But of course Gage's detachment could retreat only so far.
Soon it backed into the working party. Strangely, few of our
reporters mention this collision, and there is in fact a tendency
on the part of eyewitnesses to speak of the "vanguard" in a
broad sense, rather than of the detachments composing it.
Even our best source, St. Clair, is not as specific as we might
wish, for he notes only that "on those in my front falling back
upon me, I ran to the front to see what the matter was." If we
credit this testimony entirely (and there is no reason not to), we
find another suggestion that the retreat of the advance party
took place early in the battle: St. Clair appears not to have had
time to send an aide up for intelligence.

The various parties composing the vanguard were now inter-
twined and helpless before the enemy barrage. In all probability, the mass retreated again; but before dealing with this

question we should concern ourselves with what was going on in the main body.

How did Braddock himself react at the first sound of gunfire? British A states that he advanced to the fore, and quickly: "At the first of the firing the General who was at the head of the detachment came to the front." Furnis supports him fully: "The General who was about a quarter of a Mile Distant, immediately advanced with the Troops and drew up in an open place, when the Action became general." We have here two points—that Braddock himself led his troops to the fore, and that he did so at first firing. On the weight of the evidence, it seems that British A and Furnis are incorrect on both scores, owing perhaps to their limited perspective.

To deal with the second question first, it seems clear that Braddock's response was not instantaneous and, in fact, may have been dilatory—at least in the opinion of some. Dunbar and Cholmley's Batman both claim that before reinforcements arrived, most men in the advance party were already wounded. So does Gates, who in apparent anger claims that "the Vanguard was near ten minutes engaged before the main body came up." Indeed, it appears that Gates's estimate of ten minutes is low. Assuming that the main body did not meet the vanguard until the latter was already in retreat, it is possible that this particular action took place more than twenty minutes after the first firing. As we shall see, such an assumption is justified.

Thus far, all of the eyewitnesses we have heard from in this chapter were, at the start of action, definitely or probably in the vanguard. Naturally, they have been the ones to look to for insight into the behavior of those who bore the brunt of the early fighting. But when we ask how Braddock conducted himself at the outset, we should look first to the eyewitnesses nearest to him.

Of all our eyewitnesses, Washington and Orme are the two best situated to describe the general's reactions. The young Virginian unfortunately has nothing to say on this question, but he does implicitly back the account given by his older comrade, who is both vehement and, for the most part, precise. According to Orme, at the first firing,

the General imagining the advanced parties were very warmly attacked, and being willing to free himself from the incumbrance of the baggage, order'd Lieutenant Colonel Burton to reinforce them with the vanguard, and the line to halt. According to this disposition, eight hundred men were detached from the line, free from all embarrassments, and four hundred were left for the defence of the Artillery and baggage, posted in such a manner as to secure them from any attack or insults.[8]

Aside from his closing comment that Braddock positioned his men "in such a manner as to secure them from any attack or insults," Orme's version is clear. However, perhaps his reference to the numbers involved requires some elaboration. He does not mean that eight hundred men were to be detached from the main body and sent forth under Burton. Indeed, there were only about five hundred in that unit. Rather, he is saying that Braddock had decided to divide his army. Eight hundred, including perhaps three hundred from the main body and the entire vanguard, would march forward, Burton in command, in some sort of counterattack. Presumably, he intended to call up the rear guard, and perhaps bring in some of the flanking parties, in order that they might help the remnant of the main body to guard the baggage. In the former case, we shall see that he did indeed give such an order.

Naturally, it took time for Burton to prepare his detachment. How the main body was divided is not known, but any such division must have been complicated, and the troops cannot have been ordered and ready to march until at least ten minutes had elapsed. Even then, it would have been necessary to march them forward for about four hundred yards before they could meet the vanguard. But some, like Gates, were in no mood to be patient.

Having seen Burton safely on his way, we follow him into what was perhaps the most controversial event of the battle.

What can be established by consensus is that after he had advanced almost one quarter of a mile his forces collided with those of Gage and St. Clair, which were retreating in confusion. The point in dispute is whether his detachment was a viable fighting force at the moment of impact.

Here again, Orme gives specific testimony: "The advanced detachments soon gave way and fell back upon Lieutenant Colonel Burton's detachment, who was forming his men to face a rising ground upon the right." It might at first glance seem implausible that Burton would have halted his detachment to prepare it for an attack on the rising ground, in view of the fact that Braddock had ordered him to take command of the vanguard and then advance against the enemy. But actually the account is entirely credible in this respect, and Orme is probably relating the testimony of his good friend Burton, who unfortunately does not appear to have left a report of his own. That the collision took place beside the hillock is confirmed by Mackellar's sketch. Gates also tends to support Orme on this point, though, as we shall see, he at the same time questions his version in another area: "The main body . . . on the Van Guards being attacked moved up in a line of march [and] were flank'd on both sides by the enemy which caused an immediate confusion." This testimony suggests Burton's motive for taking a new initiative. As he advanced, his detachment was fired on, with success sufficient to threaten its viability. The most deadly volley of all probably came from the rising ground. Burton may have felt that leaving the enemy in control of such a strategic point would allow it to divide the army, once he and the vanguard had pressed on ahead. He may also have believed that his men could not successfully run the gantlet. Or perhaps he thought that by taking the hill he could divide the enemy force and throw it into confusion. In any case, the rising ground was probably the greatest strategic advantage held by the French, and we shall see that at least once more that afternoon Burton was to make a heroic attempt to seize it.

While supporting the plausibility of Orme's account in one

respect, Gates challenges it in another. The obvious implication in Orme's statement is that the vanguard was most responsible for destroying Burton's detachment as an effective fighting force. But Gates claims that the detachment was already in a confused state when it came into contact with the vanguard, because of the enemy barrage. Nor is he the only one so to argue.

Orme later encapsulated his version of the affair in a letter published in the *Pennsylvania Gazette*. In this summary, he repeated his charge that it was only because the retreating vanguard had crashed into Burton's detachment that the latter had been thrown into confusion. His letter brought a sharp response, in the form of an advertisement in a later issue of the *Gazette*:

It is thought proper to inform the Publick, that in the Account given of the late Action on the 9th of July, wherein it is said, that the Detachment of Three Hundred (which was the Van Guard of the Army) fell back on the main Body, and put it in such Confusion that no military Expedient could retrieve, is a Mistake; the main Body being in Confusion before it joined the above Detachment.[9]

Gates claims that this entry was the work of "Col. Gage and the Officers of the Van Guard." At the very least, we can easily see the hand of Gage, for his description of Burton's detachment parallels the one he gives in his appended letter to the Earl of Albemarle: "We [of the retreating advance party] found Sir John Sinclair's working party in the same confusion, as also the main body under General Braddock."

Perhaps we should clarify the issue before proceeding. Gage is not saying that the vanguard itself was not disorganized, that Burton's detachment crashed into it, or even that both units were in motion at the time of impact, although on this last point he may be aiming to imply such a condition. All he is specifically claiming is that when the forces collided, the reinforcements were already in a disorganized state. There is a question of culpability here. Gage does not want all of the blame for chaos to fall on the vanguard. Yet it is worth repeating that just because a given eyewitness may have a vested interest in making a particular point as he does, we should not take this to mean that he does not believe his claim to be true. Quite possibly Gage is accurately describing what he feels he saw, and indeed Gates supports him. Orme, on the other hand, probably was not himself an eyewitness to the incident in question. He would also be anxious to make his commander and his friend Burton look good. In this case, he would be free to believe what and whom he wished. The evidence seems to stand against him, but it is far from conclusive.

Again we should recall that no one cited so far has claimed that Burton's detachment was in motion at the moment it encountered the retreating vanguard, much less that it was itself the cause of the collision. However, one reporter insists that both were true. This is British B, who definitely had a greater store of bile in which to dip his pen than any of our other eyewitnesses. Here, drawn from what seems to have been a letter to a friend, is his description of the first moments of battle:

In the front were 500 grenadiers called Halket's grenadiers as choice men as could anywhere be seen. These men bore the first brunt of the fire in the front, till at last both Sir John St. Clair, and Coll. Gage's party were put into the utmost confusion by the Irregularly tumultuous pressing on and crowding of the men behind, who as they were hurried and pushed Irregularly forward, and commanded to march, earnestly requested to be put into some kind of order and instructed how to proceed. You'll perhaps see in some of our newspapers a foolish account from some of the triumvirate, that the foremost ranks falling back upon the rest of the army as yet not formed, threw them into a pannic and Confusion which neither the Intreaties nor threats of the officers could divest them from or persuade them to stand their ground, but this is as false and foolish a gloss as ever was Invented. The affair was quite the reverse and therefore you'll do well not to believe a word of it.

It is entirely possible that British B was not an eyewitness to the collision itself. Not knowing his place in the line of march, we cannot be certain one way or the other. My own guess is that his version is a conglomerate of wild reports, made wilder. In any case, when we weigh the evidence ranged against him, it becomes clear that he is, simply speaking, wrong. Even disregarding Orme's testimony, we have seen that Gage, Gordon, and St. Clair all claim that early in the battle the advance party retreated. To their accounts we may add those of Cameron and Mackellar, who assert, the latter through his maps, that Gage's detachment did indeed fall back. So much for British B's argument that it stood and fought. Gage, by implication, and Mackellar likewise, in his second map, also support Orme's statement that the massed vanguard was in retreat when it met Burton's unit. As we have seen, Orme can be challenged on the question of whether the vanguard was solely responsible for throwing Burton's detachment into disorder. Perhaps, indeed, Burton *was* advancing at the time of the collision. But on balance, British B, and not Orme, should be considered the author of "as false and foolish a gloss as ever was Invented."[10]

British B clearly detested Orme, the apparent head of his "triumvirate." Burton, too, may have been one of his triumvirs. It is therefore not surprising that he by implication blasts both, and particularly Orme. His account serves as a reminder that while we must be on guard against those of Braddock's army who direct their remarks to superiors, lest they mislead us through self-praise, we must not assume that we get "the truth" in private correspondence. We may get extreme recklessness, for eyewitnesses writing to friends and relatives can expect that their accounts will be believed and will not be compared critically with those of others. From British B we get not candor, but calumny.

The troops collided. Disorder spread. Here there is no ambiguity, and we can call our sources at will. Orme: "The whole were now got together in great confusion." Gordon: "Nothing afterwards was to Be Seen Amongst the Men But Confusion & Panick."

Panic. This is the key word. Did the men now panic?

That there was confusion does not mean that there was panic. It would be desirable to hear the testimony of "common soldiers" to see if they were willing to accuse their comrades of cowardice. Unfortunately, the evidence here is thin. We have only two eyewitnesses who fall into this category, and the reminiscence of one, Cameron, is almost worthless. His account of the action is straightforward enough: "Our Officers as well as Men generally behaved well." But where was he when the army telescoped? By his own testimony, he was wounded during the first moments of battle, and lost consciousness. While he lay stunned, the advance party retreated, so that when he regained his senses he found himself alone. Fortunately, he was able to conceal himself in a hollow tree nearby. The implication of his story is that he was unconscious during the few minutes that were to decide the battle. Even if he had made his escape, he was far from the action and could see only bits of it through a knothole. So much for him.

The account given by Cholmley's Batman is much more useful. He does by implication note the milling together of the troops that most eyewitnesses associate with panic: "We was drawn up in large Bodies together, a ready mark." However, by "large Bodies" he may merely be referring to troops in formation. Moreover, far from describing hysteria, he sees heroism in the conduct of his fellows: "Having only death before us made the men fight Almost longer than they was able." Nor is he alone in claiming that some of the men behaved well, or even heroically. Leslie relates that after Captain John Conyngham was wounded, his men "seeing his danger rushed between the savages and him and carried him in triumph from the spot."

On the question of whether the troops by and large panicked, French accounts are very little help. Most of them are vague in describing the conduct of Braddock's forces. Dumas himself is, however, pointed in his reference to British behavior: "The enemy was attacked on all sides, but fought with an unyielding stubbornness." Those reporters who normally rely on him echo the statement. But we must look more deeply here. Dumas was from the beginning out to make the most of his triumph. The battle represented his hour of glory. It had to be in all ways a great victory. Moreover, his main account was, as noted earlier, directed to a superior. The writer was eager to defend himself against his critics and also to win favor, perhaps a promotion. Clearly he was not going to do this by making his victory seem to have been a mere massacre. How impressed would Machault have been to read that "no sooner had we begun our counterattack than the enemy ranks disintegrated, and for three hours we butchered the helpless mass?" Naturally, it would be to Dumas's advantage to play up Braddock's army as a worthy antagonist. I note this merely to suggest a motive for mnemonic refraction. Quite likely Dumas believed what he wrote, and he may have been impressed by the fact that, no matter how poorly, the British had stood up to his forces for three hours. But this still does not suggest that his account is accurate.

Now to return to the British side. As we might expect, most of the officers at least imply that the troops panicked, and none denies it. British B, Dunbar, Gage, Gordon, and Orme are particularly pointed in their testimony. In weighing it, we should again note the question of self-interest. By blaming the disasters of that day on panicky troops, Orme could exculpate his beloved commander. By similar means, Gage could clear of any possible charges one still dearer to his heart—himself. British B, through his account of how the collision of detachments took place, managed to throw the blame for the ensuing hysteria back on Braddock and his favorites. Beyond this, all five had the bias of 'class." Provided that their recollections and integrity allowed them sufficient leeway, they were likely to blame the common soldiers rather than the officers, for the latter would represent, even in the case of Gordon, a peer group. Without challenging their testimony, let us at least look further.

Stephen is certainly specific in his account of how the men behaved:

The British Troops were thunderstruck to feel the Effect of a heavy Fire, & see no Enemy; they threw away their Fire in a most indiscreet Manner, and shamefully turned their Backs on a few Savages and Canadeans. . . . They kept in a mere huddle in spite of the most ardent Endeavours of many brave officers. . . . Shame unto the infamous Dogs!

Unfortunately, for all his vehemence, Stephen is not reliable on the point in question. He was, we should recall, a member of the rear guard. At the time the collision took place, he was probably just approaching the rear of the wagon train, which he was to help cover. Therefore, he was about one-half mile from the point of impact. Undoubtedly he saw panic-stricken men during the course of the afternoon, and heard numerous accounts, Washington's among others, of what had happened up ahead during the first minutes of battle. But he did not himself see this action.

Taking into account the question of perspective, Washington is a much better source. He may not have been at the scene when the collision took place; but, as we shall see, he was there soon after. There are other reasons for liking him as an eyewitness. He sent his various reports of the day's action not to superiors, but to friends and relatives, the one exception being Dinwiddie. Washington was not looking for favor, and indeed at this point in his life he was by no means committed to a military career, though he was leaving his options open. Certainly he was not without his biases, but they are not relevant on the point in question. As for the fact that he was young and somewhat inexperienced, this is immaterial. When an eyewitness observes panic, he knows it.

And Washington did indeed observe panic. In his recollection, at an unspecified point early in the fighting, the British regulars "were . . . struck with such a deadly Panick, that nothing but confusion and disobedience of order's prevail'd amongst them."[11] He does not claim that disintegration came about as a result of telescoping or even at the time this occurred. In fact, Orme is the only reporter to suggest that it was the collision that threw the men into a frenzy, and even he implies that the vanguard had been collapsing prior to this point. However, the implication on all hands is that panic set in no *later* than the moment when the vanguard and Burton's detachment crashed together.

Even when we take into account the bias of the officers, the weight of evidence tends very strongly toward the conclusion that most of the troops, or at least the British regulars, panicked early. First, there is the overwhelming testimony of the officers. If we ignore that—a course which could really be justified only by persuasive evidence that they are decisively misrepresenting the situation—we are still left with Washington. Finally, there is the common-sense approach. As we shall see, in about three hours of fighting, the British mounted few counterthrusts, and apparently none involving more than one hundred men—despite constant attempts to rally the troops. True, many officers were quickly incapacitated, but those remaining could certainly have mounted a significant attack, provided that there were sufficient men to follow them. In fact, however, few did follow, and the only satisfactory explanation for their timidity is panic.

We now pass on to the next question. What caused the panic? There is no simple answer. First, we should take into account the views supposedly expressed by the troops themselves. In the autumn of 1755, Shirley directed Gage and Colonel Dunbar to report on why the men had behaved as they had during the battle. The two officers later summarized what they claimed to be the testimony of the regulars who had fought. In trying to justify their behavior, these participants had purportedly stated:

1st: They were greatly Harrass'd by dutys unequal to their Numbers, Dispirited by Want of Sufficient Provisions, and not allowed time to dress the little they had, with nothing to Drink but Water, and that Often Scarce and Bad.

2d: The frequent Conversations of the Provincial Troops and Country People was, that if they engaged the Indians in their European Manner of fighting, they would be Beat, and this some of their Officers

Declared as their Opinion, and one of them to Coll Dunbar on the Retreat, for which he Severely Reprimanded him.

3d: The Want of Indians or other irregulars to give timely Notice of the Enemy's Approach, having only three or four guides for our Scouts. Lastly the Novelty of an invisible enemy and the Nature of the Country, which was entirely a Forest.[12]

The statement that the troops were taxed beyond their powers is too vague to analyze, although it may refer to the hardships of the march. Dealing with a more specific point, it may well be true that the men were short of provisions. Cholmley's Batman mentions that when, on the morning of battle, the troops halted for breakfast, few of them had anything to eat.[13] And certainly the march had been exhausting, especially for those without previous experience in the wilderness. But neither hunger nor fatigue is an adequate explanation for the mass panic, especially since these same men were apparently in high spirits just before confronting the enemy.[14]

Next we arrive at the question of what role the provincials may have played. Generally historians have had nothing but praise for the Americans who fought under Braddock, and in truth it seems fair to say that during the action they behaved much better on the whole than did the regulars. But it is also entirely possible that they played a large role in bringing about the panic that destroyed Braddock's army. We have already heard the testimony of Cholmley's Batman that the men fought on doggedly, knowing that if they were captured they would be submitted to "Barbarous Usage" by the enemy. Evidently by this he means torture, and who but the provincials, particularly the backwoodsmen, would have filled the men with such a fear? Quite likely their horrific tales so sensitized the regulars that when they were suddenly confronted by Beaujeu's Indian force they were reduced to the level of instinct—the instinct for self-preservation. British A makes this point emphatically: "The men from what storys they had heard of the Indians, in regard to their scalping; and mohawking, were so panick Struck, that their officers had little or no Command over them."[15]

The fact of the moment would not compromise with fiction. The Americans' stories were coming true. All around the troops, in every direction, was the savage enemy. Perhaps if the men had faced only a French army, even in this situation, they would have held firm. Perhaps. What can be said with certainty is that it was specifically the Indian presence that spread terror. The men knew they were out there, unseen but seeing them all too clearly, planning their destruction. Their scalps would be trophies, their torture, sport. Even in the first moments of battle, an occasional Indian might be seen as he darted from behind a tree, scalped a dead or wounded soldier who lay off to the side, and disappeared again into his hiding place. And the war cries, the incessant, infernal din! There could be no mercy here. This was indeed an inhuman enemy, implacable, demonic. The men shuddered at the sound. Leslie would later write that "the yell of the Indians is fresh on my ear, and the terrific sound will haunt me until the hour of my dissolution."[16]

The Americans, with their tales of terror, had done much to bring on the panic. But presumably they had not intended only to frighten the men. They had rather wished to counsel them in the "ways of the Indian." They were as contemptuous of Braddock's regular tactics as he was of theirs. They could not persuade him or the British officers under his command that the Indian must be fought in his own way. But they might be able to convince their comrades "that if they engaged the Indians in their European Manner of fighting, they would be Beat." If they could do this, the men might listen to their advice on how to fight.

The battle was on now. There was no time to educate. Perhaps all that remained from the backwoodsmen's stories was a residue of fear. But still they worked to save the situation—and in so doing spread further panic. British A notes that with the first firing "the American Troops tho' without any orders ran up immediately, some behind Trees, and others into the Ranks, and put the whole into confusion."[17] That some Americans moved behind trees is beyond dispute, as we shall see. But why might others have disrupted the force, apparently on purpose? Probably to tell the men to take cover. If so—and British A's claim that some Americans ran through the ranks is quite plausible—they may have done more harm than good. The men were geared not only to regular tactics, but more generally to obedience. Of course, one can scarcely claim that they were behaving as they were supposed to. But they could still hear the commands of their superiors, who were ordering them to stay in line. Then, too, while the trees might mean safety, they could also mean danger, for that was where the Indians were. There was a temptation to follow the Americans, however, and although few of the regulars did, their contrasting emotions and instincts quite possibly increased their confusion.

There were undoubtedly many factors involved in the panic, and of course not all of the troops were affected for identical reasons. Possibly there is something to the claim that "the Want of Indians or other irregulars to give timely Notice of the Enemy's Approach" was a factor in the frenzy. This suggests that because the enemy was on them so suddenly, the troops lacked time to prepare themselves mentally for combat. There is some evidence to support such an argument. Certainly the men appear to have been in high spirits as they marched north from the river, largely because of their apparent confidence that they would not be attacked, the enemy having failed to contest their crossing. Perhaps the shock of confrontation did indeed unnerve them.

The telescoping may also have played some part. As the detachments crushed together, Braddock's troops became separated from their immediate superiors, and also lost their places in the order of march. The typical British private was a product of a system of discipline aimed at developing in him a new set of instincts. His reaction to orders was to be not reasoned, but involuntary. For his company to function as a unit, he had to know his place, and this meant knowing who belonged on his right and who on his left. Suddenly, with the collision of forces, the troops became separated from their officers and their comrades. They were now lost, although surrounded by humanity. And one may well imagine that such men, inexperienced and confused, would have panicked when deprived of the steadying leadership of those in command.[18]

Of course, it was not only the telescoping that separated officers and men. Even during the first few minutes of fighting, a significant proportion of the former were killed or incapacitated. Their distinctive uniforms singled them out to the enemy. Those who were mounted were in particular danger, as one may gather from Stewart's testimony that of the twenty-nine in his unit of light horse, all but four were killed during the battle. Finally, it is possible that many of the officers recklessly—as well as heroically—exposed themselves before the enemy in a vain attempt to rally their forces. According to Dunbar, the officers, hoping to draw the troops out of the disordered mass that had resulted from collision and panic, "advanced into the front, & soon became the mark of the Enemy, who scarce left one, that was not killed or wounded." An army like Braddock's, geared to discipline and frankly opposed to individual initiative on the part of common soldiers, had to suffer considerable loss of order when the influence of a large number of officers was removed in such a brief span of time. It is noteworthy that the advance party, whose retreat marked the real beginning of disaster, was particularly hard-hit during the first few minutes. As we have seen, Gates himself claims that fifteen of eighteen officers in that detachment were dead or wounded before reinforcements arrived. We can well imagine the confusion and terror of the men as their superiors fell one by one. In the working party, St. Clair himself was among the first wounded, and, by his own testimony, he was unconscious for most of the battle.[19] Perhaps this played its part in the retreat of his detachment.

As we can see, the eyewitnesses themselves suggest various reasons for the mass panic, and common sense provides others. But time and again our reporters return to the point that the troops were shocked by the nature of the enemy. Judging from the evidence, it seems most of all to have been fear of an inhuman and unseen foe that within a few minutes destroyed the discipline Braddock had worked so hard to engender, and drove his men to huddle like sheep.[20]

What had minutes before been a proud army was now a frightened mass. Several factors—the loss of many officers, the telescoping, and panic—had brought the troops to this sorry situation. But their terror alone precluded a reordering. "Such was the confusion, that the men were sometimes 20 or 30 deep, and he thought himself securest, who was in the Center." So says British A, with both the implicit consensus of eyewitnesses and common sense to support him.[21] Enough officers remained active to coordinate a rally, were the men willing to be rallied. And now Braddock himself took the lead.

Seeing his forces on the point of total disintegration, the general rode ahead. According to Orme, after Braddock sent Burton's detachment forward, he ordered an aide-de-camp to ride to the front "to bring him an account of the nature of attack, but the fire continuing, he moved forward himself, leaving Sr Peter Halket with the command of the baggage." Orme's account is reasonable, and he was in a good position to observe what he relates. It also helps to explain why a few eyewitnesses in the vanguard mistakenly claim that the general himself, rather than Burton, led reinforcements to the front. On the basis of Orme's testimony, it is even possible to conjecture that Braddock was already on the scene at the time of the collision, though more probably he arrived shortly thereafter, likely followed by remnants of the main body.

The courage he was to show in the heat of battle would win the praise not only of his admirers, but of his critics as well. He would have been easy enough for the enemy to single out, in his gaudy uniform, on horseback, racing wildly back and forth to the perimeters of action. Bullets whistled past him. Horse after horse was shot out from under him—some eyewitnesses say four, others five.[22] Always he remounted, always he rode on, desperately trying to rally his troops. He failed in his efforts, but enough sources report that one may judge how he hoped to stem the chaos. Orme gives the clearest account: "The whole were now got together in great confusion. The colours were advanced in different places, to separate the men of the two regiments. The General ordered the officers to endeavour to form the men, and to tell them off into small divisions and to advance with them; but neither entreaties nor threats could prevail." The statement that officers advanced the colours in an attempt to help the troops sort themselves out is Orme's alone, but no one contradicts it, and it is entirely plausible. His claim that Braddock ordered the men divided into small parties—or, as some would have it, platoons—is supported by Stephen and by British A. In all probability, the general hoped to divide and redivide his men, in two or more stages, first by regiment, finally by platoon.

In his attempts to rally the forces, Braddock was well served by the officers under his command. It is scarcely surprising that the eyewitnesses who report generally have nothing but praise for the officers as a whole, considering that with few exceptions they themselves are spokesmen for that class. Some of them, like Gage, are clearly self-serving, and try to leave no doubt as to their own coolness under fire. Others, however, seem to have less to gain through their praise. They commend particular officers with no apparent motive other than to recognize courage. Thus we see Gordon singling out Burton as one who behaved with exceptional valor.[23] But probably more convincing is the fact that the army did stand its ground for more than two hours, despite the evident terror of the troops. Had the officers themselves panicked, their men, Braddock notwithstanding, would probably have followed them in headlong retreat.

As it was, the heroism of Braddock and his subordinates accomplished little. This was due primarily to the panic of the regulars and the unwillingness of the troops in general to take the offensive. If the men did not retreat, neither would they advance.

Some few do appear to have attacked—in their own way.

Early in the battle, a high proportion of the Americans had scrambled behind trees, intent on fighting Indian style. Their number included almost the whole of the rear guard. Our only indication of how the rear guard behaved during the battle comes from Mackellar, who in his second map reveals the men of that detachment "divided (round the rear of the Convoy, now closed up) behind Trees having been attacked by a few Indians." Mackellar would probably not have been in a position to know this from personal observation, but he would have received the testimony of Stephen and other officers at the scene. Although there is no way of being certain, it is probable that the rear guard, when first attacked, fought in a conventional manner, under the command of Halket. But when the colonel was killed, within minutes of his meeting with Braddock, his men reverted to the style of fighting they knew best, which they considered perfectly suited to the situation.[24]

We have seen that the majority of those Americans who had joined Braddock at Fort Cumberland were riffraff, specifically eastern-shore riffraff, not the sort who would have been familiar with forest fighting technique. Yet, those who were now fighting the Indians on their own terms appear to have known what they were doing and, in fact, seem to have been fairly successful. Of course, many, particularly those recruited by the regiments, undoubtedly panicked with their British brethren. But the proportion of Americans who not only fought Indian style but did so with apparent expertise is impressive. Perhaps Braddock had left the weaker provincial units with Colonel Dunbar and had kept the better fighters, unaware that they would use irregular tactics in a situation such as this.

The general fought their inclination. He was not about to allow the Americans, or his regulars, to vanish into the forest. Perhaps he feared particularly that the provincials would set a bad example for the rest of the men. Be that as it may, he strove mightily to get them back into line. Among our twenty-two basic eyewitnesses, only Cholmley's Batman refers to his attempts, and even he is not as specific as we might wish. Our main source in this regard is James Burd, who wrote a letter to Governor Morris in which he related an account of the action, given him by Colonel Dunbar. According to Dunbar, after the early attempts to dislodge the enemy had proven fruitless, "the Soldiers . . . insisted much to be allowed to take to the Trees, which the General denied and stormed much, calling them Cowards, and even went so far as to strike them with his own Sword for attempting the Trees." Despite the fact that this is a thirdhand account, and that Dunbar may have wanted to put Braddock in a bad light, the statement seems to be for the most part accurate.[25] The general would certainly have "stormed much" at those who took to the trees. Whether he called them cowards or struck them is less certain, but not at all improbable. He was never known to be even-tempered.

All elements in the scenario of battle were now present. The regulars were crammed into a small area and were desperately striving for the sanctuary of the center.[26] Their officers, and most of all their general, were hoping against hope to rally them. It had taken the army only about one-half hour to get itself into this sorry state. For the next two hours, the situation would remain almost static. What few developments were to come during this time would favor the enemy. And all the while, Braddock's men would be dying.

When the vanguard had retreated in confusion, it had abandoned the two six-pounders that Gage had earlier left with St. Clair on the assumption that they would not be needed. As one might expect, the French soon moved out of their hiding places at the front, seized the small cannon, retreated to a point of sanctuary, and turned them against their erstwhile owners. There is no way of knowing precisely when this occurred, but it was probably not long after the British had collapsed into chaos.[27]

This seizure of the British artillery added a new dimension to the adversary's power to kill. Historical tradition to the contrary, it is possible that Braddock, seeing his troops helpless before the enemy barrage, ordered a retreat. According to

Orme, "When the General found it impossible to persuade them to advance, and no enemy appeared in view; and nevertheless a vast number of officers were killed, by exposing themselves before the men; he endeavored to retreat them in good order; but the panic was so great that he could not succeed." British A claims, more cryptically, that "within about two hours and a half, the men were obliged to (at least did) retreat 3 or 4 times, and were as often rallied." Perhaps it was Braddock who ordered these retreats, in the hope that once clear of the worst of the enemy fire the men might regroup for a counterattack. But the panic did not abate.

Even if there was no attempted retreat, there was action. In his second map, Mackellar attempts to portray the British, with the exception of the rear guard, "joined, with little or no order, but endeavouring to make Fronts towards the Enemys Fire." Soldiers do not "make Fronts" of their own volition, though they may shoot wildly. To make a front requires coordination to a degree that can be produced only by order. Therefore, what Mackellar probably means is that at least some of the men responded when their superiors ordered them to form. Such a statement would accord very well with our other reports, for it would imply not only that the officers were ordering countermeasures, but that the men were to some extent responding. Indeed, Mackellar goes on to claim that the British sought "to recover the Guns and to gain the Hill to no purpose." In the context of other accounts, this may be taken to mean that they tried but failed. Still, even if they only *tried,* it shows some willingness on the part of the men to take offensive action.

Why did they fail? Gage provides a clue, and in this case his testimony is entirely credible.

General Braddock tried all methods to draw the men out of this confusion, made several efforts to recover the cannon, as also to drive the enemy from our flanks, as likewise to gain possession of the hill already mentioned. Some few men were at times prevailed on to draw out for this purpose, but before they had marched twenty yards, would fall back into a line of march by files, and proceed to attack in this manner, till an officer, or perhaps a man or two, should be struck down, and then the rest immediately gave way; the men would never make one bold attack, though encouraged to it by the enemy always giving way, whenever they advanced even on the most faint attack.

What Gage is saying essentially is that only a few men were willing to leave the comparative safety of their huddle in order to move against the terrifying enemy, that even they were generally not willing to follow orders to form, thinking first in terms of their own well-being, and that the slightest reverse would send them hurtling back to the security of the mass. There is considerable evidence to support his assessment, and we shall soon encounter one vivid case of the kind he describes.[28]

While the British army disintegrated, enemy ambitions rose. That morning, the French appear to have hoped only to repel the invaders. Now they seemed intent on annihilating them. Or perhaps it was not they at all who were determining the flow of battle. Perhaps the Indians were in control. For all of Dumas's trumpeting, it is quite possible that his orders were of little importance, and that the warriors raced down the British flanks of their own accord. Such a tactic was typical. As Dr. Thomas Smith wrote a decade later, the Indians always fought "scattered, and never in a compact body." Smith, himself not a military man but one with strong army contacts, also asserted that "their general maxim is to surround their enemy." Here we recognize a possible blueprint for the strategy that engulfed Braddock's army.

Our French informants unfortunately have little to say of tactics. This oversight leaves us with British testimony and the obvious drawback that we are dealing with men who did not know what the enemy was thinking. Furthermore, the clearest source, Cholmley's Batman, is not the most desirable, for he was by no means an experienced battlefield reporter. But he could at least relate his impression that the Indians in particular were seeking to surround the British.

According to him, during the first moments of battle the

advance party faced extermination: "Immediately they began to Ingage us in a half Moon and still Continued Surrounding us more and more. Before the whole of the Army got up we had about two thirds of our men Cut of [f] that Ingaged at the First." This tactic he mentions again in discussing a later aspect of the battle: "They begin to Inclose us more and more till they had Nigh Inclosed us in." Finally, viewing the last moments of action, he notes that he "expected Nothing but death for Every Oone of us, for they had us surround[ed] all but a little in the Rear, which they strove for with all their Force." Likewise, Gordon comments that at the onset of fighting the Indians "fell upon the flank partys, which only consisted of an officer & 20 men, who were very soon Cut off." This corroborates the testimony of Cholmley's Batman to some extent—apparently the Indians from the start followed a policy of divide and massacre. Common sense also suggests that the enemy sought to surround the British. After all, once the telescoping had taken place, almost the whole of Braddock's army was wedged into an area perhaps two hundred yards in length. The rear guard, although separate, was small and about half a mile behind—hardly in a position to break a cordon. To surround the beleaguered British was an obvious maneuver that the enemy forces apparently sought to effect. Their failure may have been due primarily to the artillery that the British yet retained.[29] So passed two hours, the officers attempting to rally their men, the French and Indians seeking to surround their enemy in order to administer the coup de grace, chaos the rule.

On every side Braddock's troops fell, victims of the folly of frightened men. Certainly the French and Indians were responsible for many deaths, but the evidence is overwhelming that more British soldiers were killed by their comrades than by the enemy. British D goes so far as to claim that some of those who fired at their officers did so not in confusion, but out of malice: "In Spight of what the Officers and bravest Men could do, Numbers ran away, nay fired on us, that would have forced them to rally."[30] Generally, however, the eyewitnesses suggest that the men in their panic fired wildly. British A presents perhaps the most vivid picture:

If any got a shot at [an Indian], the fire immediately ran through the whole Line, tho' they saw nothing but Trees; The whole Detachment was frequently divided into several parties, and then they were sure to fire on one another. the greatest part of the men who were behind trees, were either kill'd or wounded by our own People, even one or two officers were killed by their own Platoon.

His testimony is corroborated by such disparate sources as Washington, Croghan, Gage, and Dunbar. And possibly the most impressive support of all comes from British B, who is on so many other points a maverick:

The Confusion and destruction was so great, that the men fired irregularly, one behind another, and by this way of proceeding many more of our men were killed by their own party than by the Enimy, as appeared afterwards by the bullets that the surgeons extracted from the wounded, they being distinguished from the french and Indian bullets by their size. . . . Among the wounded men, there were two for one of these bullets extracted by the Surgeons, and the wounds were chiefly in the back parts of the body, so it must also been among the kill'd.[31]

Perhaps one incident points up more clearly than any other the extent of panic. British C relates that "Capt. Waggoner, with 170 Virginians, went up to where the Enemy was hid and routed them: But O unhappy! our Infatuateds seeing a Smoke, fired and killed him with several of his Men." He is wrong in claiming that the unfortunate captain was Thomas Waggoner, who in fact escaped from the battle unscathed. He may mean Lieutenant Edmund Waggoner, who was killed in some way, or perhaps Captain William de Peyronie, who apparently died in the tragic fashion described here. British C's account is otherwise quite plausible. Panic-stricken men, desperate to see the barest sign of an enemy that seemed invisible, would likely have shot in the direction of any puff of smoke. The Americans, concealed behind trees, were obvious targets. Such was the price of courage.

After two hours of hopeless confusion and death, the British made a final attempt to seize the strategic rising ground. Gordon provides the fullest description:

The General Order'd the officers to Endeavor to tell off 150 men, & Advance up the hill to Dispossess the Enemy, & another party to Advance on the Left to support the two 12 pounders & Artillery people, who were in great Danger of Being Drove away By the Enemy, at that time in possession of the 2 field pieces of the Advanc'd party. This was the Generals Last Order. . . . All the Officers us'd their Utmost Endeavors to Get the men to Advance up the hill, & to Advance on the left to support the Cannon. But the Enemy's fire at the time very much Encreasing, & a Number of officers who were Rushing on in the front to Encourage the men Being killed & wounded, there was Nothing to Be seen But the Utmost panick & Confusion amongst the Men.

British A and Orme present material that elaborates on Gordon's version. It was undoubtedly Burton who led the forces that attempted to seize the rising ground. When he was wounded, along with several others, his troops broke and ran. If we accept Gage's account, noted earlier, it appears that this was just one of several such attacks, all of which were stymied in similar fashion.

It was by now shortly after four o'clock.[32] The battle had raged for more than three hours. Many soldiers had already fled. These included the wagoners, who, according to several eyewitnesses, had unharnessed the horses and ridden off on them, dampening any remaining hope the British had of advancing, should they somehow break through the enemy lines.[33]

Suddenly, Braddock's army was in retreat, in a rout! Suddenly, after these long hours of chaos and death, the troops, willing to stand no more, were striving madly for the sanctuary of the river!

Why had they suddenly broken, after having for so long held their ground? The most obvious reason is that Braddock himself had fallen wounded. No fewer than eight sources note that the rout began only moments after he was shot. It would be difficult not to see some link between the two.

Mackellar gives us two other incidents that may have played a part in causing the retreat. According to him, "the British were at length beat from the Guns. The General was wounded soon after. They were lastly beat back across the Hollow way and made no farther Stand." The guns referred to are three twelve-pounders originally held by the main body. None of the evidence would suggest that the French actually turned these cannon against their former owners, as they had the six-pounders in the front, but perhaps they did; in any case, the frightening potential was there. Mackellar's reference to the "Hollow way" is to a furrow that had bisected the army at the start of battle, and over which Burton's detachment had marched in its attempt to relieve the vanguard. In his statement that the army was beaten back beyond the hollow way, Mackellar may have misunderstood what was going on. Rather than marking the onset of rout, this withdrawal appears to have been a strategic move to protect the baggage until an orderly retreat could be effected. Gage relates that

many of the men began to go off, and the General was wounded; what remained, was to endeavour to cover the retreat of the ammunition and provisions, but those that drove the horses went off with them. The men that covered the wagons went off by tens and twenties, till reduced to a very small body, which, receiving a fire from the enemy, went to the right-about, and the whole were put to flight.

Gordon provides still a third account. To his memory, after Burton had been wounded and his attempt to seize the rising ground had failed,

those officers who had Been wounded having Return'd, and those that were not Wounded, By Exhorting & threatning had influence to keep a Body about 200 an hour longer in the field, but cou'd not perswade them Either to attempt the hill again, or Advance far Enough to support the Cannon, whose officers & men were Mostly kill'd and wounded. The Cannon silenc'd, & the Indians shouts upon the Right

Advancing, the whole Body gave way, & Crossed the Monongahela where we had pass'd in the Morning.

The engineer's version is not so unique as it may seem. Like Gage, he substantially claims that many men had already fled the scene by this late hour. Gordon, in fact, suggests that a preponderant majority of those who were able had taken flight. Like Gage also, he implies that the men were in essence ordered to retreat,[34] that they might cover the guns. Gordon says "advance," but this would depend on perspective. The cannon in question were, presumably, the three twelve-pounders that Mackellar suggests had been lost before Braddock was wounded. Perhaps Gordon is mistaken in suggesting that they were still in British hands, but it is more probable that Mackellar is confused in his ordering of events, since sequence is such a common source of error.

On the question of time, it appears that Gordon is exaggerating. Virtually all other sources suggest that once the retreat began in earnest, it quickly developed into a rout. We would expect the officers to present a picture of precipitate flight, but not even Cholmley's Batman refutes them. On the contrary, he reports that the Indians "prosued us Better than a mile and Cut many of [f] in going through the River. All the wounded that Could not walk fell in the Enemyis hands but was given no Quarters." All of the reporters who refer to the retreat do so in like fashion, to the point where we can almost sense the terror of the troops as they fled, Indians at their heels, desperate hope for mere survival governing their actions. Perhaps British A gives the most vivid account. In his recollection, the men "made a most precipitate Retreat, every one trying who should be the first. the Enemy pursued us, butchering as they came, as far as the other side of the River; in crossing it they shot many in the water, both men and women, scalping and cutting them in a most Barbarous manner."

Even as the battered army fled, a few whose sense of humanity was still master to their instinct for survival stopped to aid wounded comrades. Among the fallen was Braddock—alive, but beyond consolation. If we accept a popular rumor that circulated in the wake of battle, he asked Croghan to lend him his pistols, so that he might "die as an old Roman." Croghan refused, and he, Washington, Stewart, and a few others, managed to carry the general from the scene. Orme apparently later claimed that he had tried to bribe the fleeing regulars to aid their commander, all to no avail.[35]

That the enemy pursued the fleeing forces no farther than the river was the best of what little luck Braddock's army had that day. Had it followed, Dunbar claims, a force of one hundred could have annihilated the remaining troops. British A states that the retreat could have been cut off by a mere half-dozen. The latter at least is exaggerating, perhaps for effect, but the disorder of the troops was such that Dunbar's opinion cannot be dismissed out of hand. Orme in fact states that the enemy force that did pursue, inflicting great losses, numbered no more than fifty.

Why was there no massive pursuit? The French reporters give three possible reasons. According to Pouchot, Dumas's army soon gave up the chase, "because the Indians could not wait to plunder and drink." His testimony is to some extent confirmed by Cameron, whose vantage point, though poor, allowed him to observe that "the whole Army of the Enemy fell to plundering, &c. . . . Among the Plunder they found near Two Hogshead of Rum, and the Indians, as likewise the French Soldiers, fell to drinking, and soon got themselves pretty drunk, and went off." Contrecoeur claims that Dumas could not pursue because so many Canadians had fled at the start of battle that the captain now retained only about twenty French troops. The implication here is that the Indians needed supervision that Dumas, under the circumstances, could not provide. Finally, French C relates that "our forces pursued them for some time, but sieur Dumas, having learned that General Braddock had left some leagues to the rear a corps of seven hundred men under the orders of Colonel Dunbar, ordered a halt."

Pouchot's account stands up a bit better than the other two, but this is not to say that it is correct. Contrecoeur slips on his statement that Dumas had only a score of Frenchmen still with him. We have seen that over one hundred French officers and men had joined the march that morning, in addition to 146 Canadians. Even if we take Dumas at his word, only one hundred—"one-half of our French forces"—fled at the start of battle, and these mostly militiamen. Furthermore, French casualties were light, as were those of the Canadians and Indians. According to Contrecoeur's own reckoning, only eight Frenchmen and Canadians were killed, of a total of twenty-three who died fighting the British. Furthermore, he sets the number of wounded at only sixteen, twelve of them Indians. It is fair to judge, therefore, that Dumas retained somewhere between fifty and sixty Frenchmen under his command, in addition to whatever number of Canadians had held their ground. For that matter, I have already suggested that Dumas's account of precipitate flight probably represents a considerable exaggeration, although it was one Contrecoeur chose to swallow. French C's statement that the French and Indians pursued the British for "some time" does not hold up, though his opinion that they halted because they feared Dunbar's detachment is reasonable. Of course, Dunbar was in reality about sixty miles to the rear, but the French did not know this, as Contrecoeur confirms, and they likely believed that he was much closer. It is quite possible, therefore, that Dumas feared the consequences if his forces, in headlong and disorderly pursuit, ran into a well-armed detachment of seven hundred. Besides, he apparently anticipated a counterattack, and to this end concentrated on securing the munitions and other materiel the British had left on the field. Those Indians who had pursued the fleeing British soon returned, apparently fearful that they would be deprived of their fair share of plunder. And the Indians could have guessed with reason that somewhere in the wagons was liquor. Pouchot's assertion is therefore most plausible, but the errors noted in the cases of

Contrecoeur and French C are not great enough to invalidate their claims. The three reasons given are in any case not mutually exclusive.

Dumas need not have feared a counterattack. On the western bank of the Monongahela, the scene was one of mindless terror, as men rushed to retrace the steps they had taken that morning. Perhaps even a few officers joined in the panic. Croghan says as much: "When the men were going off, many of the officers called out Halt, Halt, which the men mostly did, but the Officers continued on and got the heels of them." Taken literally, this statement is implausible. Why would the officers first call on their men to halt, and moments later themselves lead a disorderly flight? The most likely explanation is that Croghan is simply being vague in his usage. *Some* officers tried to stop the mad retreat, while *others* led it. If this is what Croghan means, it makes sense, but we should not be surprised that most of the accounts, being the work of officers, tend to note only the heroic aspect. First, there is Washington's famous description of the retreat, to and from the river, led throughout by the cowardly regulars:

At length, in despight of every effort to the contrary, [they] broke and run as Sheep before the Hounds, leav'g the Artillery, Ammunition, Provisions, and, every individual thing we had with us a prey to the Enemy; and when we endeavour'd to rally them in hopes of regaining our invaluable loss, it was with as much success as if we had attempted to have stop'd the wild Bears of the Mountains.

Most of the officers who have left detailed accounts concentrate on what happened after the army had recrossed the Monongahela, but otherwise their comments support Washington. Dunbar, Orme, British A, and Gordon all claim that once across the river the officers vainly attempted to rally their men. The last in particular gives a vivid account, in which we see once more the heroism of Burton: "Coll: Burton tho' very much Wounded attempted to Rally on the Other Side, & made a Speach to the Men to Beg them to get into some Order, But

Nothing would Do, & we found that Every man wou'd Desert us; therefore we were oblig'd to go along."

Perhaps it was just as well that the men refused to take a stand. Considering their losses, the British were by now actually outnumbered. Furthermore, the French were in possession of the cannon and a great deal of ammunition. Dumas's vigilance limited the likelihood that a counterattack would succeed. Only if the victors were indeed very drunk would the British have had a chance. Perhaps, as Cameron states, the British could have returned that night, after the French and Indians had left the field, and destroyed some of their remaining supplies, but this was all. Their defeat was itself irreversible.

So began the ignominious retreat that was to end only in Philadelphia.

Back on the field lay the wealth of Braddock's army. There was, first and foremost, the vast store of munitions, although indeed it was less impressive than that which Colonel Dunbar, at Braddock's command, would destroy before beginning his own retreat. There were also well over five hundred cattle and horses—many of which were slaughtered on the field itself—as well as provisions and valuable equipment. The wagons left behind presumably included almost all of the thirty-odd that Braddock had taken from the Little Meadows. In one of them, the French discovered the general's war chest, containing several thousand pounds. Another find was of perhaps even greater consequence. This was a collection of Braddock's private papers, including instructions to him from George II and Cumberland, and copies of his own letters. The documents enabled the French to piece together a history of his expedition and provided them with invaluable information on the respective campaigns of Shirley and Johnson. Finally, they gave them a great propaganda weapon, for now France could prove to the world that the English, while proclaiming peaceful intentions, had been preparing for war.[36]

But the greatest British losses were not inanimate. On the battlefield the fallen hosts of Braddock's army lay, soon to be joined in death by the general himself. Counting those who would die of their wounds, the British lost perhaps five hundred men.[37] Here at the scene of ignominy lay most of them, symbols of the bloodiest defeat Britain had ever suffered on the North American continent.

Those who had died on the battlefield at least did not have to endure the agonies of the wounded. Years later, Washington recalled the horrors he and the men experienced on their retreat to Dunbar's camp: "The shocking Scenes which presented themselves in this Nights March are not to be described. The dead, the dying, the groans, lamentation, and crys along the Road of the wounded for help . . . were enough to pierce a heart of adamant."[38]

At the site of their humiliation, those of the vanquished who could not flee were treated with a common callousness, the living as the dead. According to Cameron, some French officers tried—with considerable success, he implies—to stop the Indians from scalping enemy soldiers who were yet alive. His poor vantage point and the fact that he probably could not understand the French orders make him a questionable source. He may merely have noted a rumor that circulated in the wake of the battle, but if so he did it with the feeling that it was likely true, for he had no reason to be biased in favor of the French.

It is certain that the Indians kept some of their prisoners.[39] Others, however, were not so lucky. There is no way of knowing how or why they were singled out, but it is all too clear what happened to them. In the black of that night was played out the ghastly ritual that Braddock's men had feared throughout the afternoon. Some forty-four years later, Colonel James Smith recalled the horrors he had witnessed as a young prisoner at Fort Duquesne:

About sundown I beheld a small party coming in with about a dozen prisoners, stripped naked, with their hands tied behind their backs, and their faces and parts of their bodies blacked; these prisoners they burned to death on the bank of the Allegheny river, opposite to the fort. I stood on the fort wall until I beheld them begin to burn one of these men; they had tied him to a stake, and kept touching him with firebrands, red-hot irons, &c., and he screamed . . . ; the Indians, in the mean-time, yelling like infernal spirits.[40]

Five years passed. Fort Duquesne fell, to be replaced by Fort Pitt. Throughout the Ohio Valley and on into Canada, the British turned defeat into glorious victory. Then, one day in early September 1760, Colonel Jehu Eyre went riding with a friend:

Monday . . . we set off through the woods to go to Braddock's field, and on our journey we met with several Indian huts which the Indians had left; and when we came to the place where they crossed of the river Monongahela, we saw a great many men's bones along the shore. We kept along the road about 1½ miles, where the first engagement begun, where there are men's bones lying about as thick as the leaves do on the ground; for they are so thick that one lies on top of another for about a half a mile in length, and about one hundred yards in breadth.[41]

✑ FIVE ✑

Retrospect

EVEN AS DARKNESS covered the battlefield dead, even as the battered army retreated in agony, controversy billowed. Within days of Braddock's death, on July 13, those in the countryside surrounding had heard of the disaster, and they were as quick to draw conclusions as they were to load their muskets in anticipation of an Indian onslaught. As Dunbar led his pitiful troops into winter quarters—at the peak of summer— accusations followed thick and fast. With their advantages in manpower and munitions, how could the British have failed? How could they have been defeated—not defeated, but *crushed?* Now, with thousands of lives at risk, with the future of the colonies at stake, angry men sought answers.

"It is impossible to relate the different accounts that was given of our late unhappy engagement; but all tended greatly to the disadvantage of the poor deceased General, who is censured on all hands." So wrote Washington on July 28, without exaggeration.[1] The reports of eyewitnesses were bad enough. Rumors, perhaps wholly imaginary to begin with, or else wildly distorted as they passed from hand to hand, were etched sharply into the minds of a public which at first sought not to believe, hoping against hope that Braddock had not been defeated, and then, when overwhelmed by the evidence, believed all too freely.

With each account or rumor, recriminations spread. At the time, they were hurled at many targets. The British officers blamed the regulars, the regulars the Americans.[2] Cumberland drew censure for having chosen the route he had, the strategy he had, and, at least by implication, the general he had.[3] Dunbar was excoriated for having destroyed the ammunition remaining with him, thus precluding a second offensive, and above all fo having led a retreat that left western Pennsylvania stripped o defenses.[4] But, as Washington suggests, the loudest denuncia tions of all were reserved for Braddock. Likewise today. Histori ans have developed those charges which contemporaries hurle at the general, and have created some new ones as well.[5] Thi chapter is devoted to assessing their criticism.

Before discussing what Braddock has been accused of, let u see what he has not been. His contemporaries, admirers an detractors, as well as historians, have tended to ascribe to him the same virtues. Their testimony sets these forth clearly.

First, his critics. William Shirley, son of the governor o Massachusetts and secretary to Braddock, wrote an angry lette to Morris on May 23. At the time, the young man had less than seven weeks to live:

We have a G—— most judiciously chosen for being disqualified for th Service he is employed in, in almost every respect; he may be brave fo ought I know, and he is honest in pecuniary Matters. But . . . It is Joke to suppose that Secondary Officers can make Amends for th Defects of the First.

An anonymous writer, who had been behind with Dunbar a the time of the battle, shortly thereafter let his feelings b known in a letter to one of his superiors: "In the time of th Action, The General behaved with a great deal of Persona Courage, which every body must allow—but thats all that Ca be said—he was a Man of Sense and good natur'd too tho Warm and a little uncooth in his manner—and Peevish—with all very indolent." Finally, Franklin, writing more than thirt years after Braddock's Defeat, declared: "This general was, think, a brave man and might probably have made a figure as good officer in some European war. But he had too muc self-confidence, too high an opinion of the validity of regula troops, and too mean a one of both Americans and Indians."[6]

Now we come to the remarks of two who remembered Brad dock fondly. The first is Charles Lee, a major general in hi wn right and second-in-command during the Revolution. Like tephen, he was British by birth, and like him, he eventually aw his career come to ruin. But though a volatile man, he dmired Braddock, for whom he fought at the Monongahela: "There will come a day (I hope) when justice will be done to his man's memory, who has left few behind him that are his `quals, in Courage, honesty and Zeal for the Publick, his death /as a cruel stroke to us in particular, and a very unhappy troke for the Nation in general." Finally, Washington, speak-ng through William Findley, reminisced about his deceased ommander years later, during his presidency:

`rue, true he was unfortunate, but his character was much too se-erely treated; . . . he was one of the honestest and best men of any British officer with whom he had been acquainted; even in the man-er of fighting he was not more to blame than others,—that of all that vere consulted, only one person objected to it.[7]

There appears to be a consensus that Braddock may be con-:eded at least two virtues, courage and honesty. His anonymous :ritic aside, most have also seen him as dedicated. Unfortu-1ately, these favorable qualities, although they speak well of 1im as a man, tend not to be of much importance when he is viewed as a commander. That he was honest availed him little ut the Monongahela. Even his courage appears to have been valueless when weighed against the panic of his troops. Let us .ee, then, how he may be judged as a general.

In discussing Braddock's role in the battle, it is worthwhile to livide his critics into two camps, "traditional" and "modern." The nature of their differences and the usefulness of this livision will, I hope, become apparent during the course of this :hapter.

Franklin's statement that Braddock "had too much self-:onfidence, too high an opinion of the validity of regular :roops, and too mean a one of both Americans and Indians" epitomizes the traditionalist view.[8] His camp sees the general as having been an arrogant, stubborn man, too confident not only of his own powers, but of the superiority of the method of warfare with which he had become familiar back in Britain. Here we have a martinet by design, living by the book, unwilling even in the heat of battle to allow his experienced Virginians to fight the Indians in their own way. And for the Indians themselves, Braddock, according to the traditionalist view, had nothing but contempt. Of course, part and parcel of this position is the belief that the Indian method of fighting, the same one advocated by the Americans under Braddock's command, would have served him much better in battle than did his own Continental tactics.

That Braddock believed in the traditional mode of fighting is true enough, and he was certainly a disciplinarian. But to call him a martinet, as some have, is grossly unfair. The discipline enforced before and during the march was probably no more rigorous than was normal. Indeed, the British army was geared to discipline as a means of creating some semblance of a fighting machine from the riffraff who generally composed the troops—"the scum of the earth," as Wellington would call them. The rules laid down by Braddock were not exceptionally strict, nor did he enforce them with rigor. Apparently not one soldier under his command was executed, though several were caught stealing or attempting to desert. On May 14, while the troops were still in camp at Fort Cumberland, a court-martial sentenced one Luke Woodward to death for desertion, but Braddock pardoned him. The same day, he reduced the number of lashes which, by order of the court-martial, three convicted pilferers were to receive.[9]

Of course, one might argue, with justice, that even if Braddock did not enforce a discipline which was particularly harsh by the standards of his day, the soldiers who lived under it may still have been resentful. This would likely have been the case among new recruits, particularly Americans, who were not used to the rigor of the British army. They may well have considered him a martinet, and if so their opinion has since come to be accepted as fact by all but a few.

But to criticize him as a harsh disciplinarian brings up the same question raised before in relation to his supposed virtues, such as honesty. What has this to do with assessing his role in the Defeat? One anonymous contemporary suggests a link:

The flight of the men was occasioned by the great disgust they had to their officers. The soldiers from their first arrival, had showed much discontent, and the officers resolved to get the better and punished them frequently, but the more the punishments, the more the discontents increased. They say the troops were shot at from behind trees, and could not see their enemies, on which they ran away, the officers would have forced them to stand, and killed some of the men for not standing, so it became a fight between the men and officers, for the men fired on the officers that struck them, and ran quite away.

Although this is possibly only a thirdhand account, and it is garbled on some points, we can recognize in it elements of truth. We have seen that during the battle the officers sought desperately to keep their men in the field. Indeed, they themselves boasted of this. Braddock led them in their herding, and he may well have struck with his sword those who took shelter in the forest. He may also have been shot by one of his own men; and, if we take the word of British D, he was not the only officer to suffer so.[10]

Our unknown letter writer implies that because discipline was so harsh during the campaign, the men became totally alienated from their officers, including Braddock, to the point where they were more willing to fight *against* them than *for* them. This is possible, but not likely. In regard to the American soldiers, one cannot have it both ways. Either persistent regimentation and punishment had alienated them, causing them to behave badly in battle, or they performed well, in which case the question of discipline, harsh or otherwise, is irrelevant. As we shall see, and to some extent have seen, most sources suggest that the provincials performed much better than did most of their British counterparts. It is difficult, therefore, to argue that discipline had a negative effect on them, although they may well have resented it. As for the British regulars, the

evidence is more tenuous. Cameron explicitly states his admiration for Braddock, and it is doubtful that he does this merely
for effect, but one cannot assume that his attitude was typical.
There is even less to go on when attempting to judge how the
men felt about their officers as a whole. However, the battle
appears to have been lost primarily as the result of panic, and
this in turn resulted from factors other than alienation. Therefore, the question of discipline seems not to have much bearing
in their case either, and the whole issue of whether Braddock
was a martinet becomes only marginally relevant in analyzing
the engagement. But the broader question, whether the military regimen that Braddock attempted to bring to the colonies
was unsuited to the American situation, is both relevant and
provocative.

Taking next the oft-repeated claim that Braddock was contemptuous of Indians, we find that this is probably the most
complex accusation hurled against him. It has been taken two
ways. First, the simpler charge, that Braddock's contempt for
the Indian caused him to treat with disdain the possibility of
ambush. Franklin claims that he warned the general of exactly
the sort of attack which eventuated, only to be told that "these
savages may, indeed, be a formidable enemy to your raw
American militia but upon the king's regular and disciplin'd
troops, sir, it is impossible they should make any impression."
Even assuming that Braddock did make such a statement, his
actions appear to have belied the confidence of his words, for
during his march he constantly took precautions to thwart any
ambush that the French and their Indian allies might mount.[1]
Furthermore, in his recruitment of Indians there is evidence
that, at the very least, he respected them as fighters. If he had
wanted them only to reconnoiter, he would have needed no
more than fifty. But he happily anticipated the possibility that
several hundred would join his march. He must therefore have
looked on them largely as auxiliaries.

The reference to recruitment leads us to the second, more
complex, charge that Braddock was unwise in his Indian policy

Once again, we may start off with a quotation, this time from Monakatooka:

He [Braddock] is now dead, but he was a bad man when he was alive; he looked upon us as dogs, and would never hear anything that was said to him. We often endeavoured to advise him and to tell him of the danger he was in with his soldiers; but he never appeared pleased with us; and that was the reason that a great many of our warriors left him and would not be under his command.[12]

Here we have two main criticisms: that Braddock ignored the advice of his Indians, and that he alienated them, causing many to desert him. There is a corollary here, stated explicitly by many others, that the general was at best halfhearted in his attempts to recruit Indians. Let us deal with this corollary first, coupling it with the charge that he treated the Indians who did join him so badly that many of them left.

Almost from the moment he arrived in America, Braddock was involved in Indian affairs. He seems to have been particularly concerned that the British alliance with the Iroquois be maintained and strengthened, this attitude perhaps reflecting the influence of Shirley and Johnson. To the latter he wrote that he had "engag'd in the Indian affairs from the advantage they seem to be to his Majesty's Colonies."[13] There is certainly no heartwarming assertion of the brotherhood of man to be found in this statement, but there is a recognition that it was useful to have the Indians as allies.

On April 15, Braddock initiated his own attempt to recruit Indians, when he wrote to Morris:

As I am inform'd there are a Number of Indians in your Province that formerly liv'd near the River Ohio, & were driven from thence by the French, I must desire You would acquaint them that I am now on my March with a Body of the King's Troops, to remove the French from their Incroachments upon that River, & to restore that Country to our Allies, the Indians, & to protect them in the Enjoyment of it. And as those Indians must be very well acquainted wth that Country, & may be very usefull to me in the Course of this Expedition, I must desire You will prevail wth the able Men of 'em to join me at Wills's Creek, where they shall be kindly receiv'd, & in the Course of the Service furnish'd with Necessaries.

You will advise me of what You do in relation to this Affair, & of the Number of Indians that are to join me from your Province, & I doubt not your Assembly will take care of the Women & Children 'till the Return of the men, as they will be very troublesome in the Camp.

The rest of this particular story is well known. Morris forwarded the order to Croghan, who was able to recruit fifty warriors. These he led to Fort Cumberland. Braddock was disappointed in the number, but even more so in the fact that they were accompanied by their womenfolk. Actually, Croghan had been more realistic than the general, and had assumed that the Assembly would not allocate funds to support the Indian families. It was for this reason that he had brought them along. As Braddock had feared, the women soon did become "troublesome," though not for any reasons his troops would have resented. Prodigal with their favors, they soon had the men, as well as some officers, stealing provisions for them. Perhaps owing to their influence, the drinking problem in camp now increased. Finally, in order to maintain discipline, Braddock felt compelled to send them home with their men, leaving behind only Monakatooka and his small band. Croghan later lamented that "had we had fifty Indians instead of eight, that we might in a great measure have prevented the surprise, that day of our unhappy defeat." It is difficult to judge Braddock's decision without knowing how great a threat the women actually posed to camp discipline. What can be said with fair assurance is that he was not the only one who feared their influence. In fact, one of Morris's agents, Richard Peters, later claimed that he had persuaded the general to order them out of camp, for the sake of the expedition.[14]

Early in June, Braddock decided that he had too few Indian allies and asked Croghan to help him recruit some Delawares. The agent complied by setting up a conference between his commander and several chieftains, including the well-known Shingas, who later reported on the proceedings:

He and 5 other Cheifs of the Delaware Shawnee & Mingo Nations (Being 2 from Each Nation) had applied to Genl Braddock and Enquired what he intended to do with the Land if he Coud drive the French and their Indians away To wch Genl Braddock replied that the English Shoud Inhabit & Inherit the Land, on wch Shingas askd Genl Braddock whether the Indians that were Friends to the English might not be Permitted to Live and Trade Among the English and have Hunting Ground sufficient To Support themselves and Familys as they had no where to Flee Too But into the Hands of the French and their Indians who were their Enemies (that is Shingas' Enemies). On wch Genl Braddock said that No Savage Should Inherit the Land. . . . Next Morning [they] Returned to Genl Braddock again in hopes he might have Changed his Sentiments and then repeated their Former Questions to Genl Braddock again and Genl Braddock made the same reply as Formerly, On wch Shingas and the other Chiefs answered That if they might not have Liberty to Live on the Land they woud not Fight for it To wch Genl Braddock answered that he did not need their Help and had No doubt of driveing the French and their Indians away.

A crushing condemnation? If we accept it as reasonable, yes. But there is much to be said against such acceptance. First, there is Croghan's version of the conference:

I sent a messenger to Ohio who returned in eight days and brought with him three chiefs of the Delawares. The General had a conference with these chiefs . . . , and made them a handsome present, and behaved as kindly to them as he possibly could during their stay, ordering me to let them want for nothing. The Delawares promised in Council to meet the General on the road, as he marched out, but whether the former breaches of faith on the side of the English prevented them, or that they had before engaged to assist the French, I cannot tell; but they disappointed the General and did not meet him.

Here we have the testimony of one who respected the Indians, although we should be wary, in view of the fact that he was also sympathetic to the general.[15] On certain differences, such as the number of chiefs involved and their respective tribes, there is no way of choosing between the two accounts. On overall thrust, however, I would say that Croghan definitely has an edge, even though his report is less detailed.

Croghan's claim that Braddock had him distribute presents to the Indian delegates is very reasonable. Even during his short stay in America, the general had come to know the importance of gifts. When he left Dunbar behind at the Little Meadows, he entrusted to him most of the baggage, but, according to Orme, he took along "one waggon of Indian presents." Was this the sort of man who would have behaved toward the chieftains with an almost insane haughtiness? Perhaps they asked more than he felt he could grant. We have seen that in his letter of April 15, Braddock had instructed Morris to tell the Indians that the Ohio Valley would become theirs if it were reclaimed. But it is possible that he and the Indian delegates whom he met in early June had different notions of what this pledge meant. Did Shingas and his fellows demand a recognition of their hegemony in the valley? If so, Braddock was in no position to grant their wish, for the Iroquois claimed that the Ohio region was theirs by conquest. And as suggested earlier, the general seems first and foremost to have been interesting in maintaining the alliance with the Six Nations. He would likely, however, have offered the delegates more in terms of territorial influence than Shingas suggests.

These points aside, there is again the common-sense angle. Would Braddock, after having invited the chieftains to camp, have been so stupid in his treatment of them? He may not have been much of a diplomat—this question will be considered shortly. Certainly he was volatile and fully capable of an emotional outburst. But if we accept Shingas's word that he repeated his uncompromising rejection of Indian claims to the Ohio on two successive days, it appears that he did not do so in a moment of pique. We have seen that he valued the Indian alliance, if only for pragmatic reasons. No matter how we look at it, there is virtually nothing to be said for the wilder accusations contained in Shingas's account, and much to be said against our crediting them.[16]

This leaves the third and most important attempt to recruit Indians for the campaign. Ironically, Braddock's involvement

n it was minimal. Before the troops marched from Fort Cumberland, Dinwiddie promised the general that he would provide him with four hundred Cherokees and Catawbas. What he
did not tell him was that he was feuding with Governor James
Glen of South Carolina, and that both sought control of these
very tribes. At length, Glen and a Virginian trader who was
acting on his own selfish motives managed to intercept the
several hundred Indian recruits who were intent on joining
Braddock, and dissuaded them from heading north. This
strange sequence of events was doubly tragic. A contingent of
Iroquois might have been willing to join the expedition, but
upon hearing that Braddock was to be accompanied by southern Indians, whom they regarded as enemies, the Six Nations
decided to withhold aid, rather than risk a confrontation.
There is no reason to blame Braddock for either of these
misfortunes. But if he had not been the victim of circumstance,
if he had indeed been accompanied by a sizable number of
Iroquois or by the Cherokees and Catawbas, it is likely that he
would have carried the day at the Monongahela, and entirely
possible that the enemy would not even have attempted to
contest his way.[17]

The evidence therefore suggests that Braddock actively
sought Indian aid, rather than shunned it, as his critics have
charged. Possibly he did make a mistake in sending away most
of the Indians who had accompanied Croghan. As noted earlier, we lack the evidence to judge how great a threat to discipline the women actually were. But even if he blundered in his
recruitment, others did so more decisively than he.

On the other hand, I am not claiming that he was wise in his
treatment of the Indians. Perhaps he did not show them the
respect they felt they merited. But Indian diplomacy was a very
tricky business, and there were few successes at it. On this
point, it is worth noting the comments the Half King, a great
ally of the British, had made earlier concerning one of Braddock's chief subordinates: "The Colonel was a good-natured
man, but had no experience; he took upon him to command

the Indians as his slaves, and would have them every day upor the scout, and to attack the enemy by themselves, but would by no means take advice from the Indians." "The Colonel" was Washington.[18]

Finally, there is Monakatooka's charge that Braddock paid no heed to his Indian scouts.[19] It is probably simplest to discuss this in the context of a related issue. In the wake of the battle, Braddock was often accused of having ignored the advice of his subordinates, both before and during the engagement. British B in particular throws out this accusation with abandon. Regarding Monakatooka, whom he admires, he claims that the sachem had suggested that Braddock halt, presumably to wait for Dunbar before marching the last miles. British B also states that prior to the attack, when the general had ordered the troops, who were in a line of battle, to fall into a line of march, both St. Clair and Halket had opposed the move; and that early in the battle Sir John had requested of Braddock—in Italian, no less—that he retreat. St. Clair in his own account says that twice during the march he had urged that Braddock halt and wait for Dunbar's detachment. Washington and Stephen both claim that during the march they had often advised the British officers to train their men in the use of irregular tactics, and although they do not mention Braddock by name, they must have known that their arguments could not be effective without the general's support. For his part, Washington further maintains that during the battle he had begged Braddock to allow him to lead a detachment of experienced forest fighters against the enemy, only to be refused.[20]

It is doubtful that the general received all of this advice, at least as stated. In particular, British B's assertions appear to be inaccurate. For one thing, while he refers to several supposed encounters between Braddock and St. Clair, it appears from the latter's own account that on the day of battle they met only after Sir John was wounded, and that he gave no advice except to order an attack on the rising ground. St. Clair's version is by far the more plausible of the two. Furthermore, if Sir John had indeed advised a retreat, he would have mentioned in his report what in retrospect seemed a wise suggestion, for as we have seen he was never one to hide his light under a bushel.

But let us for the moment accept that Braddock did in fact receive all of the advice noted. Should he have accepted it?

The suggestion that the troops should have remained in a line of battle may indeed have merit. We have seen that they were drawn up in battle either just prior to crossing the river or on the east bank, and that this was probably done at the general's order. Such a maneuver was manageable on an open bank and was clearly called for in view of the present danger, since it was thought that the enemy might contest the crossing. For the march from the river to the battlefield, we lose our consensus. British B alone claims that Braddock ordered the return to a line of march, and only Gates claims that Burton's detachment moved up in this formation. Of course, it must be added that no one contradicts either. One problem in judging any reference to formation is that our eyewitnesses may not be consistent in their usage. A battle line was in the eighteenth century typically thought of as extending across a broad front—"the drawing up of an Army for Battle, extending its Front as far as the Ground will allow," as one writer defined it. Such a formation was clearly impossible in the forest, no matter how great the danger or sparse the trees. What British B and Gates therefore desired was some battle formation, the exact nature of which is unclear. Perhaps Braddock should have marched in different order—this will be dealt with shortly. But despite British B and Gates—and, more important, Mackellar—there is much about the general's formations, before and during the battle, that we do not know.[21]

If Sir John or anyone else told Braddock early on that he had lost the day and must retreat, this was, in retrospect, good advice; but it may not have been so at the time. Perhaps Braddock did attempt for too long to hold the field. This issue brings in another: At what point should he have acknowledged defeat and withdrawn? The historical consensus, with which I agree strongly, maintains that if during the early stages of battle he had been able to rally his men, he would probably have routed the enemy. Of course, his position deteriorated steadily, as officers and men fell. Quite possibly he held on when a more perceptive commander would have realized that the panic of his troops was such that only retreat could save them from annihilation. But there was no reason for Braddock to concede this during the early stages of battle—at least the first hour of action. So St. Clair's advice, assuming he gave it, was premature, even if prophetic.[22]

Moving on to Sir John's own statement—that he had twice advised that the general halt and allow Dunbar's detachment to catch up—it is difficult to credit him with anything but foolishness, and the same may be said for Monakatooka if he made a like suggestion. On July 3, when St. Clair made his proposal to Braddock, the general, according to Orme, called a council of war to deal with the issue. The council unanimously rejected St Clair's suggestion, citing three main problems: Dunbar's detachment was at least eleven days' march to the rear; the addition of his forces would be of little use, since the whole could not advance together; Fort Duquesne might be reinforced while Braddock waited. Even if the council did not proceed exactly as claimed by Orme—and there is no evidence to this effect—the arguments he ascribes to it are reasonable. In fact, by the time of the battle Dunbar was considerably *more* than eleven days' march behind. He was at least fifty miles to the rear, and estimates range upward to about seventy. This was not entirely his fault, since Braddock had left him only the poorest horses, as well as most of the wagons. But even if the general had sent back some of his own horses—which were none too strong themselves—he could not have brought his second division up for at least two weeks, and probably closer to three. Furthermore, one doubts that it was worth bringing up. The men whom Braddock had left behind at the Little Meadows were for the most part the dregs of his army. Perhaps we can get some insight into their quality by noting the follow-

ng anecdote, which is well substantiated. On the morning of
uly 10, the wagoners who had fled from the battlefield
orought news of the shocking defeat to Dunbar's men. Accord-
ng to an eyewitness, "about Noon of the same Day they beat to
Arms in Coll. Dunbar's Camp, upon which the Waggoners as
well as many common Soldiers took to flight in spite of the
Opposition made by the Centrys." It is difficult to believe that
men who could be terrified so easily would have behaved well
n the heat of the battle. More than likely, if Braddock had
waited for Dunbar, the only result would have been still heavier
losses. Indeed, it is possible that his second division served the
general best by remaining behind, for we have noted testimony
that one reason the enemy did not pursue the retreating British was their fear of encountering Dunbar.[23]

One last major line of advice that Braddock supposedly received also introduces the most common "traditional" charge
against him. Should he have allowed the Americans to use
irregular tactics during the battle? We may judge this with or
without reference to Washington's claim that he offered to lead
his fellow provincials in an Indian-style attack.

That the Americans fought better than their British counterparts at the Battle of the Monongahela is almost beyond dispute. In defending their role, we can cite not only legend but
eyewitness accounts as well. Washington and Stephen both
argue that the provincials behaved much better than the panicky regulars. So does Cholmley's Batman, himself not an
American, and thus free of obvious bias in this regard. Indeed,
the young servant alone among our firsthand reporters insinu-
ates that Braddock was unwise in his decision not to allow the
Americans to fight Indian style: "He always strove to keep the
men together but I belive their might be two hundred of the
American Soldiers that fought behind Trees and I belive they
did the moast Execution of Any." When we add this testimony
to that concerning the heroism of the various provincial units
that sought to dislodge the enemy from its strategic strong-
holds, we can see the justice of Washington's famous judgment

that "the Virginian Companies behav'd like Men and died lik Soldiers."[24]

Braddock himself may in his last hours have come to fee that he had undervalued the Americans. He may also, a claimed by an anonymous writer, have "cursed his own Men constantly for Cowardice, and applauded the Virginians." Per haps, as he lay dying, he even came to credit American tactics According to Washington's adoptive son, the wounded genera lamented to his young aide-de-camp, "Oh, my dear colone had I been governed by your advice, we never should hav come to this."[25]

Still, even if we accept as fact the claim that Braddock had change of heart, we are not obligated to concede that he achieved any higher wisdom in retrospect. His judgment dur ing battle may have been superior, and indeed the evidence tends toward that conclusion.

Elsewhere in this analysis it has been necessary to return to the fact that during the battle, the regulars for the most par panicked. This is another such point. Their panic made them entirely incapable of fighting Indian style. One might argue that they would possibly have behaved better if their training had been geared to irregular tactics, as it appears Washington and others had suggested. But actually, considering their in sane fear of Indians and the fact that they panicked almost immediately, before a disposition of any kind could be made, it seems doubtful that they would have made better irregular troops than they did regular.

The issue is now more limited. Should Braddock have allowed those Americans who were experienced forest fighters to use their native tactics during the battle? Again, the question is best answered in terms of the behavior of the regulars. As we have seen, the terrified troops tended to fire at anything that moved, at any puff of smoke signifying a discharge. It was due to their frenzy that they fired on and killed Peyronie and his men, as well as other Americans and perhaps Britons who tried to move against the enemy. Had they themselves gone behind trees, they would simply have fired on each other. As it was, they were almost undoubtedly responsible for most of the casualties suffered by the Americans who secreted themselves. If Braddock recognized the risk the provincials ran, this was a fine rationale for his attempts to force them back into formation, for they could not be in greater danger than they were in the woods. Even if he did not have this in mind, it justifies his decision.[26]

There is also the issue of desertion. In Braddock's day, troops deserted with incredible alacrity. Indeed, military theorists did not think that the primary function of a rear guard was to guard the army's rear, its name to the contrary. Rather, it was intended mainly to pick up and detain those from other detachments who dropped out of formation in order to desert. Seeing his troops panic under fire, Braddock may well have feared that if he allowed them to seek shelter behind the trees, they would in time desert the field altogether. Even if at first only the Americans looked to the forest for safety, it was quite possible that many regulars would follow their example. According to Washington, during the first moments of battle, "some of the Irregulars (as they were called) without direcns. advanced to the right, in loose order, to attack; but this, *unhappily* from the unusual appearance of the movement being mistaken for cowardice, . . . a running away was discountenanced." Considering the high proportion of men who actually deserted, it appears that Braddock was justified if he was among those who feared that these men were "running away." Indeed, the tendency to desert was such that it is difficult to blame the general for his apparent concern that, if he allowed his troops to melt into the forest, he might soon be without an army.[27]

Braddock may indeed have acted as he did regarding irregular tactics because he feared that they might bring about higher casualties and encourage desertion. He may well also have felt that to allow his troops to fight Indian style would lessen his chances of making the one mighty thrust that would put the enemy to flight. This last suggestion brings us back to the point that Braddock was very much a traditionalist. At the age of sixty, he was too old to change his concept of warfare. To his mind, and the mind of his era, battles were won by disciplined maneuver, not individual initiative. The great irony of Braddock's Defeat is that it was decided by a breakdown in that discipline which he had tried so hard to engender in his men. Perhaps if they had behaved better there would be less justification for his resolve not to allow the provincials to forest fight. But as it was, with the regulars firing blindly into the woods and running off in increasing numbers as the battle wore on, it appears that his decision actually saved lives, and it is justified in retrospect, even if at the time he thought only in terms of "the book."

Again on the question of taking advice from his subordinates, standard practice of the time seems to clear Braddock of the charges against him. As we have seen, during the march he actually appears to have sought counsel, for example, on the key question of whether to divide his forces. But while the battle raged he may well have felt that he himself must direct the action. Tradition would have justified such a belief, and might even have dictated it. During an engagement, the chief officer was not only to be in command, but was to be *seen* to be so.[28] Even if we ignore this line of justification, we still may exculpate Braddock on the grounds that most of the advice he has been accused of rejecting was not itself well thought-out, and that some of it, like St. Clair's suggestion that the general wait for Dunbar, was positively inane.

Thus far in this chapter I have dealt with the more common charges made against Braddock by the traditionalists. The modern school finds its chief advocate in its founder, Stanley Pargellis. According to Pargellis and several other historians who have written about Braddock's Defeat during the past four decades, the general is not to be blamed for his unwillingness to employ irregular tactics. On the other hand, they claim that he is nonetheless culpable, because he failed to use the tactics called for by Continental standards.

Pargellis himself is quite specific in his charges. According to

him, Braddock deserves criticism because he compressed his
line of march to a dangerous degree after the men had recrossed the Monongahela; failed to provide any clear instructions before ordering the main body to reinforce the vanguard;
rode to the front at the first firing, rather than holding back
long enough to judge the situation; and did not during the
battle pay sufficient heed to his subordinates. The sum total of
these arguments is that while the troops may have panicked,
Braddock's blunders had put them into such a fix that their
behavior was to be expected.[29]

Generally, I have already dealt with such charges. This obviously applies to the point of whether he was justified in ignoring the advice of his subordinates. In chapter 4, I noted points
in passing which call into question several of Pargellis's key
assumptions. Thus, we have already seen evidence that the
main body was probably about one-quarter mile behind the
rear of the vanguard—certainly not close-order. On the still
more central question of how Braddock behaved during the
first moments of battle, I have suggested that he himself did
not ride up, instead sending Burton, and that he seems to have
given definite orders, although one may assume that the lieutenant colonel was allowed some discretion on how to carry
them out.[30]

But let us deal with the broader issue of whether the general
failed to employ the tactics British tradition deemed proper.
Pargellis, in support of his view that Braddock did so fail, cites
Humphrey Bland's *Treatise of Military Discipline*. On one
ground, the choice is well taken. Bland was the standard treatise on drill procedure and field tactics, not only at the time of
Braddock's Defeat, but for almost two generations after it was
first published in 1727. It was considered definitive not only in
England, but throughout the English-speaking world, including America, and Braddock himself would probably have
known it by heart.

There are, however, two basic problems in attempting to
judge Braddock on the basis of Bland. First, the latter knew

nothing about Indian methods of warfare and had little to say on the question of how an army should react when faced with a situation like Braddock's. Second, in his treatise Bland emphasizes drill, rather than battlefield maneuver. He is by no means silent on tactics, but he is seldom precise. Instead of hard advice, he provides the reader with platitudes, perhaps epitomized by his comment that when the commanding officer finds his troops under attack, "his own judgment and experience must direct him in taking proper measures; for without he has both, those who are under his command, at such a juncture are much to be pitied, let his courage be ever so great."[3] Bland, like Braddock, symbolizes the state of the British army on the eve of the Seven Years' War. Both believed that in battle, discipline would carry the day, and this is the primary reason why they stressed drill. Likewise, both were ignorant of the exigencies of forest fighting as it was known in America. But only Braddock has borne the blame for failings common to a generation of officers.

Despite the reservations noted, two sections in Bland's work seem relevant to the problems that Braddock faced. The first is his portrayal of "street-firing," a formation to be used on a narrow road. This he describes only in the form of a drill wherein the battalion is to fire while advancing, and those who have discharged their muskets are to face left or right and march to the rear. In a lengthier portion of text, he discusses which tactics are proper for an army that is marching through brushland or forest and anticipates attack. Given this situation Bland directs that the men should march in platoons. The vanguard is to be no more than two hundred yards in front of the main body, and is expected to reconnoiter all strategic points, although in heavily wooded areas its activities in this regard are to be supplemented by small parties. Should it be attacked, the officer in charge of the main body is to detach his grenadiers, or a few platoons, to rescue those under fire. If the reinforcements become engaged, he may find himself forced to commit his entire army to action.

Judging Braddock strictly on the basis of Bland, it appears that first of all the latter would have criticized the disposition of his forces, for they did not march by platoon. We have seen that Braddock apparently attempted during the battle to divide his men into platoons, but that he was unsuccessful, as a result of the mass panic. However, the point is not particularly crucial. As a matter of fact, several eyewitnesses remark scornfully that platoon firing could not have been successful against a well-concealed enemy, and the point seems well taken. Bland might also argue that Braddock should not have committed as large a detachment as he did under Burton, at least until he had received some intelligence from the front. But even if this was a mistake on his part, one may ask whether the battle would have turned out differently, had he not sent Burton forward. Probably not. The vanguard appears already to have been in panic when the detachment was ordered out. It was certainly in a rapid and somewhat disorderly retreat. There would almost surely have been a collision in any case, and the same degree of disorder. Finally, Bland might claim that Braddock had the main body of his army too far to the rear of the vanguard. This is ironic for, as we have noted, Pargellis feels that the two were too *close*. But in judging this point we should remember that Braddock was burdened with a sizable wagon train, despite the fact that he had left the bulk of his materiel with Dunbar. A line of wagons separated the working party from the main body and divided the main body itself. Since the wagons contained tools as well as ammunition, it was vitally important to the working party in particular that they be close by. This sort of situation does not seem to have occurred to Bland. Again, he seems to have thought in terms of the Continental situation. In his idealized scheme, supply lines were always reasonable, since civilization was never too far off. The notion that an army might be isolated to the extent that Braddock's was appears not to have crossed his mind.[32]

Through the years, countless historians, professional and amateur, have pondered the question of what tactics Braddock should have used during the battle. It has been argued that he was culpable for not having attempted to seize the rising ground earlier; that he should have ordered a bayonet charge; that his proper maneuver was a feigned retreat to lure the enemy from its hiding place, preparatory to a crushing counterattack. The tactics suggested are all reasonable enough, and indeed Braddock may himself have attempted to use them.[3] But all of these require a sizable body of men to succeed, and after the panic set in he did not have such a force at his disposal.

So far this discussion has keyed on the charges against Braddock himself, but some of his subordinate officers have been attacked as well.[34] Only one of them, however, has drawn consistent criticism. This is Gage, and while it appears that the general has been dealt with too harshly, it is difficult to say the same regarding the commander of his advance party.

Some have accused Gage of having, like the Duke of Plaza-Toro, led his embattled troops in a charge to the rear. While president, Washington one evening recalled that during the retreat from the Monongahela "he overtook col. Gage three miles a head of the place in which he had halted the retreating army, and to which he sent Gage back."[35] However, Orme put the incident in a different light: "After we had passed the Monongahela the second time, we were joined by Lieutenant Colonel Gage, who had rallied near 80 men." One might also question the point implicit in Washington's recollection, that he ordered Gage to rejoin the army. How could an aide-de-camp order a lieutenant colonel to do *anything*? On this particular issue, the case against Gage is tenuous.

On other points, however, the evidence is overwhelming. Gage made four major blunders on the day of the battle. First, there was his decision not to drag along the two six-pounders after his troops had recrossed the Monongahela. Had they been in front with him, ready to wheel quickly into action, his opening barrage probably would have been more deadly, and possibly the enemy would have been thrown into chaos. As it was, with the field pieces remaining behind with St. Clair, it took some time to get them firing, and by then the enemy had dispersed into the forest. A second charge involving his actions, or lack of them, prior to the battle, is that he failed to occupy the hillock to his right as he passed it. As we have seen, this "rising ground" soon fell into the hands of the enemy, and its tremendous strategic value is reflected in the number of attempts made by Braddock's forces to capture it. That it was primarily the responsibility of the advance party to occupy such potentially strategic points reflects not only Bland's dictum, but common sense. Gage's oversight in failing to secure the knoll, coupled with his decision to leave the six-pounders with St. Clair, suggests that he was supremely confident the enemy would not attack.[36] This explains his negligence; it does not excuse it.

"When the van-guard discovers any body of men, it is to halt, and the Officer is to send back immediately and acquaint the Commanding Officer with it, and to know what particular commands he has for him." So writes Bland, and again by implication he stands as Gage's accuser. Braddock has been criticized, by Pargellis among others, for not having sent ahead to gather intelligence before acting further.[37] But we may recall in his defense that Orme at least claims the general ordered an aide-de-camp "to bring him an account of the nature of attack," although apparently because the subordinate did not return, he rode forward himself. On the other hand, there is no suggestion from either Orme or Gage himself that the commander of the advance party sent a messenger back to Braddock when he first encountered Beaujeu's party. He should have done this as soon as possible. But in fact Orme's account, which conveys the impression that Braddock remained in the dark about what was going on ahead until he himself rode forward, likewise suggests that Gage dispatched no one at all.

Seventeen years after the battle was fought, it was discussed at some length by Thomas Mante, during the course of his history of the French and Indian War. Mante's testimony is of

particular interest, since he appears to have himself served as a
commissioned officer during the conflict and may therefore be
regarded as an authority on the standard tactics of his time. It
is noteworthy, then, that he works to vindicate Braddock, even
as he acknowledges his distance from the consensus: "Few
generals perhaps have been so severely censured for any defeat, as General Braddock for this." While defending the general, he is not so kind to Gage, although his criticism is merely
implied. According to Mante, during the first moments of
battle, the

flanking parties were driven in by the enemy, and no detachments
were made from the advanced guard to repel the attack on its flanks.
Had such detachments been made in proper time, they most certainly
would have beaten off the enemy. This was by no means the General's
fault; for the advanced guard fell into confusion before it was possible
that the General could send his orders to put into execution what
ought to have been done without any orders from him.

Mante's obvious implication is that the appropriate orders
should have come from Gage.[38] Perhaps surprisingly, the latter
gives tacit support to the charge. His account may not be accurate throughout, but it is detailed, particularly on the first moments of battle. Yet he does not suggest that he attempted to
reinforce the flanking parties and, in fact, reports the orders
given to his detachment in such detail as to suggest that he did
not do so.

However, with Gage as with Braddock, we should not carry
the charges too far. The two examples of negligence cited in
the case of Gage, relevant to the period just prior to the battle,
may possibly have had some impact on the outcome, but it is
doubtful. As for his two mistakes once the engagement was
under way, they were probably of little import, regardless of
what they may suggest about his competence as a commander.
This is because in the final analysis the day was lost, not because one or more officers blundered, but because the regulars
panicked. It was they who threw away the great advantages
held by the British.

However, before rushing headlong toward judgment, let us for a moment examine the question of responsibility in terms of the issue at hand. The very thought of calling the past to account frightens some and angers others. But history is, among other things, a thought process, with conclusions the capstone. The assessment of responsibility is merely the most natural area of conclusion in a study dealing with disaster. Closely related to those who refuse to take a stand are those who with a flourish throw up their hands and shout, "Who can say?" If, after having immersed themselves in a given subject, *they* cannot say, or even suggest, chances are that they have failed to define the issues, or that the question is too complex and needs to be broken down further. On the other hand, there are the historians who delve so deeply into causation that every incident is somehow tied to Adam's fall. Having noted the extremes of the spectrum, let us aim for the center. Let us also remember that Clio, while she does not shy from reaching a verdict, is not a hanging judge.

Relative to the case in point, we must take into account one major distinction. Are we discussing Braddock's Defeat—that is, the battle—or Braddock's defeat—generally, the frustration of his aims? The latter is more complex and will be dealt with first.

We have seen that prior to early July, in fact just a few days before Braddock arrived on the scene, the garrison at Fort Duquesne was so weak that it could have offered no meaningful resistance. Therefore, one may conclude that whatever or whoever was responsible for delaying the march was responsible for Braddock's Defeat and, probably, for the fact that there was any battle at all. The general himself apparently erred in taking such a large wagon train from Fort Cumberland, though in his defense he was preparing for an extensive campaign, not one that would be turned back at the forks of the Ohio. Other causes of delay during the march, such as accident and illness, fall under the heading of happenstance.

The most serious hindrances faced by Braddock and his army were really those they faced before their departure from Wills

Creek. Chief among these—at least, if we concentrate on problems that could have been avoided—was the shortage of provisions and wagons. That the general was misled and cheated by colonial contractors is beyond question. Certainly the system of providing for an army by using the services of private and virtually unsupervised agents was a natural source of abuse, but it could not have been reformed quickly enough to help Braddock. What *could* have helped and, in fact, could have guaranteed the success of the expedition, was honesty. Beside the problem of supplies, those concerning Braddock's relationship with the colonies pale into insignificance. He was not detained for want of funds, but rather for want of provisions.[39]

Straddling our dividing line is the issue of Indian auxiliaries. Had Braddock been accompanied by a large contingent of Indian auxiliaries, the French and Langlade's followers might have considered the cause hopeless and not attacked. Even had they ambushed Braddock's forces, they probably would have been driven off. Therefore, those who thwarted the general's attempts to recruit large numbers of Indians bear a heavy burden of responsibility for his defeat.

Moving on to the battle itself, and assuming that it would be fought under more or less the same circumstances, the question of responsibility becomes fairly simple. Some historians, notably Pargellis, have criticized Braddock's disposition of forces, and have suggested that he led his men into a situation that was untenable and conducive to panic. But whatever errors he may have made, they do not appear to have been particularly egregious, and, as we have seen, most of his decisions were probably justified. As for the collapse of his troops, this chain reaction started in the front, while he remained with the main body.

Is Gage then to blame? It was, of course, his detachment that broke first and began what developed into a chaotic retreat. But there is little reason to hold him responsible for the disorder. He may well have been a poor leader, as uninspiring as he was incompetent. However, his detachment, like the army in general, disintegrated as a result of factors that were quite irrelevant to his ability. Briefly, it seems that the panic was caused primarily by the troops' almost insane fear of the unseen and alien enemy. There was also the problem of casualties among the officers, which left the men leaderless. The advance party seems to have been hit particularly hard, and early, in this respect. In view of the odds against him, Gage could not be expected to keep his detachment viable.

Braddock and his subordinates by no means put the men in an "impossible" position. Had the troops followed orders, the enemy would probably have been defeated. One must say "probably" here. Ambush was not an all-or-nothing strategy. Those who used it tended to give ground willingly in the face of a concerted counterattack. Had Braddock's men followed him in a bayonet charge they would probably have dislodged the enemy, but this is not to say that the road to Fort Duquesne would then have been open to them. They still faced difficult terrain, the sort that afforded ample opportunity for ambush. And if one maxim of Indian warfare was that they would retreat in the face of a determined counterthrust, another was that they would soon return to the attack.[40] An active pursuit might have dispersed them, but this would have been a risky maneuver, and one doubts that Braddock would have allowed it.

The point is not that the British still faced heavy going even if they repulsed the first attack. It is that in all probability they could have broken through with ease, for the enemy, in the face of a counterthrust, would not have stood and fought. Presumably, this pattern would have applied to any further possible action as well. It would not have been easy for Braddock's men, but they would probably have made it to the fort—if they had kept their heads.

The collapse of the general's army disappointed many of his peers, but surprised few. At several points in this study it has been suggested that the British officer class commonly believed that in battle the more disciplined force would usually carry the day. Their conviction was born of experience. Many an eighteenth-century battle was decided in its first moments, when some contesting army collapsed in panic and either fled the field or was surrounded and butchered. The more fearsome or alien the enemy, the greater the likelihood of collapse. During the Forty-Five, British troops were on several occasions thrown into panic by the war cries of the "wild" Scottish clansmen.[41] And few in the past had faced an enemy as frightening as that encountered by Braddock's men.

While recognizing the tendency of troops to panic, some seasoned observers chose to be fatalistic. Army recruits were generally the dregs of society, they reasoned. Such men fought, not for God, king, or country, but for a livelihood. It would, of course, be desirable for the army to get better men, but in reality this was impossible. Instead, the officers must enforce a discipline sufficiently harsh to serve as a crucible and re-form the motley recruits into a fighting machine. Sometimes they would fail, as did Braddock. But in his case, time was against him. His troops, British as well as American, were for the most part green. It would have taken an almost superhuman effort on his part to prepare them to meet any adversary, much less the sort they faced. So would the more tolerant have spoken.

Some, however, could not excuse what they saw as cowardice. Among them was James Wolfe, whose last hours would be as glorious as Braddock's were ignominious. On hearing of the debacle, he wrote:

I have but a very mean opinion of the infantry in courage. I know their discipline to be bad, and their valour precarious. They are easily put into disorder, and hard to recover out of it. They frequently kill their officers through fear, and murder one another in their confusion. Their shameful behaviour in Scotland, at Pont L'Orient, at Melle, and upon many less important occasions, clearly denoted . . . the disobedient and dastardly spirit of the men.[42]

In the end, we are faced with a choice of connotations. Were the men to "blame" for Braddock's Defeat, in the sense that we, like Wolfe, believe that they should have performed more bravely than they did? Or were they merely "responsible"? Either way, the weight of evidence places the onus on them, rather than on Braddock or other officers. It was they who would not carry out orders, who huddled together when their superiors commanded that they re-form and attack. But should we expect such culls, green in battle, fighting a fearsome and unseen enemy, to act with courage? This, the question of "responsibility" or "blame," each reader must decide for himself.

SIX

"So What?"

HERE ENDS another study of Braddock's Defeat. The list of like works is long, and undoubtedly it will continue to grow. But perhaps the time has come to ask of this affair the most profound question in the historian's reserve—"So what?"

Whether we admit it or not, all of us are to some extent antiquarians. All of us have some interest in the past for its own sake. There are, of course, those who attempt to prove that every historical splinter has significance. Perhaps, indeed, the polar ice caps would have melted had Anne Boleyn not been born with six fingers on her left hand. But most of us are willing to admit that interest alone causes us to remember that Attila the Hun died of nosebleed. For the delectation of the unabashed trivialist, I shall attempt in Appendix A to answer certain provocative questions relative to the Battle of the Monongahela, such as "What happened to Braddock's sash?"

Trivia, however, can justify only so much printer's ink. Eventually we should all be willing to ask ourselves whether a particular topic merits the attention we have given it. So let it be with the one at hand. It is surprising indeed that for all that has been written about Braddock's Defeat, apparently no one has ever discussed in print why it is worthy of attention.[1] In this concluding chapter I hope to fill that gap, by dealing first with short-term and then with long-term significance.

First, it may be said that, with the battle over, the war began. The French position in the New World was greatly enhanced by the events of July 9, 1755. Of course, the victors gained cash, arms, and provisions from the stores of the defeated army. Likewise, they won a great, if temporary, strategic advantage in the struggle for the Ohio Valley. Finally, the documents captured by Beaujeu's men, proving as they did that the British had planned a massive campaign on several fronts, stoked war fever and Anglophobia in France.

Meanwhile, the British drew their own sort of inspiration from the battle. On both sides of the Atlantic, those loyal to the Crown became obsessed with dreams of vengeance. Certainly any humiliation such as had been suffered at the Monongahela would have brought this about, especially since it had come at the hands of an ancient enemy. But the nature of the battle increased British rancor, for they claimed that their enemy had triumphed through stealth, a sort of treachery that mocked the very concept of civilization. Immediately after the battle, Leslie declared, "We have lost gallant officers and generous friends, not in battle, for that we could bear, but by murder, by savage butchery. The French dared not openly meet us; our's is the loss, theirs the disgrace." A rationale for defeat? Certainly, but that does not lessen its significance. The point is that the British and Americans now commonly looked upon France as a nation that advocated ambush rather than open battle, and ambush was commonly regarded as the recourse of cowards.[2]

The call for vengeance had an enhanced meaning for those who revered Braddock's memory. Some may be surprised that there were such people, but in fact there were many, and they seem particularly to have been Americans. We may appreciate their number by noting the considerable output of ballads and poems written in memory of the general. Such reverence soon faded. Within a few years, those who looked for heroes had new ones who were more successful, while those who remembered Braddock tended to be his critics. But during 1755, and for a year or two after, many saw each defeat of the French, each massacre of the Indians, as fit retribution for the ambush of Braddock's forces and the murder of the general. Late in September 1755, Stephen Hopkins, the governor of Rhode Island, wrote to Johnson to praise him for his victory at Lake George. Hopkins seems to have been particularly pleased that just prior to the engagement Johnson's men had driven off a band of French Indians intent on ambush:

Those who from their past Experience might be led to think they had Nothing more to do than to attack furiously, and yell hideously to make them victorious, have been modestly shewn their Error, they have been taught to turn their Backs, and leave their Brethren and Commanders behind them; They who stole a Victory from Braddock, and cheated that Hero out of his Life by Sculking, have been openly arreasted by English Warrants, and sent to Settle their Accounts with him, where Nothing will be gained by Ambuscades.[3]

It is, of course, impossible to measure the impact of vengeance. Nor should we evaluate it in isolation. The circumstances of Braddock's Defeat were such as to inspire not only vindictiveness, but terror. These twin tempers combined into a fierce hatred of the French and their Indian allies. This appears to have been particularly true in America, where the danger was greatest. Americans had always hated the French and Indians, but Braddock's Defeat hardened them still further. On the one hand, they longed for the day of final victory, when their enemy would know the bitter taste of retribution. On the other, there was the terrifying possibility that they would be overrun by an adversary that had dramatically demonstrated its inhumanity at the Monongahela. A desire for vengeance, and the specter of a horrible defeat, would spur the Americans to fight on.

If they needed any further persuasion that the enemy was ruthless, they found it in the wake of Braddock's Defeat. As Dunbar led his ignominious flight to Philadelphia, he left the frontier exposed. The result was predictable. Immediately the French began to exploit their new strategic advantage by sending Indian allies to harry out those Americans who had settled west of the Alleghenies. Their strategy was brutally successful. Homes were burnt, hundreds butchered, many more carried off. The danger was so great that it caused a major population shift, as thousands of Pennsylvanians fled to the comparative safety of South Carolina.[4]

These raids brought home to the Americans as never before a

fear and hatred of Indians. Furthermore, they seemed to show clearly that the French and Indian threats were now one. The popular belief in this newfound enemy solidarity was somewhat simplistic. Only two months after the Battle of the Monongahela, Johnson's supporters from the Six Nations played a key role in his victory at Lake George. But it is true that Britain's influence among the Indians eroded dramatically during 1755, and in fact this was due largely, if not primarily, to Braddock's Defeat. That the debacle had a great impact on the system of tribal alliances surprised few knowledgeable contemporaries. As we have seen, both the British and their French adversaries had known that in the fate of Fort Duquesne lay that of their respective influence over the powerful tribes of the Ohio Valley. Both had hoped to demonstrate that they had the power to protect their Indian allies and to punish those tribes which remained loyal to their enemy. The French had hoped further that a victory would provide the Indians who fought for them with plunder sufficient to inspire other tribes to join their cause. In the wake of Braddock's Defeat, the hopes of the French and the fears of the British were realized to the letter. Several tribes, including the powerful Delawares and the Indians of the Ohio generally, now cleaved to France. Shingas himself was among those who, before the year was out, openly espoused the French cause, and he was not shy about stating that his decision was linked to the events of July 9. According to him, while a few Delawares had actually fought for Beaujeu, "the Greater Part remained neuter till they saw How Things wou'd go Between Braddock and the French in their Engagement."[5]

Certainly the British were shocked by spiraling French influence among the tribes, and by the Indians' role in Braddock's Defeat and the subsequent massacres of settlers. But mingled with their horror was a newfound respect for Indian tactics. The provincials who had marched with Braddock had failed to persuade the general or his chief British subordinates that it would be desirable to train the regulars in forest fighting techniques. As suggested in chapter 5, Braddock's stand was probably wise, and almost certainly it did not work against him. His men were inexperienced, and he was well advised to concentrate on instilling in them a sense of discipline. But this did not mean that, given time to prepare, the British should not have altered their policy to make it accord better with the exigencies of American warfare.

Back in Britain, neither Braddock's Defeat nor other reverses seem to have made much of an impression. Military experts continued to discuss warfare in terms of past glories, particularly Marlborough's campaigns, and even Bland, in his revised edition of 1759, had nothing new to say on countering an ambush or fighting in closed country. Tactics did indeed change in the wake of Braddock's Defeat, but only in America, and only on the initiative of officers actually serving there.

Washington later claimed that as a result of the Battle of the Monongahela, "the folly and consequence of opposing compact bodies to the sparse manner of Indian fighting, in woods, which had in a manner been predicted, was now so clearly verified that from hence forward another mode obtained in all future operations." This new "mode" concentrated on combining irregular with regular tactics. The Royal Americans in particular were geared to innovation, and in 1756 Lord Loudoun, commander-in-chief, directed that members of the regiment, "in order to qualify them for the Service of the Woods, . . . are to be taught to load and fire, lyeing on the Ground and kneeling." New commands were also instituted, the most dramatic of them being "Tree all," the order given in case of ambush, to disperse the men behind trees.[6]

The inventive spirit also manifested itself in a new willingness on the part of the British to make use of rangers. As we have seen, Braddock apparently felt that only Indians should be encouraged to fight "Indian style," while Americans were to be trained in the Continental mode. He seems not to have had much use for rangers, as fighters or scouts. How different the attitude of General John Forbes, who on one occasion wrote a brother officer that he had "been long in your opinion of

equiping Numbers of our men like the Saveges . . . I was
resolved upon getting some of the best people in every Corps
to go out a Scouting. . . . And I must confess in this country,
wee must comply and learn the Art of Warr, from Ennemy
Indians or anything else who have seen the Country and Warr
carried on in itt."[7]

To this point, we have viewed those aspects of the significance of Braddock's Defeat involving changes that seem logical.
But these were not the only effects. The colonies did not, as we
might expect, react to the increased danger with a newfound
spirit of cooperation. Some did increase their military expendi-
tures and raise new militia, but the effort was small-scale,
reflecting the age-old philosophy that each should have primarily its own interests in view, and that Britain should be expected to supply the bulk of troops and funds necessary for
defense. Not even within the various colonies was there the
degree of cooperation that the crisis seemed to call for. Instead,
the peril arising in the wake of Braddock's Defeat proved
divisive, for it raised the specter of a fifth column, prepared to
capitalize on a French invasion or even to work for its success.
In Virginia, Dinwiddie suggested measures for quelling any
slave rebellion that might eventuate, this due to his fear of "the
Villany of the Negroes on any Emergency of Gov't." Horatio
Sharpe, the governor of Maryland, ordered the local justices to
inquire into rumors that blacks and Catholics were creating
disturbances. They reported in the negative, and the matter
was dropped. But in Philadelphia, the Catholics faced danger
from a different, less restrained quarter, in the wake of the
news that Braddock had been defeated:

The Mob here upon this occasion were very unruly, assembling in
great numbers, with an intention of demolishing the Mass House
belonging to the Roman Catholics, wherein they were underhand excited and encouraged by some People of Higher Rank. But the peaceable Quakers insisting that the Catholics as well as Christians of other
denominations were settled upon the faith of the Constitution, or
William Penn's Charter, and that the Government were bound to pro-

tect them so long at least, as they remained inoffensive and paid duti-
ful regard to the Establishment; the Magistrates met and with a good
deal of difficulty prevailed with the Mob to desist.[8]

Ironically, in view of their heroism on this occasion, Braddock's
Defeat was to have a greater negative impact on the Quakers of
Pennsylvania than on the Catholics and blacks of the colonies
generally. For some years the Quaker hegemony in Pennsylvania politics had been widely questioned, by Morris among
others. Because of their pacifism, the proprietorship of the
Penns had no militia and generally lacked the means to defend
itself. This was bad enough in peacetime, for even then the
frontiers were never entirely safe. Now, following Braddock's
Defeat, the scope and savagery of Indian raids reached un-
precedented proportions, and an anguished populace looked
to its Assembly for aid. In late November, the municipality of
Philadelphia petitioned the legislature:

You were lately called together upon more urgent Business than ever
came before an Assembly of this Province, and while you have been
sitting scarce a day has passed wherein you have not heard of the
inhuman Slaughter of your Fellow Subjects, & been loudly called upon
for that protection, which, by the most sacred Ties you owe to the
People. . . . Nevertheless, while you have been deliberating, much in-
nocent Blood has been spilt, a great extent of our Country laid waste,
& the miserable Inhabitants scatter'd abroad before the Savage
Spoiler.

In the face of this outcry, as well as the obvious need, the
Assembly finally did pass a weak militia bill. But it was not
enough. When 1756 proved equally disastrous for British arms,
and Indian raids continued or even intensified, pressure began
to build for the passage of legislation to place Pennsylvania on
a war footing. The position of Quakers in the Assembly became
progressively more untenable, as both the governor and their
coreligionists at home and abroad called on them to resign
their places, the former on the assumption that their
nonpacifist successors would be willing to pass the necessary

legislation, the latter so that they would not have to violate their beliefs by cooperating with the war effort. Finally, in November 1756, the pressure became unbearable, and the Quakers gave in, declaring to the Assembly the wish that their seats might "be filled by Members of other Denominations, in such manner as to prepare, without any scruples, all such Laws as may be necessary to be enacted for the Defence of the Province." So ended an era in the political history of Colonial America. Braddock's Defeat marked the beginning of the end.[9]

Thus far, this discussion has focused on what might be considered the immediate consequences of Braddock's Defeat. In some cases—the Quakers' withdrawal, the change in tactics—the impact was to be of both short- and long-term significance. On the other hand, the strategic advantages gained by the French were to be swept away, and the Indians would emerge from the war far weaker than they had entered it. But it seems fair to say that those who suffered most from the short-term effects of Braddock's Defeat were the Americans, particularly those living on the frontier.

In the long term, however, the colonies profited most, and it is really in this sense that the battle was of greatest consequence. During the decade following, British arms thrust back the French and their Indian allies. Still, the Battle of the Monongahela was not forgotten. While details of the engagement may have faded from men's minds, the residue that remained was the stuff of which myths are made. And the legends that enshrouded Braddock and his unfortunate army were to prove of greater significance than even the Defeat itself.

From the ashes of their misfortune, Americans were to draw their greatest hero. Washington had not been unknown prior to the battle, nor was it his first experience in the Ohio Valley. But during the Fort Necessity campaign, he had himself been in command, and although the odds against him had been overwhelming, a losing commander is seldom lionized, no matter how gallant his behavior or inevitable his defeat. So was it in this case. During Braddock's expedition, however, the young

Virginian was a mere aide-de-camp. Therefore, he could in no way be held responsible for the debacle. But he could be singled out for his own acts of heroism, and this is precisely what his countrymen did. The courage he displayed under fire was the sort that could scarcely be exaggerated by legend, and word of it soon spanned the Atlantic. In early 1756, Lord Halifax asked an associate, "Who is Mr. Washington? I know nothing of him but that they say he behaved in Braddock's action as bravely as if he really loved the whistling of Bullets." Such bravery would itself have impressed many, but more significant still was the fact that, despite his willingness to expose himself to the greatest danger, he was one of the few officers to escape unscathed. How was this possible? Only through divine intervention! Washington himself suggested this, when he wrote his brother that he had survived because of "the miraculous care of Providence that protected me beyond all human expectation." His adversaries may have been likewise impressed. According to his friend and phsyician, Dr. James Craik, some years after the battle he and Washington met an old chieftain, who told the future president that he and his followers had fought for the French against Braddock, and had in the beginning singled out Washington as a target, but that he, seeing the young officer remain unharmed, had told his warriors, "Fire at him no more; see ye not that the Great Spirit protects that chief; he cannot die in battle." Apocryphal? Perhaps, but still significant, for the Indian's tale suggests the aura of semidivinity that enveloped Washington in the wake of his miraculous escape from the Monongahela. This man must indeed have survived so that he might fulfill a divine mission! So thought the Reverend Samuel Davies, who undoubtedly spoke for many Americans when, during the course of a sermon delivered some five weeks after the battle, he paused momentarily to "point out to the public that heroic youth, Colonel Washington, whom I cannot but hope Providence has hitherto preserved in so signal a manner for some important service to his country."[10]

A legend that quickly became gospel was that during the battle Washington had pleaded with the general to allow him to lead the Americans in an Indian-style attack on the enemy, but that Braddock had refused, the degree of his bluntness dependent upon the reporter. As legends go, there is a great deal to be said for this one. And in any case it was commonly believed; that is the important point here. Washington came to epitomize the new, pragmatic, American method of fighting, against the blind, stodgy, Continental tradition represented by Braddock. There was more at stake here than mere tactics. Washington was seen to speak for freedom and individual initiative, Braddock for regimentation. Washington, himself a volunteer, stood for the tradition of the amateur warrior so dear to his countrymen. Braddock and his regulars were the professionals, fighting for a livelihood, rather than for home and hearth.[11]

In the wake of Braddock's Defeat, Americans by and large were not grateful to Britain for its sacrifices. On the contrary, the consensus seems to have been that the mother country had gotten in the way. If only the British had been content to supply them, they would then have driven off the enemy. As a Carolinian merchant wrote to his friend, "Our Ministry would do well to prosecute a War in America with Americans. Only they are not frightened out of their wits at the sight of Indians which by our Accounts was the case with your English Veterans. We wish they had staid at home as the advantage the Enemy have gain'd by their shamefull behaviour will put us to ten times the inconveniency in this part of the World." The provincials who had fought for Braddock were quickly lionized, not only at home, but in Britain as well. Conversely, the regulars who had failed so dismally were universally execrated, along with their general.[12] In the light of such stereotypes, it is scarcely surprising that some Americans began to wonder whether they might not be better off fighting on their own.

The Battle of the Monongahela encouraged a self-reliant spirit that would one day turn smoothly into a desire for independence. We may best understand the link if we attempt to see the battle as Americans of the time by and large would have. To them, it revealed that they could do more in their own defense than Britain could do for them. If this were so, why be bound to the mother country? There were sentimental and in some cases fraternal ties, of course, but they were already weakening by 1755. Security was a more basic motive. As long as Britain would defend them, Americans saw value in the relationship. But in Braddock's Defeat, the mother country failed dismally. One might imagine that the numerous victories achieved by British arms before the close of the decade would have more than counterbalanced any bad impressions, and in point of fact memories of the battle did fade. But they revived as friction grew in the early 1770s. Indeed, Americans might now feel that, with the French menace gone, only the Indians were yet to be dealt with, and that it was they, not the British, who knew how to handle them. This granted, what did the British connection now mean? It meant *expense*, tribute to an overlord who would not protect the colonies as well as they might protect themselves. Was the tie worth retaining? The answer came in 1776. But already more than two decades earlier, the question was beginning to evolve. According to Franklin, "this whole transaction gave us Americans the first suspicion that our exalted ideas of the prowess of British regulars had not been well founded."[13] The "transaction" was Braddock's Defeat.

APPENDICES
NOTES
BIBLIOGRAPHY
INDEX

Tangents

IN THE TEXT I have been intent on an in-depth discussion of the Battle of the Monongahela itself—background, narrative, analysis, and significance. My aim in this first appendix, however, is to travel somewhat off the beaten track, and to note some of those interesting sidelights to the career of Braddock which I felt did not belong in the text. For the most part, this section is bibliographical, but since some of the sources I mention here are not readily available, I have tried to provide some insight into what their value may be.

First, I must report that those who hope to gain some understanding of Braddock by tracing his life from the cradle are due for a disappointment. Prior to 1754, he was just a shadow figure. One can establish that he came from a military background and trace out his promotions easily enough. Lee McCardell, his only biographer, has fixed his date of birth. But almost nothing else is known of him during the long years before Cumberland chose him to head the campaign in America. McCardell manfully tries to compensate for such a lack of data by providing some insight into his milieu, but there is no way of knowing how Braddock himself reacted to it. A few anecdotes throw dim rays of light on his character, but it would be unwise to infer too much from them. Some are drawn from Walpole, who in 1754, on hearing of Braddock's appointment, sought out and related tales about him, all suggesting that the new major general was volatile and selfish, as well as debauched. About the only favorable information he could find, or at any rate was willing to pass on, was that Braddock had been a popular acting governor at Gibraltar. On the other hand, George Anne Bellamy, a popular actress of the day, whom Braddock treate'd as a daughter, provides the reader with a much more favorable impression of the unfortunate general. The anecdotes she supplies, as well as Walpole's, are treated at length by McCardell, and Winthrop Sargent recounts them as well. The latter, although on the whole critical of Braddock, gives the Bellamy testimony full play and appends much of it. He does the same with Goldsmith's discussion of the general's unfortunate sister Fanny, who in 1731 hanged herself at Bath after having wasted her small patrimony on a scoundrel. The claim that Braddock reacted with sarcasm to the news of her death may simply be malicious and is related only by Walpole, who tended to remember just the worst gossip. Still, like everything else involving Braddock's behavior prior to 1754, we cannot know for certain.

On the background to the campaign and the expedition itself, I recommend Winthrop Sargent, *The History of an Expedition Against Fort Du Quesne in 1755,* Lawrence Gipson, *The Great War for Empire,* Lee McCardell, *Ill-Starred General,* and, particularly on the march, Douglas S. Freeman, *George Washington: A Biography.* As regards Braddock's stormy relationship with the colonies and the governors' equally stormy relationships with their respective assemblies, it is worthwhile to check Arthur M. Schlesinger's fine article on the impasse in Maryland, "Maryland's Share in the Last Colonial War." Pennsylvania and Virginia politics during this period have been dealt with well and often. Two works particularly worthy of note are Robert Davidson's *War Comes to Quaker Pennsylvania 1682–1756,* especially chapter 8, and Louis K. Koontz, *Robert Dinwiddie: His Career in American Colonial Government and Westward Expansion.* The latter provides very worthwhile material, not only on Dinwiddie's attempts to rally support for the expedition, but also on the background to the French and Indian War, for the governor of Virginia played a large role in bringing the conflict about.

The individual interested in following Braddock's route from Wills Creek will find ample material to guide him on his way. The standard study of Braddock's Road has for years been and yet remains John K. Lacock, "Braddock Road." However, in respect to the last days of the march, see also Paul Wallace's "'Blunder Camp': A Note on the Braddock Road." Wallace profits from the use of several sources not available to Lacock, the most important of them being the two journals printed by Charles Hamilton in *Braddock's Defeat*. Freeman likewise provides interesting information on the road, particularly regarding topography; see *George Washington: A Biography*, vol. 2, p. 46.

When I mentioned to a friend that I was writing an account of the Battle of the Monongahela, he responded by asking, "Is it true that Braddock took his mistress with him on the march?" I have found it impossible to answer this question. It *is* true that there is a legend to this effect, and to the effect that she was one of those taken captive by the Indians (Walter O'Meara, *Guns at the Forks*, p. 121). Moreover, if we take Walpole's word for it, the general had been something of a rake in his youth. Nevertheless, I have found no evidence whatever that Braddock traveled in the company of a mistress, though presumably it would take a peculiar kind of eyewitness to verify the fact in any case. This question therefore cannot be answered with any confidence, but it does bring up a related point: Who were the women who did accompany the march? O'Meara provides some information on them (pp. 121–24). However, his suggestion that many or perhaps most of the women were looked to by the soldiers for services less creditable than washing and nursing should not be too quickly accepted. The only woman involved in Braddock's expedition about whom we know anything, Charlotte Browne, certainly set a high standard of morality. Mrs. Browne, a widow, accompanied her brother on the expedition, but went no farther than Fort Cumberland. Her account is interesting nonetheless and provides insight into the miserable conditions that the women, as well as the men, must have endured on the march to Fort Duquesne. It is contained in her diary, the relevant portions of which are published in "With Braddock's Army," edited by Fairfax Harrison.

Moving on to the battle itself, we encounter the most famous of all legends involving Braddock: that he was shot by one of his own men. Sargent claims that the story was never heard until years after the event, and that this militates against its veracity. He is wrong here, although he could not have known it, owing to the limited source material at his disposal. On August 13, 1755, John Bolling provided an account of the battle in a letter to his son. In passing, he noted that Braddock was "supos'd to have been killed by his own Men" (John A. Schultz, ed., "A Private Report of General Braddock's Defeat"). Bolling's source of information on this point is uncertain, though the rest of his account is very heavily influenced by Washington.

Several soldiers apparently claimed "credit" for having shot their commander. One was Captain Robert Allison. According to Allison, he was in the advance party on the fatal day. When Braddock refused to order a retreat, despite the hopelessness of the situation, Allison says he commanded his orderly sergeant to shoot the general, in order to save those who yet lived. The subordinate tried to shoot Braddock, but was successful only in killing several of the general's horses, thus forcing Allison to commit the deed himself, successfully. This account, which had become a family legend, is repeated in the *Historical Magazine,* vol. 11 (1867), p. 141. There is no record of any officer surnamed Allison having served on the expedition, but since the nature of his purported service is unknown, it is possible that he participated in some capacity.

In 1826, John Fanning Watson, an antiquary, interviewed Billy Brown, a nonogenarian who as a slave had served an officer in Braddock's army. According to Brown, during the battle "a soldier took aim and shot Indian. Braddock shot the soldier the soldier's Brother shot Bk. he was on foot. the soldier offered to give himself up." Brown identified the man in question as one Pritchett. Seven years after this interview, Watson conversed with another supposed survivor of the battle, William Butler. "I asked him particularly *who* killed Braddock, and he answered promptly one *Fawcett,* brother of one whom Braddock had just killed in a passion; this last, who killed Braddock, was in the ranks as a non-commissioned officer; the former was a brave major or colonel." Watson accepted the stories, identifying "Pritchett" with "Fawcett" (see entries for Brown and Butler in Appendix E).

Here we for the first time encounter the main "claimant"—"Old Tom Faucett." Faucett, a backwoodsman, did indeed serve in the battle. We know this because he was listed among the deserters after the event. He certainly lived on for many years, and in fact Butler claimed to have seen him in 1830, though most evidence suggests that he had died somewhat earlier than this. Be that as it may, he seems to have been alive in 1812 to deliver the following diatribe to Braddock's skeleton, which he had helped to unearth:

You tried to put shame on th' names o' brave men. We was cowards, was we, because we knowed better than to fight Injuns like you red-backed ijits across the ocean is used to fight; because we wouldn't stand up rubbin' shoulders like a passel o' sheep and let the red-skins made sieves outen us! . . . And them boys—th' ole Virginny Blues—you made git from behint th' trees and git kilt; and them others you cussed, . . . and cut down with yer saber, my own pore brother, Joe, amongst 'em!—Why, ef I hadn't stopped ye with a shot, ye'd had us all massacred and scalped! (see Appendix E)

Even if Faucett did not deliver this particular speech, it seems clear that on numerous occasions he claimed to have shot Braddock. The problem is that on others he insisted he had not. Drink appears to have loosened his tongue. Did it also loosen his memory?

Sargent devotes a great deal of space to analyzing Faucett's story, and to tearing it apart (pp. 244–53). In particular, he notes discrepancies in the various versions. So does John S. Ritenour (*Old Tom Fossit*), who after surveying the evidence puts his subject down as a drunken illiterate who told his tale for the sake of notoriety (pp. 113–20).

Others are not so sure. William Lowdermilk (*History of Cumberland*) claims that the discrepancies noted by Sargent could

be ascribed to the fact that Faucett tended to forget or confuse certain details as he aged (pp. 187–88). He implies acceptance of Faucett's story, while others, such as James Hadden,
accept it with conviction (*Washington's Expeditions* [*1753–1754*]
and Braddock's Expedition [*1755*], pp. 114–15). Hadden's case is
particularly interesting, since apparently without realizing the
implications he notes that Tom Faucett's brother Joseph, the
man whom Braddock had supposedly killed, survived the
battle, married, and had children (p. 125).

Needless to say, there is no way to prove that Braddock was
not killed by one of his own men. However, the fact that there
are so many different accounts, given by various individuals,
and that virtually every known version contains elements that
are implausible at best, militates against accepting the legend.
The popularity of this tradition should, however, serve as a
reminder of just how unpopular Braddock was for fully three
generations after his defeat: For one of his men to claim that
he had shot him might have been merely a boast.

After his wounding, by whatever hand, Braddock was carried
from the field in his sash, which had been designed for this very
purpose. His fate we know. That of his sash is less certain. What
appears to have been the same item, stained with the general's
blood, was in 1846 presented to Zachary Taylor as a tribute to
his deeds during the Mexican War (Wills de Hass, *History of the
Early Settlement and Indian Wars of Western Virginia*, pp. 129–30).
In 1909, Miss Sarah Knox Wood, a descendent of President
Taylor's, allowed the Maryland Historical Society to exhibit the
sash, which was then in her keeping (*Maryland Historical Magazine*, 5 [1910], pp. 73–74). It is now on display at Mount Vernon
(Elswyth Thane, *Mount Vernon: The Legacy*, p. 92).

And what of Braddock's cannon, some of which, thanks to
Gage's blunder, had from the very start of battle been turned
against the British? Montcalm used them in August 1756, during his successful attack on Fort Oswego. This has been frequently noted. Not so well known is the fact that two years later
the British regained them, when they took Fort Frontenac

E. B. O'Callaghan, ed., *Documents Relative to the Colonial History of the State of New York,* vol. 10, pp. 484, 821, 829). In a small way, this restoration symbolized the turning of the tide. With Forbes's conquest of Fort Duquesne later that year, the wheel came full circle.

✍ APPENDIX B ✍

Bibliographical Survey

BERNARD OF CHARTRES, an eleventh-century philosopher, once compared scholars living in his own time with the ancients by describing the former as "dwarfs, mounted on the shoulders of giants." Modest? Certainly. Self-abasing? No, not really. For he went on to say that, being so positioned, "we can see more and further than they."

Those who have studied intensively Braddock's campaign and defeat include several of the greatest historians this nation has yet produced—George Bancroft, Francis Parkman, and Lawrence Henry Gipson. It is primarily on the basis of their research, and that of others approaching them in stature, that I have completed my own study of the battle. My hope is that, like Bernard, I enjoy a vantage point that permits me to see a bit further than my predecessors. In this appendix, I shall attempt to show how Braddock historiography has evolved, and how far earlier historians were able to see.

Some may consider Braddock's Defeat to be too limited a topic to merit an essay such as this. Such might be the case if we were to see it merely as a battle, and at that as one which by no means decided a war. But historians have seldom done this. Rather, most have seen it as something of a morality play, whose protagonists were not Beaujeu and Braddock, but *Washington* and Braddock, each personifying a nation and a system. As Pargellis writes, "To almost everyone . . . this episode stands as a conflict between Old World and New World ways, with the outcome justifying the New."[1] Let us therefore proceed, but likewise recall that we view scholarship through but a narrow aperture.

The symbolic aspect of the battle was most clearly drawn

during the nineteenth century, when narrative achieved its highest expression. While Bancroft and Parkman were penning their epics, across the Atlantic, James Anthony Froude was proclaiming Shakespeare the greatest of all English historians. But this was not only an age of stylistic excellence. It saw also a rapid advance in historical scholarship. In both the method and the basis of telling, the study of Braddock's Defeat developed in a microcosmic relationship to the whole.

Very nearly a century passed between the battle and the first treatment of it scholarly enough to merit the term "history." This does not mean, however, that it was seldom written of during the interim. Shortly after the campaign had come to its disastrous end, interested individuals began to sift through the published accounts, embellished them with rumor, and published reports of the action. A few of them, like Thomas Mante and John Entick, worked with care. But even though contemporary to the event, none of them really had much to go on, for the printed versions were few. Furthermore, most writers were quite credulous and were thoroughly willing to accept fiction as fact, particularly if it tended toward the glorification of Washington or the detriment of Braddock. This tendency grew with the years. As memories became more clouded, gullibility increased, and history gave way almost entirely to legend. Some of the myths involving the Battle of the Monongahela remain with us today, the notion that Braddock was ambushed being perhaps the most common.

In 1839, Jared Sparks completed *The Life of George Washington,* which included the first nineteenth-century analysis of the battle worthy of special notice. Of the general's character, he gave a mixed, but on the whole a negative, review:

General Braddock was a brave man and an experienced officer; but, arrogant and obstinate, he had the weakness, at all times a folly and in his case an infatuation, to despise his enemy. Ignorant of the country, of the mode of warfare in which he was engaged, and of the force opposed to him, he refused counsel, neglected precautions, and thus lost his life.

Sparks was no mean scholar, though his contempories over-rated him in this respect. He himself visited Braddock's Field and examined every inch of the terrain. On his tour, he discovered several "deep ravines" in the area and concluded that the French and Indians had concealed themselves within them—not a foolish inference, although I have suggested it to be on the whole incorrect. More surprising is his statement that Braddock was, indeed, ambushed. Sparks had access to the comments of only two of our twenty-two basic British eye-witnesses, Orme and Washington, and neither provides much insight into the first moments of battle, which involved primarily the advance party. On the other hand, Sparks also had at his disposal three French accounts, that he had discovered in the archives of Paris. Although he does not give details, one was certainly by the anonymous writer whom I have designated "French B," and it is in fact Sparks who first related Beaujeu's famous speech to the Indians. But it cannot be said that he otherwise made very good use of his find. Though the French reports clearly show that Braddock was not ambushed, Sparks chose to cling to tradition. His tendency to be credulous is likewise manifest in the fact that, like John Fanning Watson, he interviewed William Butler, a centenarian who claimed to have fought under Braddock, and furthermore blithely accepted the old man's damaging testimony that the general had positively refused to allow an Indian band to join his march.[2]

Despite the tenuous nature of his sources, Sparks set a pattern that was to endure for the remainder of the century. Virtually all writers would echo his "compromise" portrayal of Braddock as a brave man who would perhaps have been a competent tactician had he been fighting in Flanders rather than in America. They would see the general as a martinet, a bigot in his attitude toward provincials, and, most damaging of all, a pigheaded person who refused to take the advice of those wiser than he, most notably Washington. Younger historians would mirror Sparks in other ways as well. As noted in chapter

3, throughout the nineteenth century and into our own, most writers took it for granted that the enemy had fired on Braddock's troops from the security of trenches. Although this was an old tradition, it received its main impetus from Sparks. It fitted in well with an overall negative assessment of Braddock, because historians could claim that if only the general had ordered sufficient reconnaissance, he would have known of the trenches and could have planned accordingly. And why had he not? They would answer, because he was overconfident, contemptuous of the enemy, and so mindless of the value of Indian scouts that he turned many away, while ignoring those who did accompany him.[3]

With the publication in 1852 of the fourth volume of Bancroft's *History of the United States,* we move into a higher sphere. It has become fashionable to criticize Bancroft as one who allowed his political leanings and patriotism to get the better of his scholarship. Biased he was, but he was also a scholar of the first order. His years of research in British, French, and American archives are everywhere reflected in his great *History,* and in no area more than in his study of Braddock's expedition. Through him, our attention is for the first time drawn to several of the most important sources on the campaign and battle. Sparks had known of Orme's letter to Morris, but it is Bancroft who first refers to the captain's journal, including his maps, and in fact his account of the battle draws most heavily on this source. He also notes Gage's letter, which had recently been published—a source that only he and Parkman, among major historians of the century, used. Furthermore, he cites three French accounts, which he had probably heard of through Sparks and which would be published later in the decade. He makes far better use of these than had Washington's famed biographer. Bancroft's list of second- and third-hand reports is likewise impressive, and more so because he looks at them with a critical eye. Perhaps he is a bit free in accepting anecdotes favorable to Washington, but on the other hand there is nothing here of Butler's dubious reports. His research was mature enough that he could afford to dispense with such material.

Bancroft's learning is admirable. So is his account of the battle, which is the most original of his century. Although no admirer of Braddock's he does not see the general as totally, or even primarily, to blame for the debacle. Among the officers, he singles out Gage as a blunderer. But the central cause of defeat was in his opinion the panic of the troops: "Had the regulars shown courage, the issue would not have been doubtful." The implications of this statement are significant. There is nothing here of the popular concept that Braddock's real mistake lay in not using irregular tactics. In fact, Bancroft has very little to say about the American troops. He says that the British would have carried the day using standard Continental tactics, if only the regulars had kept their heads. Nor does he claim that Braddock stumbled into an ambush. Rather, he accepts the consensus view implicit in the French accounts he had examined, to the effect that both sides were surprised by their sudden confrontation. He also takes French B's suggestion that Beaujeu's troops fought from behind trees. Bancroft makes no reference to trenches, and indeed he appears to have considered the entire question of reconnaissance immaterial. One last conclusion he draws from his French accounts—that Beaujeu was truly heroic. Although Sparks had touched briefly on the French captain, it is Bancroft who first glorifies him, Dumas receiving some lesser praise.[4]

Bancroft's account might have exerted more influence than it did if not for the fact that only three years after it appeared in print Winthrop Sargent produced his monograph on the Braddock expedition. The book won great acclaim on both sides of the Atlantic and was quite popular, appearing as it did in the centenary of the battle. Sargent was only in his thirtieth year when his finest work appeared. He was to die young and is today remembered primarily for this one study, which is still generally considered definitive in its field.

Sargent does not appear to have been familiar with much

material on the battle, that Bancroft had not known of, the one major exception being the "Seaman's Journal," a version of which had been published in London the year before. Sargent appended that version, as well as long excerpts from a second. More important, he published Orme's journal and also the three French accounts referred to by Bancroft, those of French A, French B, and Lotbinière. He also became familiar with the reports by Pouchot, Croghan, Leslie, and British D, but he did not make much use of any of them and indeed appears to have examined the last only after his study had gone to press.

In his portrayal of Braddock, Sargent evinces some ambivalence. Like Sparks, he considers the general to have been volatile and stubborn, though courageous. But unlike his predecessor he defends Braddock for having been critical of Americans. To Sargent's mind this bias had developed in response to the apathy that provincials had commonly displayed toward his mission.

Sargent's account of the battle is taken from two sets of sources. His version of the initial clash between Beaujeu's detachment and the advance party is drawn primarily from the "Seaman's Journal," with additional material coming from the French accounts. Otherwise, his main source is Orme. Although Bancroft had made use of Orme's journal, it is with Sargent that Braddock's aide-de-camp becomes clearly established as the most important informant of all, as regards Braddock's campaign in general and the Battle of the Monongahela in particular. Sargent's account of the telescoping and resultant panic derives directly from Orme and helps to exculpate Braddock, since it focuses blame on the regulars. But Sargent does not take this point to its logical conclusion. Having described the panic in detail, he then turns around and suggests an involved feint that he felt Braddock should have used to draw out the enemy. Regarding the general's role in the Defeat, he seems on the whole to be a witness for the defense. On the basis of his own observations, he repeats Spark's claim that the enemy fired from trenches. However, while claiming that Braddock had not treated his Indians well, he suggests too that those who did accompany the march were recalcitrant and usually unwilling to reconnoiter, so that their commander could scarcely be blamed for not knowing of the ditches that lay across his route. On the key question of whether Braddock should have listened to Washington's plea that the men be allowed to fight Indian style on the fateful day, Sargent does not take a clear stand. Indeed, he has surprisingly little to say about the behavior of the provincial troops. This may again derive from his reliance on Orme, who says nothing whatever about them.

During the eighty years after Sargent produced his great work, only one historian made a significant contribution to the study of Braddock's campaign or defeat. This was Parkman, one of the few products of his century to rival Bancroft in stature. In his classic *Montcalm and Wolfe,* first published in 1884, Parkman included some fifty pages on the Braddock expedition, about twenty of which may be said to revolve around the battle itself. Clearly this is a topic that interested him, and his account of the engagement is vividly drawn.

Parkman refers to the traditional British sources, first- and secondhand, and stands as the apparent discoverer of Mackellar's maps. Moreover, he makes use of a small volume of French reports, published by John D. G. Shea in 1860, and on this basis becomes the first major historian to refer to the accounts of Godefroy and French C. More important, he introduces two documents discovered in the course of his archival research—the reports by Dumas and Contrecoeur. One should not overestimate the significance of his contributions. French A in particular had followed the accounts of the two captains so closely that the information itself was not new. But Dumas's stirring account of the first moments of battle—and especially of his own heroism—is the stuff of theater, and Parkman uses its dramatic potential to the full. For the first time, Dumas emerges as Beaujeu's equal in greatness.

Parkman made use of more accounts of the battle than did

any other nineteenth-century historian, but it cannot be said that he used them better. His narrative of the action is famous, but somewhat tarnished by his tendency to go beyond the sources for dramatic effect. This is not to say that he misrepresents his material, but rather that he embellishes it. So had countless historians before, so have countless since. But it seems that both Bancroft and Sargent "stick to the facts" somewhat better than does Parkman.

Parkman's narrative ability tends to reach its summit when propelled by soaring patriotism. So it is with his description of the battle. Leaving most of his sources behind, he draws on Washington, Burd, and legend in glorifying the heroism of the provincials in the wake of the regulars' collapse:

The men of the two regiments became mixed together. . . . Both men and officers were new to this blind and frightful warfare of the savage in his native woods. . . . The Virginians alone were equal to the emergency. Fighting behind trees like the Indians themselves, they might have held the enemy in check till order could be restored, had not Braddock, furious at a proceeding that shocked all his ideas of courage and discipline, ordered them, with oaths, to form into line.

However, if Parkman implicitly condemns Braddock for having refused to allow the Americans to fight Indian style, he supports him on other fronts. Like Sargent, and even more pointedly, he sees Braddock's problems in reconnaissance as deriving not from his mishandling of the Indians, but from their own recalcitrance. In any case, he does not see the scouting problem as decisive. He agrees with Sparks and Sargent that the enemy used natural trenches as hiding places, but suggests that many, if not most of them fought from behind trees. The thrust of his account is that Braddock lost, not because he was fighting in an area of which he should have received intelligence and had not, but rather because his troops panicked.

Parkman's portrayal of Braddock is among the more sympathetic of the century. He suggests the usual flaws in the general's character—stubbornness, surliness—and, like most of his contemporaries, he judges Braddock unfit to have led a campaign in the American wilderness, owing to his ignorance of Indian tactics. But he notes that "whatever were his failings, he feared nothing, and his fidelity and honor in the discharge of public trusts were never questioned." Such praise for his courage and honesty is not new. Neither is the historian's claim that Braddock for the most part conducted his march well, taking all due precautions. It is rather Parkman's emphasis of these positive points that leaves the impression that he is on the whole more sympathetic to the general than Sparks, Bancroft, or Sargent had been. Perhaps this is again the result of Orme's influence, and it is noteworthy that Parkman puts the captain himself in a very favorable light.[5]

More than fifty years passed between the publication of *Montcalm and Wolfe* and that of the next major work involving Braddock's Defeat. In the realm of our subject, this long interval was a time of mighty narrative and weak scholarship. At best, the writers by and large rehashed Sargent, and even then they liberally sprinkled his account with folk legend. This shoddy workmanship did not derive from any diminution of interest in the battle, but rather from the desire to press it into a chauvinistic context. Braddock was now generally cast as a total fool—perhaps a brave one—who, after blundering into an ambush, was too pigheaded to allow the Americans under his command to save the day by using Indian-style tactics against the enemy. Thus did the haughty, regimented, traditionalist Old World come into conflict with the individualistic, innovative New, to the disgrace of the former.[6]

But the torrent of rancor finally abated. In 1936, Stanley Pargellis produced two works that have strongly influenced subsequent research on Braddock's Defeat. During the course of his research among the Cumberland Papers at Windsor Castle he discovered a number of documents relevant to the battle, which he published in *Military Affairs in North America 1748–1765*. Now for the first time the public came to know of the eyewitness accounts by Gordon and St. Clair. And in his article, "Braddock's Defeat," Pargellis became the first to make reference, albeit brief, to the report by Gates, and the first to incorporate Stephen's account, then little known, into a discussion of the battle.[7]

Pargellis leaned rather too heavily on weak sources, and this led to questionable conclusions. His arguments are dealt with in chapter 5, and again in Appendix C. It is nevertheless true that he made an invaluable contribution, not only by adding considerably to the store of material on Braddock's Defeat, but in his approach to the various accounts bequeathed to or discovered by him. Earlier writers on the battle had seldom dealt critically with their sources. Perhaps at most they had judged a particular version to be untrustworthy, and in such cases they had made little if any attempt to determine whether certain aspects might nonetheless be worthy of acceptance. They had also tended to credit everything contained in accounts they liked, particularly when the text was quotable. There are few instances in the earlier narratives where we can see evidence that a given historian is noting contradictions among his various sources and choosing one viewpoint as most plausible. Admittedly, there are several reasons for this. One of the most important is that throughout the nineteenth century writers had comparatively few eyewitness accounts to work with. But the main consideration was probably stylistic. If one were to compare versions, it would be necessary either to disrupt the narrative—which, in the age of Parkman, would have been considered gauche, to say the least—or else to argue out in a footnote each disputed point, and thereby produce a book that was only one-quarter text. Pargellis was the first willing to sacrifice the fluidity of his narrative for the sake of accuracy. He was not always consistent in the means by which he judged credibility, and in the scope of an article he could not discuss each eyewitness to the extent desirable, but there is no question that he, more than any other historian, pointed the way toward more careful handling of source material. Unfortunately, only a few have followed his lead.

Pargellis's thesis has experienced the same mixed success as his methodology. Briefly, in his article he argues that Braddock was justified in his resolve to fight the battle entirely on the basis of Continental tactics, but that he misapplied them and was therefore to blame for the disaster. Most historians have accepted the first point, but not the second. That is, they tend to feel, for one reason or another, that the general could not have won by allowing his troops to fight Indian style, but they also insist that the regular tactics he advocated were sound. As one might suspect, they for the most part place blame for the Defeat not on Braddock, but rather on incompetent subordinates, or, more often, on panicky troops. On the strength of this conviction, the pendulum has swung dramatically. Braddock, long maligned, has been portrayed in an increasingly favorable light, perhaps too much so.[8]

Among major historians, probably the staunchest defender of the general has been Gipson, who in 1946 produced *The Great War for Empire: The Years of Defeat, 1754–1757,* the sixth volume of his magnificent series, *The British Empire Before the American Revolution.* As one might expect in a book whose theme is defeat, there is a good deal here about Braddock. The thrust of Gipson's argument is that the disaster at the Monongahela resulted primarily from several key blunders by Gage, of great importance being his decision not to occupy the hillock on the right before encountering Beaujeu's troops, and then, more disastrous still, prematurely ordering a retreat. He seems justified on the first point, but not on the second, for while the retreat of the advance party certainly had disastrous consequences, it is by no means clear that Gage ordered it. On the telescoping, and generally on the battle, Gipson relies primarily on Orme, and indeed he makes no significant contribution to our list of sources. But he does set the tone for a generation that would admire Braddock. To his mind, the general was vigorous and humane: "His military conceptions and his tactical arrangements were sound and most errors of judgment in connection with the campaign were committed by others . . . ;

yet his correspondence is remarkably free from any censure of his fellow officers."[9]

Only two years after Gipson's work appeared, Douglas Southall Freeman came forth with the second volume of his life of Washington. Freeman's interest in Braddock is evident in the fact that he devotes fully one hundred pages to the expedition of 1755, including almost forty on the battle. But the significance of his study certainly does not lie in the area of quantity. Here length connotes thoroughness, not only in treatment, but in research. Freeman uses all of the significant sources on the battle known in his day. Moreover, he uses them extremely well, and is also the first to refer to Roucher's account, although he does not work too much with it. Regarding Braddock himself, Freeman is favorably inclined, but more critical than Gipson, perhaps reflecting Washington's own ambivalence. Still, when it comes to analyzing the general's role in the battle and the march preceding it, he provides the most admirable defense yet produced. This defense reflects the systematic nature of Freeman's scholarship. He lists the various charges leveled against Braddock and answers them individually. A simple format indeed, and yet one that had never been used previously, possibly because, again, it was inconsistent with the dictates of style. Although just one section, albeit a lengthy section, of a multivolume work, Freeman's study of Braddock's expedition and defeat stands head and shoulders above others written in this century. Here we have not only narrative, indeed excellent narrative, but scholarship of the first order, and a new concept of how to handle the issues arising from the subject.[10]

In 1958, more than two centuries after his death, Braddock finally became the subject of a full-length biography. Lee McCardell, who had made something of a hobby of studying the rather mysterious officer, entered the historical lists with *Ill-Starred General: Braddock of the Coldstream Guards.* McCardell's research is admirable. He is the first writer in the field to have ferreted out Cameron's memoir, and he makes use of virtually all relevant sources in print at the time, primary and secondary. Unfortunately, he is not particularly discriminating in his use of them, seldom differentiating between a solid eyewitness account and even the wildest rumor. His study of the battle hearkens back to the age of narrative. There is no real analysis here or elsewhere. The action simply flows, and McCardell's numerous sources provide a wealth of battlefield quotations. As one might expect, the end result is very readable, but it does not rank high in the realm of scholarship.

The present work has served to introduce several new sources and to draw attention to others which, though in print, have hitherto been ignored by historians. But the stress, I hope, has been on analysis. I have attempted—with what success the reader may judge—to carry the handling of our materials further down the road suggested by Pargellis. To encourage continued analysis, I have appended all eyewitness reports of the battle. Others may use them to embellish my account or, if they find cause, to alter it. Certainly the wealth of testimony provides many more angles than could be handled in the text.

In emphasizing critical method, I am by no means suggesting that we should put the age of narrative behind us.[11] I do feel, however, that no matter how the historian finally tells his story, he owes it to his audience to prepare it carefully, and this must involve not only gathering sources, but analyzing them. I furthermore believe that the "mass" audience is becoming progressively more sophisticated, and that contrary to the suggestions of some, it is no longer frightened by footnotes or by a frankly critical approach to source material. For the sake of narrative, the historian may well choose to do his analysis behind the scenes. But it seems to me that the historian's craft has advanced to the point where, regardless of subject, the writer cannot toss his materials around with abandon and yet win for his product the accolade of "history." This, too, is a legacy of the giants.

Orme's Reliability

FROM 1755 to the present, Robert Orme has remained our chief source of information on Braddock's expedition and the Battle of the Monongahela itself. Some four decades ago, however, Stanley Pargellis accused the captain of having misrepresented the action in order to protect Braddock's reputation, as well as his own. In this appendix, I discuss Orme's importance as an eyewitness and judge his credibility.

As soon as he had recovered sufficiently from the wounds he had suffered in battle, Orme began to dispatch a series of letters presenting his account of the affair. These letters fell into two categories. First there were those intended for publication, in hopes that they might sway the public. These versions were printed in no fewer than seven newspapers, on both sides of the Atlantic, during the late summer of 1755.[1] The second category includes letters aimed at individuals, specifically superiors and colonial governors. In this case, too, he was prolific, and some of the addressees passed on copies or extracts of his accounts.[2]

According to the captain, he wrote at the behest of his late commander. In his letter to Fox, he states that "the General the Day before his Death Order'd Me as soon as I was Able to transmitt to You, Sir, An Account of the Unhappy Action." Quite likely the order did not involve Fox alone. Whether the dying general looked for vindication, or merely a just account of the battle, one cannot know. Orme himself certainly worked toward the former end, and possibly the latter as well. In the process, he may likewise have sought out his own vindication. St. Clair might wash his hands of all responsibility for the fiasco by claiming that during the last days of the campaign Braddock had continually ignored his good advice. Orme could scarcely get away with that. Everyone of any importance on the expedition knew that he had been Braddock's chief favorite and had held tremendous sway with him. Only by vindicating the general might he vindicate himself.

We have seen the end product of his labors. Orme's narrative boils down to a simple proposition: Braddock had served nobly throughout the campaign and battle; the disastrous defeat was entirely the fault of his panicky troops. Although heaping praise on the officers, Orme implies that if any were at all to blame, it was those of the vanguard, who had allowed their men to retreat into Burton's detachment.

From his day to ours, the captain's account has had tremendous impact. The historiographical survey I appended previously gives some indication of his persistent influence.[3] Yet, as we also saw, the fact that historians have by and large accepted his portrayal of the battle has not prevented them from criticizing Braddock. This is due to two aspects of the action that Orme passes over. First, being himself in the main body at the commencement of firing, he has nothing to say about the fighting up front, and therefore does not contradict the legend that the attack constituted an ambush. As I suggested in Appendix B, historians like Sparks who have assumed that Braddock was indeed ambushed tend to be hard on the general for what they see as his failures in reconnaissance. Orme likewise has nothing to say about the behavior of American troops, and this has left historians free to accept the legend that they fought heroically and might well have routed the enemy had not Braddock forced them from cover.

Orme was himself a persuasive sort. This we may judge by comparing two letters Morris wrote to Shirley. In the first, undated but apparently written in late July, the governor of Pennsylvania states:

The Defeat of our Troops appears to me to be owing to the want of Care and Caution in the Leaders, who have been too secure, and held in too great Contempt the Indian Manner of Fighting; even by Capt.

Orme's Account they were not aware of the Attack. And there are others that say the French & Indians lined the Way on each Side and in the Front behind Intrenchments that we knew Nothing of till they fired upon us.

Yet, by September 5, Morris had changed his tune: "My good friend, Capt. Orme, is now with us. . . . Capn Orme is going to England, and will put the affair of the Western Campaign in a true light, and greatly different from what it has been represented to be."[4]

This is not to say that everyone accepted his story. Daniel Dulany, perhaps his most vocal critic, claimed in a newsletter of 1755:

As Orme is gone home, I take it for granted his account of the action will be published there, and, perhaps, may give the public a different impression of the conduct of the expedition than a disinterested and candid narrative would do. He absolutely governed Mr. Braddock, and his influence and insolence became so notorious that there is hardly any one in the army who cannot give instances of them. . . . His influence all America has reason to deplore, his insolence to resent, and his enmity to fear, if he has yet the power of hurting us by his representations.[5]

If we accept Pargellis's opinion, Orme was disbelieved by individuals far more influential than Dulany. He claims that the captain was refused a promotion in 1756 and that this resulted from an unwillingness on the part of superiors to accept his account. The first claim is true enough, and indeed Orme was both surprised and disappointed by the rebuff. But in writing to Washington of his misfortune, he implies not that he had been discredited, but quite the opposite:

Letters from America had made the Generals Character as odious in this Country as there but since my Arrival and my having writ a true and impartial Narrative of the Affair the Opinions of Men are altered and his Character will be rather revered than disapproved. . . . I thought I should have returned but am not included in the American Promotions[;] except the Pleasure of once more seeing my dear George I am as well contented.

Even if his last statement suggests sour grapes, it is frankly far-fetched to assume that he had failed to secure promotion because his superiors disbelieved him. Orme was himself involved in a serious scandal at the time. Despite the fact that he was apparently already married, and a father, he had wooed and won the daughter of Viscount Townshend. Later that year they were to wed, and he was to retire to the comfortable life of a country gentleman. Townshend was not amused by the affair, and he would have had sufficient influence to block any promotion Orme might otherwise have received. It is possible that he did so, and possible also that Orme himself overestimated his chances for advancement. After all, Braddock's death had deprived him of his most important patron. Perhaps, too, he failed of promotion because the army needed a scapegoat, and he was looked on as an obvious choice. But presumably the powers that be would have made more than they did of the rebuff if this had been a major factor. In any case, if he were chosen as a scapegoat, it would more likely have been because it was felt that he had abused his influence over Braddock than that his account misrepresented the action.[6]

Next we come to a more direct accusation by Pargellis. According to him, Orme was the central figure in a conspiracy to cover up the general's blunders which had brought about the disaster:

Braddock's reputation he valiantly tried to save by throwing the blame for the defeat elsewhere. He could not throw it on the officers, for they, being literate men with powerful correspondents, would deny the allegation. His solution was to praise to excess the "unparallelled good Behaviour" of the officers, and to put the blame, unreservedly upon that poor dumb ox, the British private soldier. Gage, to excuse his own negligence, reached the same answer. Gordon on the other hand, who had listened to Orme's blandishments, ran to the cover of Cumberland's protection.... St. Clair said just enough to make it clear to Cumberland where he stood. Gates contented himself with hinting that things were not what they seemed. Stephen knew nothing

f these wheels within wheels. . . . No evidence shows that
Washington] was consciously involved in a rather unscrupulous
cheme and that he covered up his complicity.[7]

Despite this neat listing, there is really no proof of a conspiracy.
Pargellis presents no evidence, and I know of none, to show
hat Orme in any way sought to influence Gordon. Furthermore, the accounts by the reporters noted are quite individu-
lized, again militating against any "conspiracy" theory. This
applies as well to most of the reports that have surfaced during
he period since Pargellis wrote. Uniformly, the writers have
supported Orme's basic thesis. But this should not suggest a
cover-up. Among reporters favoring his essential view is Furnis, who hated him and would not have followed his lead.

Pargellis tends to see Washington as a yokel, who accepted
blindly whatever his friend Orme told him. It is true that the
Virginian was younger than his fellow aide-de-camp, and probably a less experienced observer. But while he might have left it
to the captain to provide a detailed account of the battle, he
could certainly have understood and judged the most basic
aspects of it, and it is primarily these which Pargellis discusses.
Washington undoubtedly knew how his friend was portraying
he engagement, and he seems to have agreed with him. Recognizing his support, Orme wrote boldly on August 25, reply-
ing to a letter in which Washington had noted unhappily that
criticism of Braddock was rife:

The Part of your Letter mentioning the Reflections upon the General
gives me much uneasiness tho' I feel a Contempt for the Detractors
which alleviates in some Degree my Concern[.] I know the ignorant
and rascally C D. is one promoter through Resentment and Malevo-
ence, and the thick head Baronet another intending to build his Character upon the Ruins of one much more amiable than he can be. For
my Part I judge it a Duty to vindicate the Memory of a Man whom I
greatly and deservedly esteemed and I think every Man whom he
regarded should be his Advocate keeping litterally to Facts which must
always improve the goodness of his Disposition. I am convinced the
Affection he bore you as well as your Integrity and good Nature will

make you assiduous in removing those abominable Prejudices the gen-
erality of People have imbibed and publish.[8]

Conspiratorial? Hardly. Rather, the comments of one man to
another whom he felt with confidence would think as he did.
Orme and Washington had seen the battle from the same perspective. They had both been present when Braddock ordered
Burton's detachment forward, they both had witnessed the collision of troops, or had been on the scene within minutes. Most
important, both had seen their fill of panic, a panic that had
cost the general both victory and life, despite his heroic attempts to counter it.

Probably the best way to judge Pargellis's accusations against
the captain is simply to compare the latter's account of the
action to others written by eyewitnesses, as was done in chapter
4. It seems to me that such a comparison shows Orme to have
been both honest and accurate. The only points where he is
directly challenged involve the first moments of action:
whether Braddock himself rode up; whether Burton's detachment was in disorder prior to the telescoping; whether it was in
motion at the moment of impact. As I have suggested, the
telescoping may well have taken place before he was on the
scene, in which case he was relating testimony he had heard,
most probably from his friend Burton. Even so, the evidence
against him is not particularly strong. Regarding Braddock's
actions, the reporters who claim that the general himself rode
forward were in the vanguard and therefore had a poor perspective. If we accept Peyton's testimony, the case for Orme's
statement that Braddock merely ordered Burton's detachment
ahead is overwhelming. I feel that this would be unwise, but
even if we reject Peyton we are left with Washington. He as
well as Orme knew of Braddock's initial orders. He would have
known if the captain were misrepresenting them in his accounts. Again we may refer to Orme's letter. If Washington's
friend were a liar, would he have so brazenly attempted to
portray himself as a champion of integrity to one who knew the
truth as well as he?

Orme compares favorably with most other eyewitnesses, not only in terms of the credibility of his narrative, but also in his interpretation of the action. It is true that he associates the onset of chaos with the telescoping more than do others, but this is of limited importance. Orme's central thesis, that the disaster of July 9 was caused by mass panic, and that the panic of the troops could not be justified by reference to any blunders on the part of the general, not only withstands the scrutiny of the remaining eyewitnesses, but actually is strengthened by it.

We may feel that Orme and his fellow officers protest too much in blaming the men, and clearly their accounts reflect the biases of their class. But one must present overwhelming evidence if he hopes to discredit their testimony. Pargellis has not done this, and I strongly doubt that anyone ever will. Furthermore, judging from the testimony discussed at length in chapter 4, it appears that the reason such evidence is not forthcoming is simple and does not hinge on the undoubted fact that most of the troops were illiterate. Rather, it is this: Even if they embroidered, in their central argument Orme and his peers told the truth.

APPENDIX D

British Eyewitness Accounts

A Note on Transcription

IN TRANSCRIBING the documents appended here, I have ob
served the following rules: the letter thorn is rendered as th
superscript letters are brought down to the line; letters consis
tently capitalized are made lower-case, except where modern
usage calls for the capital. Aside from the last, these practice
are applied to printed, as well as manuscript sources. They ar
used in the text and in all appendices.

British A

[A fair copy of this report has already been transcribed and
published by Charles Hamilton (*Braddock's Defeat* [Norman
University of Oklahoma Press, 1959], pp. 40–58). However, the
following is drawn from my own transcript of an earlier draft
Hardwicke no. 136, document no. 5, Manuscripts and Archive
Division, New York Public Library, Astor, Lenox and Tilder
Foundations. The Hardwicke draft is not as full as that printed
by Hamilton; it does not include the closing passages on the
retreat, or the list of officers to be found on pp. 53–58 o
Braddock's Defeat. The earlier portions of the respective drafts
as well as the accounts of the battle itself are, however, almost
identical. There are only three noteworthy differences between
the reports of the engagement. First, the Hardwicke draft, un
like Hamilton's, specifies that Gage marched with *two* compa
nies of grenadiers. Second, the line which in the Hardwicke
version reads, "it was proposed to strenghten the flanks, bu
rejected," in *Braddock's Defeat* concludes, "but this was unhap
pily rejected." Finally, where Hardwicke reads, "tho' certainly a

very bad way as we were situated," Hamilton's fair copy has,
'which could not have answered all as the Enemy were situated." The portions of the Hardwicke draft quoted here corre-
spond to *Braddock's Defeat,* pp. 49–52.]

Wednesday July the 9th. as we were to cross the Monongahela that day, and so near the Fort as we were drawing, it was
found absolutely necessary to detach a Party to secure the
crossings. Accordingly Lt. Col: Gage with 300 Men, the two
Companies of grenadiers and two peices of Canon, marched
before daybreak, and before the Road was cleared. at Day
break the whole Detachment marched tho' slowly, having a
great deal of trouble with the Road; after about 5 miles we
came to the first crossing of the River which was extreamly fine,
having a view of at least four miles up a River, undoubtedly
pleasing, the breadth about 600 yards; near this first crossing,
our advanced party had scared some Indians from their holes;
finding many spears, and their fires newly burning; from this
crossing, to the other was near two miles, and much the finest
of the two: on the other side of the second crossing, the advanced Party had halted at Frazier's House, close to the Bank,
which was very steep, and took two hours to make it passable
for the Carriages. The general now thinking the dangerous
Passes were over, did not suffer the Advanced Party to proceed
any farther than just the Distance of a few yards from the main
body; it was proposed to strengthen the flanks, but rejected.
between 12 and one, after we had marched about 800 yards
from the River, our first flank upon the left was fired upon,
and every man killed or wounded. the Alarm soon became
general, and the fire was very brisk from Right to Left; the
Indians were every one of them planted behind Trees, and
fired with the utmost security; the ground from where the
Enemy fired, and were posted was rising and advantagious.
upon our right were a Couple of Immense large Trees, fallen
on each other, which the Indians were in possession of, and
annoyed us from very much; but an officer and a party of men

soon dislodged them, and by pretty brisk fire, kept our Right tolerably easy; The Guns which were all rather to the Left, fired both Round and grape shot, and with great Execution. The Indians, whither ordered or not, I can't say, kept an incessant fire on the guns, and kill'd the men very fast. The Indians from their irregular method of fighting, by running from one place to another, obliged us to wheel from right to left, to quit the guns, and then heartily to return and cover them. At the first of the firing the General who was at the head of the detachment came to the front, and the American Troops tho' without any orders ran up immediately, some behind Trees, and others into the Ranks, and put the whole into confusion. The men from what storys they had heard of the Indians, in regard to their scalping; and mohawking [toma-hawking], were so panick struck, that their officers had little or no Command over them, and if any got a shot at one, the fire immediately ran through the whole Line, tho' they saw nothing but Trees; The whole Detachment was frequently divided into several parties, and then they were sure to fire on one another. the greatest part of the men who were behind trees, were either kill'd or wounded by our People, even one or two officers were killed by their own Platoon. such was the confusion that the men were sometimes 20 or 30 deep, and he thought himself securest, who was in the Center. during all this time the Enemy kept continually firing, and every shot took place. The general had given orders that they should fire in Platoons, which was impossible to be Effected, tho' certainly a very bad way as we were situated. within about two hours and a half, the men were obliged to (at least did) retreat 3 or 4 times, and were as often rallied. we found at last, that we should never gain the day, unless we dislodged them from the Rising ground, upon which Lt. Col: Burton with the grenadiers attempted the hill; for some time we were in hopes of their success, but some shot killing two or three of them, the rest Retreated very fast, leaving their officers, entreating and commanding but without any Regard to what they did.

The Indians were scalping at the beginning of the affair, which we heard was a sign of their being dubious of success but it is certain they never gave ground.

General Braddock who was in the heat of the action the whole time, was greatly exposed, he had 4 Horses shot under him, and Balls through several parts of his cloaths: at the latter end of the unlucky affair, a shot hit him in the Body, which occasioned his death three or four days afterwards.

Sir Peter Halkett was killed at the beginning, and many other officers; after they had Retreated from the Hill, the men made some stand, and the Canon kept a tolerable good fire, but very soon for want of sufficient guard to it, the men were obliged to desert them. during this time the Waggoners who imagined things would turn out badly, had taken the gears from their horses and galloped intirely away, so that if fortune had turned in our favour, we had not one horse left to draw the train along. however after about four hours incessant fire and two thirds of our [men] killed or wounded, they as if by beat of Drum, turned to the Right about, and made a most precipitate Retreat, every one trying who should be the first. the Enemy pursued us, butchering as they came, as far as the other side of the River; in crossing it they shot many in the Water, both men and Women, scalping and cutting them in a most Barbarous manner.

On the other side of the River most of us halted to consider what to doe, but the men being so terrified desired to go on, nay indeed they would, melancholy situation! expecting every moment to have our Retreat cut off (which half a Dozen men would very easily have done) and a certainty of meeting no Provisions for 60 miles.

Retreated to Col. Dunbar, 12 miles beyond Gist's Plantation, which Plantation is 50 miles from the Place of Action.

Killed. 385.   Wounded. 328.   not Wounded. 523.

Commentary

Aside from Cholmley's Batman, British A is the most important of our anonymous reporters. His account is both full and accurate. Although he is apparently in error in stating tha Braddock early on rode up to the front, this mistake seems t derive from his faulty perspective. British A was probably to ward the front himself. His mention of wheeling right and lef seems to be in reference to the advance party, and his excep tionally detailed report on this point suggests that he was him self of that detachment. So does his reference to Croghan' opinion (see his account) that the fact that the Indians wer scalping from the first showed them to be pessimistic. Croghan would presumably have rejoined the advance party during th first moments of fighting and might have given an optimisti assessment then, but not for long.

On the other hand, British A's inaccurate version of the earl moments of fighting, and particularly his claim that the enem first revealed itself when it fired on the flanks, rather than tha it appeared to the fore and soon *ran down* the flanks, indicate that he was to the rear of the advance party. Despite a fev errors such as those noted, British A is generally reliable. He i also honest. He does criticize the troops for their panic, but h also notes that they made a stand after their retreat from th rising ground. As for his attitude toward Braddock, he i mildly critical, here and elsewhere in his journal. While show ing no great admiration for the Americans, he suggests tha Braddock's reliance on traditional platoon-firing tactics was un wise in vew of the circumstances.

British B

[This is reprinted from "Braddock on July 9, 1755," ed Richard Walsh, *Maryland Historical Magazine*, 60 (1965), pp 421–27. The original is on permanent exhibit at the Marylanc Historical Society and is ms. 2018 in the Colonial Collection. I lacks the first and last pages, which explains its abrupt openin and closing. The account here represents Walsh's complete transcript.]

... affairs and the ordering of a march than such a young-ster as he. The General, upon this said with some vehemence, 'Gentlemen, you are hot.["] Col. Dunbar told his excellency that he left it to him to judge, who had most reason, that 'twas true he was old, but he thought his age should rather protect him, than expose him to the ridicule of that young man in his excellencie's hearing.

A little after this Scuffle and several others of less conse-quence, too tedious and triffling to relate, the general marched before with twelve pieces of artillery fifty five waggons with a great part of the ammunition and baggage, twelve hundred men of the choice of the army, and the artillery chest, and left Dun-bar behind, with about 800 men and 72 waggons, to bring up the heavy artillery, and the rest of the baggage and ammunition.

Before he reached the Monongahela, our Indian friend, the half king, with some of his tribe, had once or twice reconnoi-tred the french fork and brought the general Intelligence, that the Enimy were very strong there being, as he could judge, about 2200 french Regulars and irregulars, with a white flag, and about 3000 of their Indian friends and allies. After this advice, which several of the scouts agreed in, not-withstanding the repeated solicitations of the old officers, to regulate the march and be more circumspect, the general let them go on, in the same confused manner as before, and the triumvirate still kept laying their wages of 100 guineas to five shillings, and did not stick to charge those with cowardice, who talked of watching the enimy, or guarding against their designs.

When they approached nigh the Monongahela, Dunbar with his party, was by this time 50 miles behind (you will probably see this called ten miles in some of the triumvirates letters published in our newspapers) and Monacatucha the half king preferred his advice, that they should proceed no further, but Incamp and fortify the army on this side the Monongahela, alledging, that if they proceeded towards the fort they must of a necessity be all

surrounded and cut off by superior numbers, having no safe
place of retreat, but this good advice was disregarded.

Upon the 9th day of July the army crossed the Monongahela
twice about eleven o'clock in the morning, that river, which is a
branch of the Ohio, making a great bend or Circumflexure in
this place, which is about seven miles on this side of fort
duQuesne, as Sir John St. Clair, and Sir Peter Halket, were
apprehensive that the Enimy would attack them at the passing
of this river (which they really intended, but happened to come
a little too late) they with some difficulty persuaded the General
to form the army into battle order; in this order they marched
so, about a quarter of an hour after they had passed the river
but soon was ordered again to resume the line of march, and
got into their wonted Confusion. Sir John at this appeared
uneasy, and solicited the General again to form the army into
the line of battle but to no purpose. Sir John alledged to the
General pointing to a valley with a small rising hill upon each
side, scarce half a mile distant from the front, that the enimy
would attack him there. The General asked him by what Intelli
gence he knew that. He replied by the same Intelligence as his
Excellency had had of the Indian Sachem, which when the
General made slight of, Sir John assured him, that were he his
enimy and knew his numbers and disposition as well, as he was
assured the french knew it, he would himself undoubtedly
attack him in that very place, and he judged that the french
officer or officers would in common prudence pursue the same
scheme. The general still slighted this advice, and Sir John
begged that he would only suffer him with an advanced party
of two or three hundred men to go and reconnoitre the fort
and bring him proper Intelligences, which request was refused,
so on they marched in the same confused manner, with artillery and baggage, and in effect as Sir John had conjectured,
they were surprized with a very hot and heavy fire, both on
their front and flanks, from a party of french, concealed in a
parcell of high weeds and brush on the left hand, and a great
number of Indians from the rising of the hill on every hand.
This put them into a terrible confusion and the men dropt very

ast. Leutenant Coll. Gage led a party in the front, to cover Sir
ohn St. Clair, who followed him with his pioneers to clear the
woods. The remainder of the army were behind with the General in a confused disposition. In the front were 500 grenadiers
alled Halket's grenadiers as choice men as could anywhere be
.een. These men bore the first brunt of the fire in the front, till
at last both Sir John St. Clair, and Coll. Gage's party were put
nto the utmost confusion by the Irregularly tumultuous press-
ng on and crowding of the men behind, who as they were
hurried and pushed Irregularly forward, and commanded to
march, earnestly requested to be put into some kind of order
and instructed how to proceed. You'll perhaps see in some of
our newspapers a foolish account from some of the triumvi-
ate, that the foremost ranks falling back upon the rest of the
army as yet not formed, threw them into a pannic and Confusion which neither the Intreaties nor threats of the officers
could divest them from or persuade them to stand their
ground, but this is as false and foolish a gloss as ever was
Invented. The affair was quite the reverse and therefore you'll
do well not to believe a word of it.

While affairs were in this disorder Sir John St. Clair again
awaited the general, and told him that he was certainly being
defeated, if he did not speedily make as regular a retreat as
possible, and endeavor to save the Remainder of the army; this
was not regarded, and Sir John was ordered again to his post.
Sir Peter Halket, and Lieut. Coll. Gage came also to the general. Sir Peter proposed, that he should be allowed 200 men, to
take possession of an advantageous post which he perceived the
enimy had just left. The general called him fool, and old
woman, telling him that he was fitter to be led than to lead,
ordered him to go to his station, and give his advice when it
was asked. Sir Peter (that good and worthy man) modestly
replied, that he valued not his own life, if the giving of it up
would better the cause, and he was grieved to have the bad
prospect before his eyes, of the certain destruction of so many
brave men who deserved a better fate, and returning to his
Station was in a few minutes afterwards shot dead. Coll. Gage

asked his excellency what he was to do; the reply was to go and mind his business. The Coll. obeyed saying as he went away, that he could but die at the head of his men, for it was out of his power to do any service. Soon after the Confusion and destruction was so great, that the men fired irregularly, one behind another, and by this way of proceeding many more of our men were killed by their own party than by the Enimy, as appeared afterwards by the bullets that the surgeons extracted from the wounded, they being distinguished from the french and Indian bullets by their size, as they were considerably larger for the bore of the Enimis' muskets of which many were picked up was very small. Among the wounded men, there were two for one of these bullets extracted by the Surgeons, and the wounds were chiefly on the back parts of the body, so it must have been among the kill'd. Captn. Mercer marching with his company to take possession of an advantageous post, was fired upon by our men from behind, and ten of his men dropt at once. Capt. Polson lost many of his men by irregular platooning behind him, on which he faced about, and intreated the Soldiers not to fire and destroy his men. They replied they could not help it, they must obey orders, and upon one or two more fires of this sort, Capt. Polson himself lost his life, being shot directly threw the heart. He jumped at one Spring a great distance from the ground and then fell. In fine, between the two fires of friends and enimies, that whole company was destroyed but five; the Hundred Grenadiers were also by this time all killed but Eleven, three of whom were mortally wounded. A party of these fellows had got behind a large tree which had fell down, and making use of it for a Breast work, made considerable havock among the Indians. These fellows the Generall ordered to be called off, by his aid de Camp Washington who obeyed the order with reluctance. Sir John St. Clair had now received a desperate wound from a musket ball that went thro' his shoulder, followed with a large profusion of blood. He immediately rode up to the general and Speaking to him in Italian, told him that he was defeated, and all was ained, to whom, when the general made some scornful reply, ir John told him, that by the fresh bleeding of his wound, he id not expect to survive many minutes, and therefore could ave no Interest in dissembling, or saying what he really did ot think. Sir John was immediately carried off by his Servant, e having tied him on the horses back, as he was thro loss of lood unable to keep the saddle. The general by this time had ad five horses killed under him, and his aid de Camp Washagton, two, whose upper coat was intirely shot to tatters with ausket bullets, and yet he not hurt. Soon after this the general as wounded with a musket ball, which went thro his right rm, his side and lodged in his lungs, and Washington applying o the Soldiers to carry him off the field; the[y] absolutely efused. At last some good natured waggoners and other eople carried him off in a sort of bier or litter upon their houlders, he being a gross heavy man was not able to bear the ogging of a waggon or motion of a horse. Six hundred private oldiers and upwards now lay dead and disabled on the field, esides officers. The men had now fired away all their stock of ammunition, and many of them took the cartridges of powder and shot from the dead and wounded, and used that also. There was no other shift now, but a speedy flight; great numbers of the officers were killed; all those of the artillery were killed or wounded but one. The artillery baggage, ammunition, military chest, with all the general's plate, of which he had a complete service, money letters from the Governors, papers of Instructions, fell into the hands of the enimy, amounting, as is hought to 500000 Lb Sterling. The flight was precipitated and confused, many were killed and scalped by the Indians in repassing the Monongahela; almost all the poor women belonging to the Camp were slaughtered by these savages; multitudes of the wounded men dropt down on the Roads, and many died that were not wounded, thro hunger faintness and weariness, the men on that day the battle was fought, having eat little or nothing for two days, and drank only water, under an excessive hot sun. In short, the poor remainder of them, that reached

Coll. Dunbar's camp, appeared like spirits more than men, and their wounds alive with maggots. The General died on the Road on the 13th of the month, more out of vexation and grief, as is said, than of his wound, which his surgeon believed were not mortal. He held one Council of war before his death in which it was determined, and orders given accordingly to Coll. Dunbar, to destroy all the Remainder of the artillery baggage and ammunition, and this ridiculous order was soon put in execution. The General was buried in a coffin made of Bark, with little or no Ceremony, a little on the other side of the Great Meadows. About an hour before his death he resigned his command to Coll. Dunbar, who marched Immediately with the broken Remains of the forces, back to fort Cumberland on wills' creek, where the wounded officers and men were left, and in a few days from thence took his rout towards Pensylvania, where he is now arrived. Soon after this defeat, the Indians began to perpetrate their Butcheries on the Back of Virginia and Maryland, and still continue to do so, cutting off numbers of families. The french are now fortifying at the great meadows, and our Countrys here, are in a most deplorable situation.

Before I make any remarks upon this unaccountable transaction, I shall give you the particulars of Sir Peter Halkets death. Just after he had left the general, as I have above related, he rode to the head of his men and riding about to give necessary orders, he was observed by an Indian fellow, who sat disabled in the field by a shot in his knee; this savage levelled his piece at Sir Peter as he rode about, which one Capt. Ghist, a capt. of the Militia and huntsman perceiving who had just discharged his musket, he made haste to reload, in order to prevent the danger with which Sir Peter was threatened, but could not make such dispatch but that the Indian had shot Sir Peter down, before he was in readiness to oppose him. Ghist however immediately step'd up and blew out the miscreant's brains; Sir Peter's Servant went up to his master's body to see if he was not mortally wounded, or if dead, to take proper care that the body was decently disposed of, but the poor fellow, in that Instant was shot, and fell upon his master, a worthy example of duty and fidelity. Thus fell Sir Peter Halket, in the Service of his king and country, a gentleman much lamented by all that knew him here, of a sweet affable conversation, and . . .

Commentary

It is unfortunate that the lengthiest and in some respects the fullest account of Braddock's Defeat is also easily the least reliable. British B cannot be placed on the scene of battle; he reports with equal inaccuracy events that took place all over the field. In the text and notes of this study we have already seen some of his grosser inaccuracies. To mention all of his minor mistakes, such as the fact that it was Halket's son, rather than his servant, who died with him, would cause us to spend far too much time on a document that is actually worth comparatively little.

The errors are in fact so numerous and in many cases so great that I wonder if British B actually was an eyewitness. I agree with Walsh that he was almost certainly an American; from his references to "our Countrys here" and the like, he may furthermore have lived on the frontier. However, he does not appear to have been addicted to Indian-style fighting. He does mention Washington, Polson, and Mercer in favorable contexts, but his real heroes appear to have been St. Clair, Gage, and, obviously, Halket, three who were not only British, but traditional in their tactics. Due to his acquaintance with them, and his clearly partisan attitude, I would guess that he was at least a member of the expedition. It is possible, however, that he was one of those left behind with Dunbar. Note that in his—admittedly truncated—letter he does not claim to have been present at the battle. He does, of course, relate events from the field, but on whole so inaccurately that he may merely have been reporting wild rumors, especially those which tended to the disadvantage of Braddock and his favorites. Still, there is no hard evidence to disqualify British B as an eyewitness, and anyway he has little impact on our overall concept

of the battle, for his wild claims are in most cases overwhelme
by the evidence presented by more reliable reporters.

British C

[The following is an "Extract of a Letter from an Office
about the late Battle in America," originally printed in th
Whitehall Evening Post of October 9–11, 1755. I am using th
reprint in N. Darnell Davis, "British Newspaper Accounts o
Braddock's Defeat," *PMHB*, 23 (1899), p. 321.]

In advancing towards the Enemy the Fire in Front was thic
and heavy; and two of our Parties, one of three hundred, th
other of two hundred Men, falling back, caused such Confu
sion and Pannick that no military Expedient thought of had
any effect upon our Men; who, after firing away, in the mos
irregular Manner, all their Ammunition, ran quite off, leaving
to the Enemy the Artillery and Baggage. The main Body wa
with Col. D——, or the whole Army would have been de
stroyed: Loss of Horses and Want of Carriages for the
Wounded, made us destroy Ammunition and superfluous Pro
vision. The whole Artillery is lost. The Troops are so weakened
by Deaths, Wounds, and Sickness, that it is judged impossibl
to make any farther Attempt for the present. It is affirmed
that the military Chest, with £25,000. to pay the Army, and al
the General's Papers, are lost. Capt. Waggoner, with 170 Vir
ginians, went up to where the Enemy was hid and routed them
But O unhappy! our Infatuateds seeing a Smoke, fired and
killed him with several of his Men.

Capt. Polson, another brave Virginian, with his Company
attacked the Enemy a little before the Retreat was beat, which
they hearing, surrounded these brave Fellows, and cut the
Captain and most of them to Pieces. It is with Regret I send
this sad Account.

P.S. D——'s hasty Retreat seems still a great Mystery.

ommentary

This account is brief but meaty. Generally it is plausible, hough I have noted the error involving Waggoner. As is the ase with British B, I am somewhat concerned that the officer ho prepared this account did not really witness the battle. he fact that he occasionally speaks of Braddock's forces in the rst-person plural should not confuse us. This would have een conventional usage for one who supported the cause for hich the army was fighting. I am bothered by his haziness ver the causes of Dunbar's retreat and his mistaken belief that he colonel's detachment had represented the "main Body" of raddock's army. If British C was indeed involved in the battle, e was probably in the main body, and in Burton's detachment, onsidering the perspective he gives on the collision. But he ould have picked up Orme's account of the telescoping from ny of several newspapers, and other material from random ources. The fact that even in such a brief report he includes etails on the activities of two provincial captains and their roops suggests that he was himself an American, with at least ome respect for irregular tactics. On the whole, his account is vorth noting. If he was indeed an eyewitness, his comments elp to boost Orme's credibility. If not, we have enough reli- ble sources to minimize the likelihood that we will accept his oint when he is mistaken.

British D

[The excerpt that follows is taken from *The Expedition of Ma- or-General Edward Braddock to Virginia, with the two Regiments of lacket and Dunbar. Being Extracts of Letters from an Officer in one f those Regiments to his Friend in London* (London, 1755). I am ising a reprint by Archer B. Hulbert, in *Braddock's Road and Three Relative Papers,* Historic Highways of America, 4 (Cleve- and: A. H. Clark Co., 1903), pp. 163–65.]

The General seems very anxious about marching through the Woods, and gave very particular Orders; Powder and Bullet were given out, and every Thing fit for Action; two Lieutenant-Colonels were ordered to command the advanced Party. The General followed with the Gross of the two Regiments from *Europe,* the *Americans* followed, and the Rear was brought up by Captain *Dumary's,* and another Independent Company. We marched on in this Manner without being disturbed, and thought we had got over our greatest Difficulties, for we look'd upon our March through the Woods to be such. We were sure we should be much above a Match for the *French,* if once we got into the open Ground near the Forts, where we could use our Arms. We had a Train, and a gallant Party of Sailors for working our Guns, full sufficient to master better works than those of the *French* Forts, according to the Intelligence we had of them. Then we march'd on, and when within about ten Miles of Fort *Du Quesne,* we were, on a sudden, charged by Shot from the Woods. Every Man was alert, did all we could, but the Men dropped like Leaves in *Autumn,* all was Confusion, and in Spight of what the Officers and bravest Men could do, Numbers ran away, nay fired on us, that would have forced them to rally. I was wounded in one Leg, and in the other Heel, so could not go, but sat down at the Foot of a Tree, praying of every one that run by, that they would help me off; an *American Virginian* turned to me, Yes, Countryman, says he, I will put you out of your Misery, these Dogs shall not burn you; he then levelled his Piece at my Head, I cried out and dodged him behind the Tree, the Piece went off and missed me, and he run on; Soon after Lieutenant *Grey,* with a Party of *Dumary's* Company came by, who brought up the Rear; the Firing was now Quite ceased, he told me the General was wounded, and got me carried off. When we arrived at the *Meadows,* we found Colonel *Dunbar* did not think it expedient to wait for the *French* there, but retired, and carried us, the wounded, with him to *Will's Creek.* I have writ till I am faint.

Commentary

In *The History of an Expedition Against Fort Du Quesne in 1755: Under Major-General Edward Braddock,* Pennsylvania Historical Society, Memoirs, 5 (Philadelphia, 1855), Winthrop Sargent suggests that the author of this account may have been an "ignorant camp-follower" (p. xii). Ignorant British D may have been, but he was no camp follower. The strong anti-American bias evinced in his various letters indicates that he was British, and men do not venture across the Atlantic in order to become camp followers. That he was literate suggests that he was not a common soldier, although as we have seen a few privates like Duncan Cameron could read and write. British D was in all probability what he claims to have been, a British officer. His account is highly personal and not very detailed, but in no respect implausible. Indeed, on points that he alone makes he deserves the benefit of the doubt.

Duncan Cameron

[Cameron's account is extracted from his autobiographical sketch, *The Life, Adventures and Surprising Deliverances of Duncan Cameron,* 3d ed. (Philadelphia, 1756), pp. 10–12.]

We march'd from *Wills-Creek* under the Command of General *Braddock,* a brave old experienced Officer, in whom we had a great deal of Confidence, and his Dependance was chiefly upon us Regulars that he brought from *Ireland,* being 1000 Men compleat, which with above 1200 of New-rais'd, and Three Independent Companies, made in the whole upwards of 2500 Men, besides Officers; we had 200 Baggage Waggons, about 1500 Pack Horses, and a fine Train of Artillery. The Way was very rugged till we got over the *Alleghany* Hills, when gradually it grew better as we proceeded. At the Place call'd the *Little Meadows,* our General ordered about 1200 Men to be pick'd out for a hasty March to the *French* Fort *Du Quesne* on

the Fork of the *Ohio;* I happen'd to be one of 800 old Regular
pick'd out for that Purpose; we march'd forward with hast
Marches, having about 80 Waggons, the chief Part of the Ar
tillery, with necessary Ammunition with us; leaving Col. *Dunba*
to bring up the Remains of the Army, &c. On the 9th of *July* w
cross'd the *Mononghale* (a Branch of *Ohio*) in two Places, an
soon after the second Crossing, when our advanc'd Guard ha
got about one Mile from the River, a Firing began in the Front
The Enemy were advantagiously posted on two Hills, one o
each Side of our Way, which Hills joined in our Front: Th
Firing as a Signal began in the Front, and immediately wa
follow'd from behind the Hills and Trees all-along each Flank
Our Troops keeping in regular close Order, not a Shot o
theirs, posted to such Advantage, could be well shot amiss; an
yet they shot too high: Our Officers as well as Men generall
behaved well; and all the Blame that can be properly laid, is i
not having proper Scouts out to have prevented our falling int
such an Ambush; however, our Army was defeated by a Num
ber equal if not superior, posted as well as their Hearts coul
wish. Near 400 of our Men were left dead on the Spot, betwee
2 and 300 wounded got off, about 100 were left wounded no
able to get off. Among the Kill'd to our very great Grief, wa
our brave Colonel Sir *Peter Halket,* and his Son. As soon as th
Remains of our Army had recross'd the River, and got out o
Gun-shot, the *Indians,* a merciless Crew that compos'd Part o
the *French* Army, began immediately to scalp the Dead an
Wounded; this I heard and saw, though escap'd being seen b
them; for I being one of the first that was wounded, and wa
for a while pretty much stunn'd, was left among the Dead o
the advanc'd Guard of our Army; when our Army retreated
the Enemy follow'd close, by which Means the Ground wher
the Battle began in the Front was deserted for a Time both b
Friends and Enemies, and in that Time I made shift to ge
away and hide myself at some small Distance in a hollow Tree
and I had not been long there before these ravenous Hell
hounds came yelping and screaming like so many Devils, an

fell to work as before-mentioned: About a Foot above the Entrance into the Tree I was in there was good Foot-hold for me to stand on, upon which I stood, and against my Face there was a small Knot-hole facing the Field of Battle, by Means of which I had a fair Prospect of their Cruelty: But Oh! what a Pannic was I in, when I saw one of those Savages look directly at the Knot-hole, as I aprehended, gave a Scream, and came directly up to the Tree? But what Inducement he had for doing it I cannot tell, for he went off again without shewing any Signs of his discovering me. The whole Army of the Enemy fell to plundering, &c. Though I must do the *French* Commandant this Justice, that as soon as possible he could, he put a stop to the *Indians* scalping those that were not yet quite dead, and ordered those Wounded to be taken Care of. Among the Plunder they found near Two Hogsheads of Rum, and the *Indians,* as likewise the French Soldiers, fell to drinking, and soon got themselves pretty drunk, and went off, as I aprehended, at Night to the French Fort, without carrying off, much of their Plunder, neither could they do it by reason of their Intoxication: They did not leave so much as a Guard on the Field of Battle; neither did they pursue our Army farther than the River; so that if our People had halted but Half a Mile from the Field of Battle, they might have returned at Night, and destroyed most of the Baggage. At Night when the Coast was clear, I got me out of my Hiding-place.

Commentary

Even more than British D's account, Cameron's is personalized and anecdotal. The reporter himself is honest enough, but during most of the battle his perspective for viewing the action was, to say the least, poor. His usefulness is limited to discussing the first moments of battle and some of the background to it. His admiration for Braddock as well as Halket seems to have been genuine, but we cannot say whether this attitude was typical of the regulars. His assessment of the strength of the army before and after it was divided is fairly accurate, but several other reporters, notably Orme, were in a better position to know and give more precise figures.

John Campbell

[This very brief account represents the bulk of a letter from Campbell to Morris, July 17, 1755. My source is *Minutes of the Provincial Council of Pennsylvania*, 6 (1851), p. 481.]

I thought it proper to let you know that I was in the Battle where We were defeated, And we had about Eleven Hundred and Fifty private Men besides Officers and others, And we was attack'd the 9th Day about Twelve o'Clock and held till about Three in the Afternoon and then we were forced to retreat, when I suppose we might bring about 300 whole Men besides a vast many wounded; Most of our Officers were either wounded or killed; General Braddock is wounded but I hope not mortal, and Sr. John St. Claire and many others, but I hope not mortal. All the Train is cut off in a manner.

Commentary

I have included this account primarily because there is no valid criterion for not doing so, "worth" being too subjective a quality to use as a yardstick. Besides being brief, the report is not very accurate. The most that can be said in rating it is that it may indicate that immediately after the battle, when Campbell was sent off with his message, there was some hope that Braddock might recover. If the general did not indeed seem to be a dying man, this would in part justify Dunbar's acceptance of his order to destroy the ammunition. British B also suggests that Braddock's wounds may not at first have seemed mortal.

Cholmley's Batman

[The following key account is extracted from a transcript on pp. 27–32 of *Braddock's Defeat*, edited by Charles Hamilton. Copyright 1959 by the University of Oklahoma Press.]

Wednesday July the 9th. The Advance Party Marched at two in the Morning, Consisting of two grannadier Companies and a hundred Patallion. My Master Commanded the Pattallion. We marched to take Possession of a Pass Over the River which is Called Muningahele River, we haveing all the morning two pieces of Cannon which was very troublesome to get forward before any Road was Cut which there was not at that time for the working party being b'hind at that time. A Bout Eight in the Morning we Came to the River after Marching Near Seven Miles. When we Came Close to the River some of our men saide they saw great many of the French Indiens on the Other side of the River. Some saide their was not Any but to be Shure Colonel Gage who Commanded the Party Ordered the Cannon to be taken of the Carriges and to be drawn Over by the men, Ready to Ingage if accation. The men all marched Over in line of Battle with the Cannon till they Came to the Other side of the River where we had a Bank to Rise Eight yards parpendiquler that we was Oblig'd to Sloape before we Could Rise the hill. The River is betwixt two and three hundred yards Over and not much more than knee deep. After we had Rose the Bank we had not a Bove two hundred yards to Frayzors Plantation where we marched and our Command went no further at that time. So as soon as we arived their, the Sentryes was posted and Every thing made secure. The men that had any thing to Eate they Eate it for their Breckfast, it being then about half an hour after Nine, but I believe where there was one that had any thing to Eat their was twenty that had Nothing. Some men had Nothing most of the day Before. My Master Eat a little Ham that I had and a Bit of gloster Shire Cheese and I milked the Cow and made him a little milk Punch which he drank a little. About half an hour after ten the working party Came Over the River and a Bout a[t] Eleven the grand Army begins to Come Over. As soon as they Came to the River we Rec'd Orders to march on again. Sir John Sincklare asked Colonel Gage if he would take the two piece of cannon with us again. Colonel Gage

Answered, no Sir I think not, for I do not think we Shall have much Occasion for them and they being troubolsome to get forwards before the Roads are Cut. So we began our March again, Beating the grannadiers March all the way, Never Seasing. There Never was an Army in the World in more spirits than we where, thinking of Reaching Fort de Cain the day following as we was then only five miles from it. But we had not got above a mile and a half before three of our guides in the froont of me above ten yards spyed the Indiens lay'd down Before us. He Immediately discharged his piece, turned Round his horse [and] Cried, the Indiens was upon us. My Master Called me to give me his horse which I took from him and the Ingagement began. Immediately they began to Ingage us in a half Moon and still Continued Surrounding us more and more[.] Before the whole of the Army got up we had about two thirds of our men Cut of that Ingaged at the First. My Master died before we was ten Minuits Ingaged. They Continualy made us Retreat, they haveing always a large marke to shoute at and we having only to shoute at them behind trees or laid on their Bellies. We was drawn up in large Bodies together, a ready mark. They need not have taken sight at us for they Always had a large Mark, but if we saw of them five or six at one time [it] was a great sight and they Either on their Bellies or Behind trees or Runing from one tree to another almost by the ground. The genll had five horses Shot under him. He always strove to keep the men together but I believe their might be two hundred of the American Soldiers that fought behind Trees and I belive they did the moast Execution of Any. Our Indiens behaved very well for the Small Quantity of them. Their was a man and his Son thought to have killed a Bout sixteen men. The father, after [having] Spent all his Ammunition, lay down his gun till he went to get a fresh Supply. In the mean time one of our men found her and to hinder the Enemy for having Any service from her he knocks her Round a tree and bent her like a Bow. Soon after the man Comes and finds his piece all Bent. He was seemingly very Angry. He afterwards said he should do the same. He spyes a French Indien that had shot several Shots from behind a tree. He Immediately Called his Son to Shout at him, which he did and shot him dead. They begin to Inclose us more and more till they had Nigh Inclosed us in. If it was not for their Barbaras Usage which we knew they would treat us, we should Never have fought them as long as we did, but having only death before us made the men fight Almost longer than they was able. There was about three Quarters of an hour before we Retreated. I expected Nothing but death for Every Oone of us, for they had us surround all but a little in the Rear, which they strove for with all their Force. But our men knowing the Conciquance of it preserved the pass till we Retreated. The generall was wounded and a great many Officers was killed with about five hundred private men, and about four hundred wounded out of Better than twelve hundred. The Ingagement began before one and Ended half an hour after four, when we Retreated. They prosued us Better than a mile and Cut many of in going through the River. All the wounded that Could not walk fell in the Enemyis hands but was given no Quarters. My Masters horse Rec'd a Ball in the Shoulder and after that the genll['s] horse was Shot and I mounted him of my Masters. Near half an hour after their was Other horses Ready. I advised him to mount another As he was wounded. I was a fear'd he should fail with him; but I did not leade him above half an hour Before a Ball Struck him in the Rib and he died Immediately. I had seven horses in the field and one Cow and they was all lost but two horses. When we Retreated we marched all Night and the Next day without any thing to Eat or drink Except water untill we Came to guests Plantation before we halted, it being Better than Sixty Miles, and then we had Eight miles to Colonel Dunbar Party but it being so late, then Eight O Clock and the men so forteagud, not being a hundred Ariv'd at that time made us halt their that Night.

Commentary

Cholmley's Batman stands as our only first-rate source on the battle writing from the point of view of the common soldier. In surveying the day's activities prior to the attack, this report is quite possibly the finest of all. On the engagement itself, Cholmley's Batman is, however, a less informative reporter than we might wish. First, he becomes too anecdotal. He is, after all, not a practiced observer and is not likely to give a broad view of the fighting. Instead, as we might expect, he relates various vivid events he saw or heard of on the fateful day. Second, he becomes less precise on matters involving large bodies of men. For example, he mentions that "they Continualy made us Retreat," but since his perception of time is hazy for that portion of his account dealing with the battle, we cannot be certain who is retreating here, the advance party, the vanguard, or the entire army. Cholmley's Batman merits a high rating for honesty, but not always for accuracy.

George Croghan

[I am including here the bulk of a letter from Charles Swaine to Richard Peters, written August 5, 1755. The letter has been printed once before, in the *Philadelphia Evening Bulletin,* September 15, 1849, p. 1, col. 6. However, this is my own transcription, from the Peters Papers, Historical Society of Pennsylvania, Manuscript Dept., 4, pt. 1, p. 38.]

Mr. Croghan came over on Saturday to Shippensberg, he had a free sight of the Enemy as they approached, says they were about three hundred the French in shirts, & the Indians naked, that they were lead by three French officers with hats in their hands and with which they gave a signal for the firing. He was informed 400 Onandago Indians came to the Fort the day before, that there were 100 Delawares, 60 Wiandots, 40 Puywas, 500 Pawwaws, the Shawnees who lived about Logtown, and some of all other tribes, that some of the Wyandots now going down to Philadelphia were in the action against us; but says the attack was not made by above three hundred, but it was intended to dispute every inch of Ground between the river and the Fort, that the Indians had all the plunder and next day went off—all the prisoners and wounded who could not get off the Field were killed in cold blood and only one man and three Women got into the Fort. The firing was over excepting a few shot now & then a Quarter of an hour before our people retreated, & the enemy had fired for some time at such distance that the Bullets came in quite dead—that the Indians never expected a [British] defeat, by reason they began to scalp immediately but when the Grenadiers, (who gave the fire at 200 yards distance, instead of receiving it) began to retreat, than the Indians hollowed and began to act vigorously— many of our people fired twenty-four rounds and never saw the enemy, not above two hundred and Fifty were left dead on the Ground, and it is supposed one hundred and Fifty were killed by our own people & it appears to me, that had there been any officers to have rallied the men on retreating even at last the Enemy would not have got the six cannon and mortars, & perhaps they might have Advanced toward the Fort, for when the men were going off, many of the officers called out Halt, Halt, which the men mostly did, but the Officers continued on and got the heels of them. the unfortunate General Braddock was intirely deserted in the waggons with only his servants and a person or two more, & it was some time before they got a party of men to Guard him. There is an anecdote which possibly you have heard as to the greatness of his despair & his wanting to die as an old Roman, & endeavouring to lay hold of Croghan's pistoles, this you may credit, as I privately inquired of Croghan as to the Truth of it.

Commentary

Croghan is a source well worth listening to. Of our eye-witness reporters, he is easily the most competent judge of the sort of battle he is describing here. It is unfortunate that his account of the battle itself is so brief. However, what he does present is important and apparently reliable. Most points he makes are corroborated by others, and the only one which is implicitly disputed by the consensus—that the officers in the end panicked—has been discussed in the text. Because of his experience and the fact that he has less of an ax to grind than have most eyewitnesses, Croghan is the sort whose word may generally be allowed to stand, even when uncorroborated. An exception should naturally be made when he is citing rumor. Roucher remains a far superior source on the composition of the Indian forces that joined the French, partly because Croghan's estimate of their numbers is too high, mainly because the Frenchman was in a better position to know. Another point inviting caution is that Swaine may in some cases be giving his own opinions. The most obvious case of Swaine's intervention is his handling of the retreat: "It appeares to me, that had there been any officers to have rallied the men. . . . " Perhaps Croghan himself was not as critical of the officers. For the most part, however, it appears that Swaine has reported faithfully the observations of his friend.

William Dunbar

[This account has never been in print, nor have I ever seen a reference to it. The manuscript of which the following is a transcript is Hardwicke 136, document no. 6, Manuscripts and Archives Division, New York Public Library, Astor, Lenox and Tilden Foundations. As the reader may note, Dunbar's account follows the one by British A in the Hardwicke Papers. The two reports are in different hands, probably neither that of the eyewitness himself. Both are rather rough. Ms. 6 is headed "Extract of a Letter from Lieutenant Dunbar—Wills Creek 20th July 1755."]

On Wenesday the 9th Inst, We were advanced within 9

miles of Fort du Quesne, & in order to reach it were to pass
the Monongahela in 2 different places. by 2 in the Morning
Col: Gage with the 2 Companies of Grenadiers, to wch I belonged, with 150 Men besides was ordered with 2 six pounders, to cross the River, & cover the March of the General wth
the Rest of the Army. This We executed witht any disturbance
from the Enemy, and when we had yet possession of the Bank
of the sd crossing, we were remained drawn up, till the general came with the rest of the Army, & passed the River in a
Column. The Ground from thence to the French Fort, we
were told was pretty. good, & the woods open, but all upon
the ascent [.] Col: Gage was then ordered with his advanced
Party to march on, and was soon followed by the general. We
had not marched above 800 yards from the River, when we
were allarmed by the Indian Hollow, & in an instant, found
ourselves attacked on all sides. their methods, they immediately seise a Tree, & are certain of their Aim, so that before
the Genl came to our assistance, most of our advanced Party
were laid sprawling on the ground. our Men unaccustomed to
that way of fighting, were quite confounded, & behaved like
Poltrons, nor could the examples, nor the Intreaties of their
officers prevail with them, to do any one [what was ordered.]
This they denied them, when we begged of them not to throw
away their fire, but to follow us with fixed Bayonets, to drive
them from the hill & trees, they never minded us, but threw
their fire away in the most confused manner, some in the air,
others in the ground, & a great many destroyed their own
Men & officers. When the General came up to our assistance,
men were seized with the same Pannic, & went into as much
disorder, some Part of them being 20 deep. The officers in
order to remedy this, advanced into the front, & soon became
the mark of the Enemy, who scarce left one, that was not
killed or wounded; when we were first attacked, It was near
one o'Clock, & in this Confusion did we remain till near 5 in
the Evening, our Men having then thrown away their 24
Rounds in the manner above mentioned, & scarce an officer

James Furnis

[The extract printed here is the bulk of a letter from Furnis to the Board of Ordnance, written at Fort Cumberland on July 23, 1755. The whole has been transcribed from Furnis's letter book in the William L. Clements Library, Ann Arbor, Michigan, by Edward G. Williams, and appears in his "Treasure Hunt in the Forest," *Western Pennsylvania Historical Magazine*, 44 (1961), pp. 388–89.]

On the 9th Instant the General at the Head of about 1200 Men—crossed the Manongahela near Fort DuQuesne. the rear of the Army had scarce forded the River before the advanced Party consisting of 250 Men Commanded by Lieut. Colo. Gage, received a smart fire from behind the Trees which put them into some disorder, upon which the General who was about a quarter of a Mile Distant immediately advanced with the Troops and drew up in an open place, when the Action became general, but the Enemy had greatly the Advantage, by securing themselves behind Trees—in such a manner, as they could not be seen, while our people by keeping together in a Body were a Butt for them to fire at, and only threw away their Ammunition the Action began about half an hour past One, and continued untill a Quarter past Four, when the Troops gave way, and all methods taken to rally them prov'd ineffectual, so that we were oblig'd to leave all our Artillery and Horses in the Field and to cross the River in great Confusion, several of the Indians pursued us into the Water, and came up with and scalp'd some of the stragglers, but the main body keep'd the field in order to secure the Artillery and Baggage expecting we might rally which was very lucky, for the Soldiers were struck with such a Pannick that a small body might have cutt off what remained, we are at present uncertain of the number of the french and Indians, but they are computed at about three or four Hundred—and our loss kill'd and wounded about Eight hundred. at this time Colo. Dunbar was in the Rear with the rest of the Army, Horses and Provisions about 54 Miles distt. not being able to proceed for want of Horses. —On the 11th in the Evening the General with most of the wounded Arrived at the Camp, and the next day gave orders to destroy the Stores which were there, and a great Quantity of Provisions, least they should fall into the hands of the Enemy, who we then expected would pursue us, the greatest part of the Drivers having gone off with their Horses, on the first Alarm of our defeat.

Commentary

A meaty report, well worth our scrutiny. Furnis is obviously not very precise in his description of the battle, and not everything he says is correct, a point that has been noted in the text. However, his position in the army lends credence to other aspects of his testimony. He would certainly have been in a better position than most to know why the ammunition that Dunbar was holding was destroyed. On the other hand, the reader benefits from the fact that Furnis was in many ways the "odd man out." He presumably would have had close contact with Thomas Ord, his immediate superior, but in view of his probable civilian status, he would likely not have been friendly with more than a few officers, and perhaps not with any. In addition, considering his role in the army, the battle he portrays was certainly not his to win or lose. No one would have blamed him for the defeat, no matter how he described it. Since he was not close to the officers, and was not himself in a position where he might be considered culpable, he had less reason to cover up his superiors' conduct than they had. This raises his credibility rating. His errors seem to be due not to dishonesty or a biased interpretation, but rather to faulty perspective.

Thomas Gage

[This lengthy and important account is the full text of a letter Gage wrote to the Earl of Albemarle, dispatched from

Fort Cumberland on July 24, 1755. I am reproducing the letter from the only version in print, Thomas Keppel, *The Life of Augustus Viscount Keppel* (London, 1842), pp. 213–18. In his transcription, Thomas Keppel has apparently modernized spelling and punctuation.]

We are arrived here with the remainder of our army, since our unfortunate defeat on the 9th instant, within a few miles of Fort Du Quesne. As I imagine you would be glad to have some particulars of that action, I will give you the best account I can draw from so confused an affair.

General Braddock marched from this place with all his forces, escorting the whole convoy of provisions, ammunition, &c., to a place called the Little Meadows, about twenty-three miles from hence; and finding he had made but very slow progress, chose a detachment of 1200 men, and proceeded towards the French fort as fast as possible, taking with him two six-pounders, four twelve-pounders, and four howitzers; the remainder was left under the command of Colonel Dunbar, to follow with all convenient speed.

The night before the action, I received orders to march the next morning by three o'clock, with two companies of Grenadiers, and 150 men; to pass the Monongahela, —and to march on the other side, till I should come opposite the place where Frazer's house formerly stood, then repass the river, and post myself on the most convenient spot I should find. These orders were executed without any opposition from the enemy; and I remained on the post we had taken till Sir John Sinclair, who followed me with the working party, came up to me, and the General with the main body was passing the last ford. I then received orders to march on till three o'clock. We had scarcely marched a quarter of a mile from the river, when the guides, who were the only outscouts we had, brought word that the French or Indians were coming. Upon which, the guard in our van came to the right-about, but, by the activity of the officer who commanded them, were stopped from running in, and prevailed on to face again. The detachment was ordered to fix their bayonets, and form in order of battle, with intention of gaining a hill upon our right, which was partly already possessed by an officer's party that was scouring our right flank. The first was obeyed in a good deal of hurry, but none of them would stir to the posts assigned them. Though I had all the assistance that could be expected from the officers, not one platoon could be prevailed upon to stir from its line of march, and a visible terror and confusion appeared amongst the men.

By this time, some few shots were fired on the parties who were on the right and left flanks, on which the whole detachment made ready, and notwithstanding all the opposition made by the officers, they threw away their fire, when, I am certain, scarcely two of the men could be seen by them. This fire killed several of our men on the flanking parties, who came running in on the detachment, as did also the vanguard, which completed our confusion. The enemy took advantage of it by coming round us covered by trees, behind which they fired with such success, that most of the officers were in a short time killed or wounded, as also many of the men, and the rest gave way. We found Sir John Sinclair's working party in the same confusion, as also the main body under General Braddock. The same infatuation attended the whole; none would form a line of battle, and the whole army was very soon mixed together, twelve or fourteen deep, firing away at nothing but trees, and killing many of our own men and officers. The cannon was soon deserted by those that covered them. The artillery did their duty perfectly well, but, from the nature of the country, could do little execution.

General Braddock tried all methods to draw the men out of this confusion, made several efforts to recover the cannon, as also to drive the enemy from our flanks, as likewise to gain possession of the hill already mentioned. Some few men were at times prevailed on to draw out for this purpose, but before they had marched twenty yards, would fall back to a line of march by files, and proceed to attack in this manner, till an officer, or perhaps a man or two, should be struck down, and then the rest immediately gave way; the men would never make one bold attack, though encouraged to it by the enemy always giving way, whenever they advanced even on the most faint attack.

In this manner the affair continued about two hours and a half, when many of the men began to go off, and the General was wounded; what remained was to endeavour to cover the retreat of the ammunition and provisions, but those that drove the horses went off with them. The men that covered the wagons went off by tens and twenties, till reduced to a very small body, which, receiving a fire from the enemy, went to the right-about, and the whole were put to flight.

The General was saved by the dexterity of his servants, but all other marks of our disgrace were left upon the field; all our artillery, ammunition, and provisions fell to the enemy's share. It was impossible to rally any body of men for a considerable time, and the General was defended by very few but officers in his repassing of the river. Some bodies of men were with difficulty rallied at different distances, who waited till the General came up, and then marched on with him all that night and all the next day, when we were joined by two companies of Grenadiers, and some provisions from Colonel Dunbar's detachment, and the whole joined the next day.

I have given your Lordship the best account I am able of this shameful affair, and refer you to the public account for a list of the killed and wounded. General Braddock died the fourth night after the action. Sir Peter Halket was killed in the field. I hope that his Royal Highness [Cumberland] will think me worthy of succeeding Sir Peter in his regiment, as I was the eldest lieutenant-colonel in the action, and should have been appointed colonel to it by General Braddock, had he lived a few days longer. I likewise flatter myself of his protection for the officers of the regiment succeeding to the commissions vacant by this action, as I can with truth assure you, no officers ever behaved better, or men worse. I can't ascribe their behaviour to any other cause than the talk of the country people, ever since our arrival in America—the woodsmen and Indian traders, who were continually telling the soldiers, that if they attempted to fight Indians in a regular manner, they would certainly be defeated. These discourses were prevented as much as possible, and the men, in appearance, seemed to shew a thorough contempt for such an enemy; but I fear they gained too much upon them. I have since talked to the soldiers about their scandalous behavior, and the only excuse I can get from them is, that they were quite dispirited, from the great fatigue they had undergone, and not receiving a sufficient quantity of food; and further, that they did not expect the enemy would come down so suddenly. . . . Most of the wounded are in a fair way of recovery. I received a slight wound in my belly, which is almost well. Poor Nartlo was killed.

Commentary

As I suggested in the text, Gage seems to have fallen victim to his own self-interest. Prudence dictated that in his account he attempt to exculpate himself, for having been in a key position of command he was naturally in line for a great share of the blame for the fiasco. He could not remove criticism from his shoulders by laying it on Braddock's. First, both Keppel and Cumberland had been good friends of the general's and might resent attacks on his memory. Second, he wanted to claim Braddock's favor. The other obvious scapegoat was the men. By blaming them, he freed himself from any possible imputation of misbehavior or incompetence.

It is suspicious that he describes the battle in the way that most favors his case—suspicious, but not surprising. But while there is more reason to challenge his integrity than there is in the case of most other eyewitnesses, this does not mean that his report should be tossed aside. The account he gives of the activities of Braddock's army during the last hours before battle seems to be reliable, as far as it goes. So is much of what he says on the engagement itself, as is shown by comparison with other accounts. But we must be particularly wary in dealing with him. When he makes a statement that can be interpreted to his own advantage, he is not worth the benefit of the doubt. One final point: We should note how closely his own comments on the soldiers' excuses for their misbehavior, and his reference to the fact that there were only a few guides, tally with the report he and Dunbar prepared for Shirley. The report may in fact have been entirely his own creation. And although he probably spoke to some of the soldiers about their conduct, Gage appears even more than most to have been the sort to remember only what he wanted to.

Horatio Gates

[To my knowledge, this account has never been in print and is in fact referred to only by Stanley Pargellis, in "Braddock's Defeat." Gates's comments are extracted from a letter he wrote to Colonel Robert Monckton. From the reference to Gage's advertisement in the *Pennsylvania Gazette*, we can gather that Gates wrote to Monckton on September 5, 1755. Monckton then forwarded the account, or a portion of it, to Major John Hale, who on November 27 included the following extract in a letter he sent to John Calcraft, an army agent in London who was, ironically, joint executor and a major beneficiary of Braddock's will. I am quoting only the Gates extract from Hale's letter. The original is in the Loudoun Papers, LO 687, The Henry E. Huntington Library.]

As to a history of our Campaign I shou'd be very glad to repeat it to you but am very cautious of writing one as there is so much hazard in letters, they make no scruple of opening both publick and private and here is so much curiosity in this town, (N York) thus far I will inform you Sr that there has not been one true account publish'd as yet a great deal of pro & con in the news papers and yesterday Col. Gage and the Officers of the Van Guard contradicted Captn: Orme's publick letter by an advertisement which you will see in the Philadelphia [sic] Gazette. a few who were the Generals favourites gratefully strive to save his fame by throwing the misfortune of the day on the bad behaviour of the troops, but that was not the case, the main body of the army instead of being form'd in a line of battle, on the Van Guards being attacked moved up in a line of march were flank'd on both sides by the enemy which caused an immediate confusion and so great was the disorder that there was no setting it to rights and from that instant all was lost. the Vanguard was near ten minutes engaged before the main body came up of which time the enemy made so good use that fifteen out of eighteen Officers were kill'd and wounded and half of the 300 men that composed it, in this fell poor Stone I cannot say how as I was unluckily shot through the left breast sometime before he got his wound, I am not quite recover'd, the ball having cut some string that has deprived me of the use of my left arm. Floyer was shot through the hand which join'd to an extream shatter'd constitution was the death of him he was buried at Wills creek.

Commentary

Gates's brief account obviously lacks details of the battle. Virtually all of his noteworthy testimony has been examined in the text. His version is clearly anti-Braddock, and angrily so at that. However, we should note what he does *not* say. He does not claim that the troops did not panic, only that the unwise tactics used by Braddock were primarily responsible for whatever panic there was. Likewise, he does not say that European tactics were inadequate in view of the circumstances, only that Braddock's particular orders were ill chosen. In fact, he seems to suggest that he is generally in agreement with Gage's account of the battle, at least as opposed to Orme's. Yet Gage clearly condemns the troops and implies approval of Braddock's tactics. It made well be that Gates, like British B and St. Clair, had it in for Braddock and Orme, and looked for any stick with which to beat them. We cannot, however, be certain hat Gates bore his commander a grudge. Only his tone and his inconsistencies suggest the possibility.

Harry Gordon

[This lengthy and extremely important account is reprinted from the version appearing in Stanley Pargellis's *Military Affairs in North America 1748–1765* (New York: D. Appleton-Century Co., Inc., 1936), pp. 104–09. Charles M. Stotz has also printed he report: "A Letter from Wills' Creek—Harry Gordon's Account of Braddock's Defeat," *Western Pennsylvania Historical Magazine*, 44 (1961), pp. 129–36. Gordon's letter is dated July 23, 1755.].

On the 11th of June we March'd from this fort with such a rain of provision & Amunition Waggons, that the first days March Convinc'd us that it was impossible to Get on with so many Carriages so heavily loaded. The General Diminish'd the Carriadges By putting the greatest part of the provisions on Pack horses, & sending Back two of the 6 pounders with their Amunition; in this Reformation we March'd as far as the Little Meadows, which are only Distant 15 miles from our first Camp yet took us five Days to Get up all our Carriages, the Roads Being steep & horses very weak.

At the Little Meadows the General order'd another Reform, which Reduc'd us to a Pick'd Body of Eleven hundred men & officers; our Carriadges consisted of two 6 pounders, four 12 pounders, four Howits's, 3 Cowhorns, & 75 Rounds of Amunition, 3 or 4 provisions Waggons, which made our whole train of Carriadges three or four & thirty. We Left the Little Meadows the 19th of June with a Resolution of pushing on Directly to fort Du Quesne, & to leave Coll: Dunbar with the rest of our Army & Carriadges to Get up in the Best Manner he cou'd. We Came on Extreamly well, Considering the Difficulty of making the roads, which was so Great, that Altho' Every one us'd their Utmost Endeavor & only halted four Days on the Road, it was

the 8th of July Before we Cou'd Get within 10 miles of th
french fort.

on the 8th we Cross'd the Long Run which was a sma
Rivulet that runs in to the Monongahela about 12 miles fror
the F: fort. We were Oblig'd to Cross it many times in th
Space of two Miles, in which Distance we came along a Narro
Valley At the widest a Quarter of a Mile, very much Con
manded on Both Sides by Steep hills. In this March Ever
proper precaution was taken to secure us. By Detaching all th
men that cou'd be Spar'd from the Advanced party, that da
Commanded By C: Burton on our flank the General Likewis
orderd 350 men to take possession of the heights on Each Side
& the Grenadier Company of Sir P: H Regt., the Advance c
the Advanc'd party, to Gain the Rising Ground, which Shut u
the Valley in our front. No Enemy appear'd, & we Encamp'
on the last Mention'd Rising Ground, which Brought us withi
a Small Mile of the River Monongahela.

in our Next Days March we must Either Go along th
Narrows, a very Difficult pass, on the Right Side Entirel
Commanded By high ground & on the Left hemm'd in b
the Monongahela: A Small Consultation was held, & it wa
carryied to Cross the Monongahela at the Nearer End of th
Narrows, to keep along the South Side, & to Cross it agai
Below where turtle Creek runs in, & without the Narrow
As there was Danger Imagin'd, the 2 Compys of Grenadier
with 150 men of the two Regts Commanded By Coll: Gag
were Order'd to March By 2 o'Clock of the Morning of th
9th to take possession of the Banks of the second Crossing c
the River; two of the light 6 pounders were sent along wit
this party; the rest of our Little Army March'd at fou
Cross'd peaceably, & Came up with Coll: Gage about Eleve
o'Clock in peaceable possession of the furthest Banks of th
Last Crossing. Every one who saw these Banks, Being Abov
12 feet perpendicularly high Above the Shore, & the Cours
of the River 300 yards Broad, hugg'd themselves with joy a
our Good Luck in having surmounted our greatest Di

ficultys, & too hastily Concluded the Enemy never wou'd dare to Oppose us.

In an hour which Brought the time about Noon, the Bank was slop'd & passable for Artillery and Carriadges; Coll: Gage with the same Advanc'd party was ordered to [march] forward; the covering party of the Carpenters & Pioneers followed immediately in his Rear, after them then came two 6 pounders, their Ammunition Waggon, & a Guard in their Rear, after them follow'd the Main Body in their Usual Order of March with a strengthen'd Rear Guard of 100 men. ⟨this Order of March was in My Opinion the⟩

The flank partys of the Advance & Main Body were No Stronger than Usual & Coll: Gage's party march'd By files four Deep our front had not Got above half a Mile from the Banks of the River, when the Guides which were all the Scouts we had, & who were Before only about 200 yards Came Back, & told a Considerable Body of the Enemy, Mostly Indians were at hand, I was just then rode up in Search of these Guides, had Got Before the Grenadiers, had an Opportunity of viewing the Enemy, & was Confirm'd By the Report of the Guides & what I saw myself that their whole Numbers did Not Exceed 300.

As soon as the Enemys Indians perceiv'd our Grenadiers, they Divided themselves & Run along our right & Left flanks. The Advanc'd party Coll: Gage order'd to form, which Most of them Did with the front Rank upon the Ground & Begun firing, which they contined for several Minutes, Altho' the Indians very soon Dispers'd Before their front & fell upon the flank partys, which only consisted of an officer & 20 men, who were very soon Cut off. The Indians Making their Appearance upon the Rising Ground, on our Right, occasion'd an Order for Retiring the Advanc'd Body 50 or 60 Paces, where they confusedly form'd again, & a Good many of their Officers were kill'd & wounded By the Indians, who had got possession of the Rising Ground on the Right. There was an Alarum at this time that the Enemy were attacking the Baggage in the Rear, which

Occasion'd a second Retreat of the Advanc'd party; they had not Retir'd But a few paces when they were join'd By the rest of the troops, Coming up in the greatest Confusion, & Nothing afterwards was to Be Seen Amongst the Men But Confusion & Panick. They form'd Altogether, the Advanced & Main Body in Most Places from 12 to 20 Deep; the Ground on which they then were, was 300 yards Behind where the Grenadiers & Advanc'd party first form'd. The General Order'd the officer to Endeavor to tell off 150 men, & to Advance up the hill to Dispossess the Enemy, & another party to Advance on the Left to support the two 12 pounders & Artillery people, who were in great Danger of Being Drove away By the Enemy, at that time in possession of the 2 field pieces of the Advanc'd party. This was the Generals Last Order; he had Before this time 4 horses killed under him, & now Receiv'd his Mortal wound. All the Officers us'd their Utmost Endeavors to Get the men to Advance up the hill, & to Advance on the Left to support the Cannon. But the Enemy's fire at the time very much Encreasing, & a Number of officers who were Rushing on in the front to Encourage the men Being killed & wounded, there was Nothing to Be seen But the Utmost panick & Confusion amongst the Men; yet those officers who had Been wounded having Return'd, & those that were not Wounded, By Exhorting & threatning had influence to keep a Body about 200 an hour Longer in the field, but cou'd not perswade them Either to attempt the hill again, or Advance far Enough to support the Cannon, whose officers & men were Mostly kill'd & wounded. The Cannon silenc'd, & the Indian's shouts upon the Right Advancing, the whole Body gave way, & Cross'd the Monongahela where we had pass'd in the Morning, with great Difficulty the General & his Aid de Camps who were Both wounded Orme and Captain Roger Morris were taken out of a Waggon, & hurryed along across the River; Coll: Burton tho' very much Wounded attempted to Rally on the Other Side, & made a Speach to the Men to Beg them to get into some Order, But Nothing would Do, & we found that Every man wou'd

)esert us; therefore we were oblig'd to go along; we march'd
ll night, & never halted till we Came to Guests's which was
ear 60 Miles from the place of the Action, we halted that
ight there, & next Day join'd Coll: Dunbar's party which was 6
niles further.

Thus Sir I have sent you an Account of those transactions
ntirely consisting with my own Certain knowledge. I was
ever a Critick, therefore leaves it to you to make what Re-
narks you see proper. As you are a Much Better Judge in these
Matters than I shall Ever pretend to Be, only One thing cannot
scape me, which is, that had our March Been Executed in the
ame manner the 9th as it was on the 8th, I shou'd have stood a
air Chance of writing from fort Du Quesne, instead of Being
n the hospital at Wills's Creek.

I am a Good Deal hurt in the Right Arm, having Receiv'd a
hot which went thro', & shatter'd the Bone, half way Between
he Elbow & the wrist; this I had Early, & altho' I felt a Good
leal of pain, yet I was too Anxious to allow myself to Quit the
ield. . . .

On the Road I propos'd fortifying a Camp at Licking Creek
0 miles to the Westward of the Crossing of the Yohiogany, a
ery advantagious Situation, & which Cover'd the Richest part
f the Country which Lyes Betwixt Guest's & that, or at least I
magin'd we might have Been join'd By Coll: Dunbar's party at
Guest's, where a good Camp might Easily Been had, which
ortified with two or three Redoubts in front cou'd have Been
lefended By our Numbers (above 1000 fit for Duty) against
ny force our Enemys cou'd Bring against us.

Instead of all this Nothing wou'd Do, But Retiring, & De-
troying immense Quantitys of amunition & Stores, with which
Last all our Instruments & Stationary wares shar'd the fate. . . .

I shoud be Extreamly oblig'd to you if you would be kind
Enough to Remind H:R:H [Cumberland] of my former peti-
ion for a Commission in some Regtt. I have Reason to Believe
hat had General Braddock Liv'd I shou'd have Been provided
for in some of the Regts here.

Commentary

Gordon is not an infallible source. In terms of pure reliability he is probably outranked by Dunbar. He can occasionally be tripped up on details, such as the numbers of the enemy and the distance from the river to the battlefield. More important, he becomes rather hazy once he has described the first few moments of battle. For example, he claims that the retreating advance party collided with "the rest of the troops." If he means this literally, his account is incorrect, since the advance party collided first with the working party, and then the two of them combined fell back on Burton's detachment, which may or may not have been in motion. It is more likely, however, that he is guilty only of using imprecise terminology, for he soon remarks that "They form'd Altogether, the Advanced & Main Body." In other words, at this point he is equating the advance party with the vanguard as a whole, something he has not done earlier in his account. He in any case omits the collision between the advance party and St. Clair's detachment. His discussion of the battle as a whole is delivered in this imprecise fashion.

Despite such lapses, however, his account remains one of our most important. Unlike Gage, he does not seem to have distorted what he observed on the battlefield. Indeed, although he is likely trying to blow his own trumpet, he does not have Gage's motive to cover up, since he need not worry that he may be blamed for the defeat. Furthermore, he seems to have been in an excellent position to observe the first moments of fighting, better perhaps than any eyewitness except Gage or Croghan. On the early stages of battle, prior to the retreat by the advance party, he is apparently our most reliable reporter, in view of his honesty and precision. The fact that the latter fades when he discusses the remainder of the engagement does not prevent him from being considered one of our four or five most useful informants.

Philip Hughes

[This "Extract of a Letter from Fort Cumberland, dated July 23" appeared in *The Public Advertiser,* October 31, 1755. I am ısing the reprint in Davis's "British Newspaper Accounts of Braddock's Defeat." The writer does not identify himself, beond the fact that he is a chaplain. Davis notes that there were wo chaplains on the expedition, Hughes of the Forty-Fourth ınd John Hamilton of the Forty-Eighth. Further research shows hat Hughes was wounded in the battle. Hamilton is not listed ımong those who saw action, and in fact he probably remained »ehind with Dunbar. It is with considerable certainty, therefore, hat I identify the author of the following as Hughes.]

I believe I am the first Chaplain who ever saved a Pair of Colours, which I took within fifty Yards of the Cannon, when he Enemy were Masters of them. The French and Indians rept about in small Parties so that the Fire was quite round us, ınd in all the Time I never saw one, nor could I on Enquiry ind any one who saw ten together. The Loss killed and wounded 864. The French had 2000 Men, besides Indians, we ıad six Indians, and they at least as many hundreds, We narched near 400 Miles in three Months, cut 350 thro' Woods, ınd for the last 200 saw no House but this dirty Fort. Rum 20's ı Gallon, the worst brown sugar 4s 6d a Pound, a Year old Calf ;old to Sir Peter Halket and our Mess at 3.£. after the 25th of [une a Dollar for a Pint of Rum, so you may judge of our Distress. The whole Country is a Wood.

Commentary

One point relevant to the battle has been discussed in the ext. Otherwise, Hughes's sad remark on the high cost of rum recalls the complaint of the soldiers, related in the report by Gage and Dunbar, that during the march they had had "Nothng to Drink but Water." Hughes's account is on the whole ınimportant, but it certainly conveys an honest, if naive, impression of the battle. Many inexperienced man, especially those regulars who had never seen action, undoubtedly shared his exaggerated estimate of the enemy's strength, and it is likely that this belief contributed to the panic.

Matthew Leslie

[I am reproducing Leslie's brief account from Samuel Hazard's *Register of Pennsylvania*, 5 (1820), p. 191. Hazard describes his transcript as a "Copy of a letter from Major Leslie to a respectable merchant of Philadelphia." Leslie, who was almost certainly not a major at the time he wrote this letter, had several contacts within the mercantile community of Philadelphia, but to suggest an addressee would be nothing but guesswork. Nor do we know where the letter was written. It is dated July 30, 1755.]

You have heard the disastrous termination of our expedition, with the loss of our General and most of the army. What could bravery accomplish against such an attack, as sudden as it was unexpected? the yell of the Indians is fresh on my ear, and the terrific sound will haunt me until the hour of my dissolution. I cannot describe the horrors of that scene; no pen could do it, or no painter delineate it so as to convey to you with any accuracy our unhappy situation. Our friend, Captain John Conyngham is severely wounded, his horse fell on the first fire, and before he could be disengaged from the animal, which had fallen on him, received a wound on his arm; and his life was saved by the enthusiasm of his men, who seeing his danger rushed between the savages and him and carried him in triumph from the spot. I need not tell you that the Captain is indebted for his life to the love his men had for him. Many had sacrificed their lives before he could be extricated from the horse. If you have an opportunity please to communicate the sad intelligence to our friends in Ireland. Tell them I live, but that my feelings have been dreadfully wounded. To tell you what I did, I cannot; suffice it that I acted as all brave men placed like me in a similar position, would act.—We have lost gallant officers and generous friends, not in battle, for that we could bear, but by murder, by savage butchery. The French dared not openly meet us; our's is the loss, theirs the disgrace.

When we meet I will give you particulars. Captain Conyngham is doing well. I hope we shall soon be under your hospitable roof in Philadelphia.

Commentary

Leslie is among the most likable of our reporters. His compassionate account should remind us that in the wake of the battle not all officers looked first to their self-interest. In a less subjective vein, it appears that while he gives the impression of reliability, his account is too anecdotal and personalized to serve as a basis for any check on accuracy.

Patrick Mackellar and Robert Orme: Maps

[Orme's first sketch (map 2), showing the disposition of the army as a whole, has been reprinted often since George Bancroft published it. I am reproducing it, as well as Orme's detail of the advance party (map 3), from Sargent, *History of an Expedition* (facing pp. 218 and 352, respectively). Mackellar's sketches and commentary (maps 4 and 5) are drawn from Pargellis, *Military Affairs,* pp. 114–15.]

Commentary

It is almost certain that all four of these maps are the work of Mackellar. The first two are associated with Orme because they were enclosed with his journal. However, as we might expect, he did not draw them. In a letter that he sent to Napier accompanying the journal, he protests that "I am sorry the plans are not finished, but am to have them to-morrow night" (Sargent, *History of an Expedition,* p. 282). Orme would have had one of the four engineers prepare the sketches, and Mackellar is the most likely candidate, in view of the great similarities between maps 2 and 4. As for Gordon, his right arm was badly damaged during the battle, and there is little chance that he would have recovered quickly enough to draw the maps Orme had ordered. Whoever drew them, the captain undoubtedly

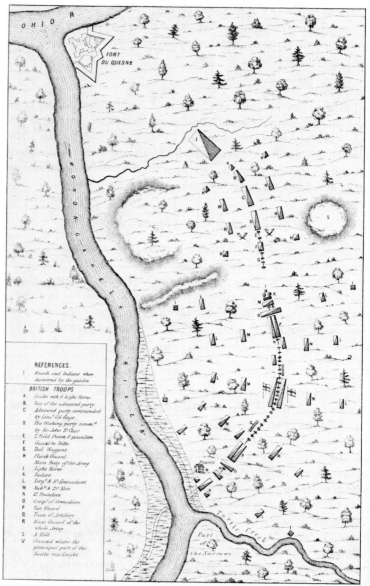

Map 2. Orme's Sketch of the Battle

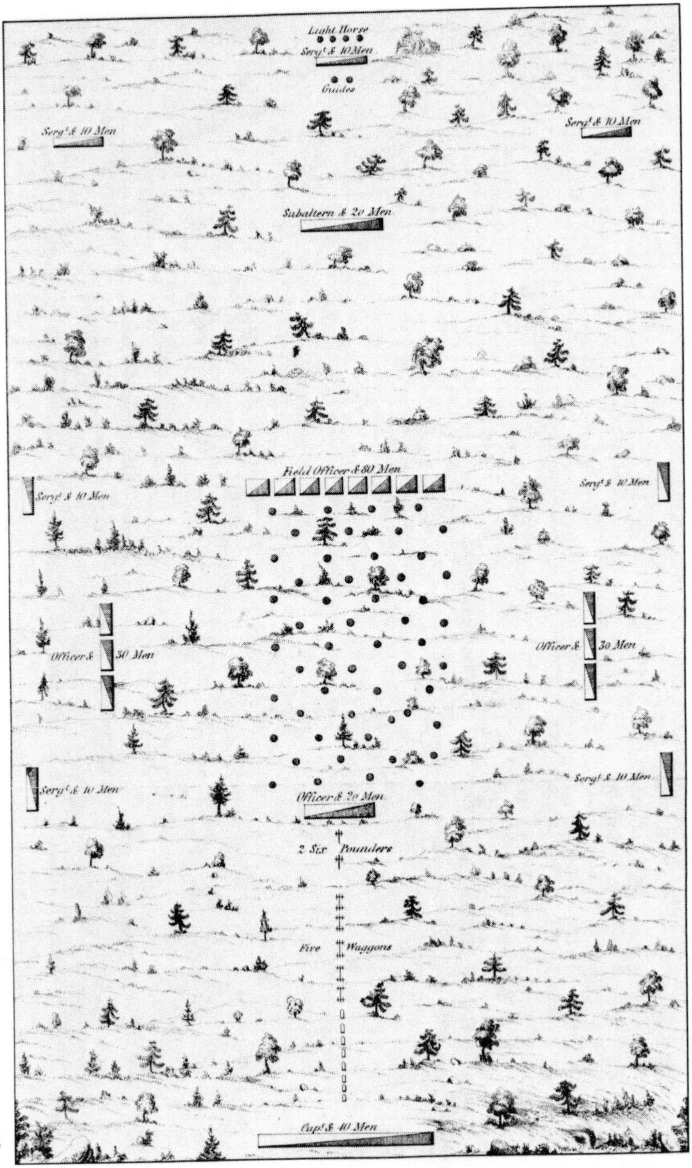

Light Horse
Serg.t & 10 Men

Guides

Serg.t & 10 Men   Serg.t & 10 Men

Subaltern & 20 Men

Field Officer & 80 Men
Serg.t & 10 Men   Serg.t & 10 Men

Officer &   30 Men   Officer &   30 Men

Serg.t & 10 Men   Serg.t & 10 Men

Officer & 20 Men

2 Six Pounders

Fire   Waggons

Capt.t & 10 Men

Map 3. Orme's Detail of the Advance Party

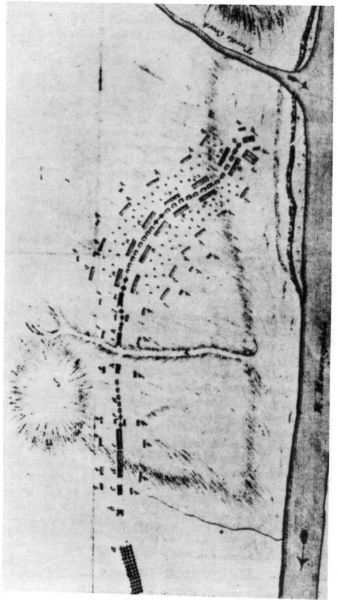

Map 4

Map 4. Mackellar's Sketch of the Beginning of the Battle

A Sketch of the Field of Battle of the 9th July upon the Monongahela, seven miles from Fort du Quesne, between the British Troops commanded by General Braddock and the French & French Indians commanded by Monsr de St Pierre, shewing the Disposition of the Troops when the Action began.

Explanation of Map 4.

British Troops, the long Lines express the Number of Files

French and Indians

Cannon

Howitzers

Waggons, Carts and Tumbrils

Provision and Baggage Horses

a. French and Indians upon their march to attack the British, when first discover'd by the Guides
b. Guides and six light Horse
c. Van-Guard of the advanced Party
d. Advanced Party commanded by Col Gage
e. Working Party commanded by Sr Jn St Clair D.Q.M.G.
f. Two six pounder Field Pieces
g. Carts & Waggons wt Ammunition & Tools
h. Rear Guard of the Advanced Party
i. Light Horse
k. Sailors and Pioneers
l. Three 12 pounder Field Pieces
m. General's Guard, Foot & Horse
n. Main Body in Divisions upon the Flanks of the Convoy, wt the Cattle, Provision & Baggage Horse between them & the Flank-Guards
o. a 12 pounder Field ps in the rear of the Convoy
p. Rear-Guard
q. Flank-Guards
r. a Hollow Way
s. a Hill which the Indians took possession of soon after the beginning of the Action
t. Frazer's House

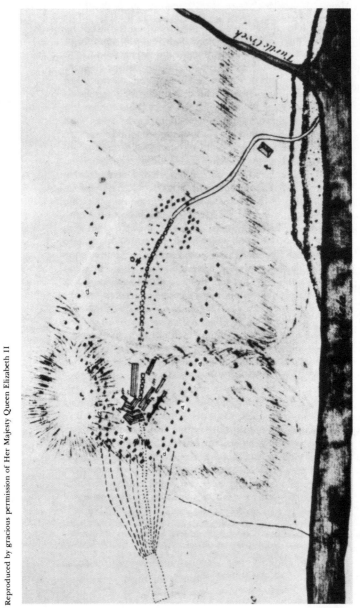

Map 5

Map 5. Mackellar's Sketch of the Battle at Two o'Clock

A Sketch of the Field of Battle &c, shewing the Disposition of the Troops about 2 a Clock when the whole of the main Body had joined the advanced and Working Partys, then beat back from the Ground they occupied as in Plan No 1 [map 4].

Explanation of Map 5

a. The French and Indians skulking behind Trees round the Brittish

f. The two Field Pieces of the advanced Party now abandoned

c, d, e, h, i, k, m, n, q. The whole Body of the British joined, with little or no order, but endeavouring to make Fronts towards the Enemys Fire

l. the three 12 pounder Field Pieces of the main Body

o. The rear Field Piece. 12 pounder

p. The Rear Guard divided (round the rear of the Convoy, now closed up) behind Trees having been attacked by a few Indians

N.B. The Disposition on both sides, continued about two hours nearly as here represented, the British endeavouring to recover the Guns (f) and to gain the Hill (s) to no purpose. It was proposed to take possession of this Hill before the Indians did, but unhappily it was neglected. The British were at length beat from the Guns (l). The General was wounded soon after. They were lastly beat back across the Hollow way (r) and made no farther Stand. All the Artillery, Ammunition, Provision & Baggage were left in the Enemys Hands, and the General was with difficulty carryed off. The whole Action continued about three hours and a half. The Retreat was full of Confusion, but after a few Miles, there was a Body got to rally.

Engaged	in the Field	kill'd	wounded
Genl Braddock			
Officers Staff included	96	26	36
Sergeants Corporals & private men	1373	430	484
Total	1469	456	520
Monsr de St Pierre			
French	200	8	
Indians	600	20	
Total	800	28	

N B The Number of the French & Indians is not yet certain

had considerable influence over their preparation. He may
likewise have had a say in the preparation of the two sketches
known to have been drawn by Mackellar, though in their case
other officers may also have made suggestions.

In any case, none of the maps sharply contradicts another.
There are slight differences in the stated disposition of troops
prior to battle. Regarding the number of flanking parties, I
have accepted Orme's version as more plausible, for Mackellar's map implies that these units totaled considerably more
than four hundred men. A more important discrepancy favors
Mackellar. This involves distance. The advance party certainly
was not as spread out as is suggested by Orme's second map. It
may be added that the troops at the time of battle were much
farther from Fort Duquesne than Orme would have us believe,
but the Mackellar map proper gives no indication as to where
they were relative to it, so there is no contradiction here. The
same severe skew is apparent in the sketch reproduced by
Freeman (see chap. 4, n. 1), which is probably a rough version
of the first Orme map. There is a possibility that in both
Mackellar is simply departing from scale.

Robert Orme

[This major account is excerpted from Orme's journal (Sargent, *History of an Expedition,* pp. 352–57). Other reports by
Orme are noted in Appendix C. I agree with Sargent's opinion
(p. 282) that Orme addressed his journal to Napier. He did so
in the expectation that the addressee would then forward the
account to Cumberland. According to the letter that Orme sent
with the journal, the maps he had intended to include were not
yet complete. Apparently they were inserted later. The fact
that the maps were still to be finished indicates that he mailed
his report within a few weeks of the battle, and certainly before
the close of summer 1755. The manuscript journal is now in
the British Museum, no. 212 King's Mss. In his rendering,
Sargent has apparently modernized spelling.]

[July 8th.] Lieutenant Gage was ordered to march before break of day with the two companies of Grenadiers, one hundred and sixty rank and file of the 44th and 48th, Captain Gates's independent company, and two six-pounders, with proper guides; and he was instructed to pass the fords of the Monongahela and to take post after the second crossing, to secure the passage of that river.

Sr John St Clair was ordered to march at 4 of the clock with a detachment of two hundred and fifty men to make the roads for the artillery and baggage, which was to march with the remainder of the troops at five. . . .

July 9th. The whole marched agreeably to the Orders before mentioned, and about 8 in the morning the General made the first crossing of the Monongahela by passing over one hundred and fifty men in the front, to whom followed half the carriages. Another party of one hundred and fifty men headed the second division; the horses and cattle then passed, and after all the baggage was over, the remaining troops, which till then possessed the heights, marched over in good order.

The General ordered a halt, and the whole formed in their proper line of march.

When we had moved about a mile, the General received a note from Lieutenant Colonel Gage acquainting him with his having passed the river without any interruption, and having posted himself agreeably to his orders.

When we got to the other crossing, the bank on the other side not being yet made passable, the artillery and baggage drew up along the beach, and halted 'till one, when the General passed over the detachment of the 44th, with the pickets of the right. The artillery waggons and carrying horses followed; and then the detachment of the 48th, with the left pickets, which had been posted during the halt upon the heights.

When the whole had passed, the General again halted, and they formed according to the annexed plan.

It was now near two o'clock, and the advanced party under Lieutenant Colonel Gage and the working party under Sr John

St Clair were ordered to march on 'till three. No sooner were the pickets upon their respective flanks, and the word given to march, but we heard an excessive quick and heavy firing in the front. The General imagining the advanced parties were very warmly attacked, and being willing to free himself from the incumbrance of the baggage, order'd Lieutenant Colonel Burton to reinforce them with the vanguard, and the line to halt. According to this disposition, eight hundred men were detached from the line, free from all embarrassments, and four hundred were left for the defence of the Artillery and baggage, posted in such a manner as to secure them from any attack or insults.

The General sent forward an Aid de Camp to bring him an account of the nature of attack, but the fire continuing, he moved forward himself, leaving Sr Peter Halket with the command of the baggage. The advanced detachments soon gave way and fell back upon Lieutenant Colonel Burton's detachment, who was forming his men to face a rising ground upon the right. The whole were now got together in great confusion. The colours were advanced in different places, to separate the men of the two regiments. The General ordered the officers to endeavour to form the men, and to tell them off into small divisions and to advance with them; but neither entreaties nor threats could prevail.

The advanced flank parties, which were left for the security of the baggage, all but one ran in. The baggage was then warmly attacked; a great many horses, and some drivers were killed; the rest escaped by flight. Two of the cannon flanked the baggage, and for some time kept the Indians off: the other cannon, which were disposed of in the best manner and fired away most of their ammunition, were of some service, but the spot being so woody, they could do little or no execution.

The enemy had spread themselves in such a manner, that they extended from front to rear, and fired upon every part.

The place of action was covered with large trees, and much underwood upon the left, without any opening but the road, which was about twelve feet wide. At the distance of about two hundred yards in front and upon the right were two rising grounds covered with trees.

When the General found it impossible to persuade them to advance, and no enemy appeared in view; and nevertheless a vast number of officers were killed, by exposing themselves before the men; he endeavored to retreat them in good order; but the panick was so great that he could not succeed. During this time they were loading as fast as possible and firing in the air. At last Lieutenant Colonel Burton got together about one hundred of the 48th regiment, and prevailed upon them, by the General's order, to follow him towards the rising ground to the right, but he being disabled by his wounds, they faced about to the right, and returned.

When the men had fired away all their ammunition and the General and most of the officers were wounded, they by one common consent left the field, running off with the greatest precipitation. About fifty Indians pursued us to the river, and killed several men in the passage. The officers used all possible endeavours to stop the men, and to prevail upon them to rally; but a great number of them threw away their arms and ammunition, and even their cloaths, to escape the faster. About a quarter of a mile on the other side of the river, we prevailed upon near one hundred of them to take post upon a very advantageous spot, about two hundred yards from the road. Lieutenant Colonel Burton posted some small parties and centinels. We intended to have kept possession of that ground, 'till we could have been reinforced. The General and some wounded officers remained there about an hour, till most of the men run off. From that place, the General sent Mr Washington to Colonel Dunbar with orders to send waggons for the wounded, some provision, and hospital stores; to be escorted by two youngest Grenadier companies, to meet him at Gist's plantation, or nearer, if possible. It was found impracticable to remain here, as the General and officers were left almost alone; we therefore retreated in the best manner we were able. After we had passed the Monongahela the second time, we were joined by Lieutenant Colonel Gage, who had rallied near 80 men. We marched all that night, and the next day, and about ten o'clock that night we got to Gist's plantation.

Commentary

For a discussion of Orme's reliability, see Appendix C.

Francis Peyton

[Peyton's letter is reprinted from John L. Peyton, *The Adventures of My Grandfather* (London, 1867), pp. 244–49. Like Keppel and Sargent, J. L. Peyton has apparently modernized spelling and punctuation; this is the least of our worries. If genuine, Captain Peyton's account is the earliest known, having been dated July 13, 1755, from the Great Meadows.]

Never did I undertake to write a letter when so overwhelmed with grief and disappointment. Our expedition has failed! Our commander is dead! Our noble General Braddock! He died this day from his wounds. Alas! who could have anticipated such a disaster—such an extraordinary and disgraceful defeat as that which we have sustained on the Monongahela river.

I will endeavour to give you some connected account of our military operations since the letter I wrote you from Monakatuca Camp [July 6].

Well, my dear mother, after leaving that spot our whole army arrived at the Monongahela river and crossed it on the 9th July. It is a bright and beautiful stream of about 200 yards width at that point, but varying both in width and depth; sometimes rattling playfully over the rocks which form its bed, and sometimes flowing silently under the rugged roots and branches which stretch half across it. It was very shallow where we crossed, as I suppose it generally is during the dry season. We crossed it in the first place full of hope and confidence; we have recrossed it in shame and confusion! I was acting as adjutant of Colonel Burton's regiment. According to his orders I had formed in columns of companies to the right of the main force, which was on the opposite side of the stream. The scouts reported the French and Indians in great force near at hand; therefore our whole army was drawn up in line of battle. The General issued the order to advance. We did so; and had not proceeded 500 yards when we heard quick and heavy firing along nearly our whole line. In order to ascertain the force of the enemy, and their exact position, General Braddock called a halt; and directed that our regiment, with the vanguard of 800 men, should move forward to reinforce the pickets and reconnoitre the enemy's position. Lieutenant-Colonel Burton placed himself at the head of the regiment, and advanced in gallant style. We had proceeded hardly one quarter of a mile, when we came upon our pickets retreating in confusion, bringing terrified and exaggerated accounts of the enemy's force. This threw the vanguard into disorder, which disorder quickly spread among our men. Suddenly we beheld the savage enemy advancing toward us; for we had not been able to see them through the thick forest in which we were. The confusion greatly increased, and our men were now falling wounded and dead in all directions from the brisk fire which the Red Skins opened upon us. Colonel Burton and the other officers exerted themselves to the utmost to induce the men to stand their ground, and return the enemy's fire; or to advance upon, and dislodge them from their hiding-places. But in vain; panic-struck they retreated upon the baggage in the utmost precipitation and confusion, and had hardly come back to it before the French and Indians attacked us in this position. Every man among us must have been destroyed, and I should never again have addressed a letter to you, my respected mother, had it not happened that four pieces of cannon were stationed in reserve at that point. These were promptly manned, and chiefly by officers, who thus succeeded in keeping back the foe. Notwithstanding we held them in check, a murderous fire was kept up upon us and our whole line. Nearly all of our horses and drivers were killed, and those who were not, fled; for still our treacherous foe could not be seen through the trees and thick undergrowth: and excepting the road which we had cut, there was no opening whatever.

General Braddock seeing that it was necessary to advance and dislodge the enemy, rode forward with his staff to the front. He endeavoured to reanimate their courage, and induce them to advance, dashing forward through the thick forest to show his indifference to danger. But, oh! that I should have to write it—he failed, and while thus exposed was shot down, dangerously wounded. So also was the brave Colonel Burton, while many officers were killed. This greatly increased the panic, and in spite of our efforts to retire in good order, we found it impossible to control the men, who fled. The only regiment in which there was any steadiness was the 48th. At the head of this, Colonel Burton, notwithstanding his wound and loss of blood and consequent prostration, endeavoured to advance. He was aided by Colonel Washington and Colonel Lewis who had rallied around them a body of Western Virginians. These men protected themselves by the trees while they fired—after the fashion of the Indians— and thus prevented an advance of the enemy. But for all that their efforts were futile, the 48th refused to advance, but stood firing helplessly at the forest trees behind which the enemy were concealed, until they had expended all their ammunition; after which, in spite of the officers, they broke and fled towards the river in the wildest confusion; many of them throwing away their arms and accoutrements. In spite of being thus forsaken by the panic struck 48th, the brave Western Virginians whom Colonels Washington and Lewis had formed behind the trees—after the Indian mode of fighting— retreated, but in order, from tree to tree, loading and firing as they drew back, upon such of our snake-like enemy who showed themselves in advancing. The Colonial Volunteers thus prevented pursuit, and saved the remnant of the British army from destruction. Meanwhile, Colonel Washington had

had the wounded General Braddock carried to the rear, and carefully tended.

The whole of our retreating force recrossed the river in safety; and on the 11th we reached Gist's Plantation, where our wounded were attended to, and the army rested for a short time. We then continued our retreat to Rock Fort, near Colonel Dunbar's, and thence to this point which we have only reached this evening.

The whole retreat has been indeed conducted by Colonel Washington, whose remarkable talents have gained the confidence of the other and senior officers. His principal and most efficient aid in this humiliating task has been Captains Andrew and William Lewis, of Augusta, (county) who have lived all their lives on the frontier, and perfectly understand the Indian character. Thus, my dear mother, you will perceive that to the volunteers of my native Virginia, we entirely owe our escape.…

I have been with the wounded general during some or other portion of each day. He endured agonizing pains of body, and, if it were possible, still greater anguish of mind at the failure of the campaign. Indeed, it appeared to be a relief to him that he would not survive so grievous a disaster. He entertained the hope that his king and his country—since he had laid down his life in their service—would shield his memory from any unjust or ungenerous imputations connected with this most fatal enterprise.

It is a source of much pride and pleasure to me, to witness how rapidly our friend and neighbour, Colonel George Washington, has grown in the estimation of all, by his wisdom and prudence; and by the great ability he has displayed in extricating the army from an unfortunate and dangerous situation. He is spoken of in terms of praise by all—both colonial and English officers, and particularly by General Braddock, whose last breath was drawn while sounding his praise, and exhorting obedience to his orders. Though Colonel Washington does not belong to the British army (for, like myself, he was a volunteer in this expedition), has, indeed, never been to England, or received any regular military training, he has the faculty of inspiring confidence in officers and men alike: particularly—if any can be singled out—is he admired by Colonel Burton. All agree that in future campaigns against the Indians, it will be better to conduct them under officers born and bred in this country; and not by persons despatched from England, however competent the latter may be considered. They cannot understand America so well as the natives, who have already learned the way to fight the savages around them. And in this age the Indian craftiness has been quickened by their French allies.

Commentary

If this account is wholly imaginary, it is not the only one. Almost a decade before the appearance of *The Adventures of My Grandfather,* William Makepeace Thackeray produced *The Virginians,* a novel that included the "testimony" of one George Warrington, a survivor of Braddock's Defeat. In preparing Warrington's report on the battle, Thackeray drew most of his information from Sargent, text and documents. The resultant account (1900 ed., pp. 428–30) is incorrect on numerous points, but, as one might expect, it is told with flair. Of course, so is Francis Peyton's. The point is, however, that while Thackeray wrote as a novelist, and everyone knew that his account was fictitious, John L. Peyton wrote as a historian. In the introduction to *The Adventures of My Grandfather,* Peyton writes that he had recently come into possession of a collection of family papers. Some of the documents had been mutilated during the Civil War, and therefore in preparing his manuscript, Peyton tells us (p. v), "I have been under the necessity, in cases where the meaning appeared tolerably clear, of supplying a few lines to fill the hiatus. If this should, in any instance, have caused obscurity or anachronism, I hope this will be a sufficient explanation, especially as it has arisen from a strong wish to render the narrative not only agreeable to my family, for whose gratification it is especially designed, but interesting to the public." Peyton never specifies which documents he has altered, or where. I strongly suspect, however, that if the letter in question exists at all he has virtually rewritten it.

There is, indeed, no evidence that Francis Peyton accompanied Braddock. This should not surprise us, since if he were really a volunteer of the campaign, his name would not have appeared on the various lists of officers who took part in the battle. If we give John Peyton the benefit of the doubt, and assume that his ancestor fought at the Monongahela and did write the letter ascribed to him, we are still faced with major problems in judging his account. The letter itself is in some ways strange. For one thing, what son would recount such a gruesome experience to his mother and not so much as mention whether he had been wounded? The style of the letter is likewise a cause for suspicion, suggesting more a historian of the mid-nineteenth century than a country gentleman of the eighteenth century.

But the main cause for concern is that the account reads remarkably like a rehash of Orme, with other material drawn from the "Seaman's Journal" and Sargent's narrative. Wherever Peyton is original, his statements are trite, dubious, or plain wrong. Enough material exists so that we can say with certainty that the "savage enemy" did not advance toward the British. Similarly, the claim that the "whole retreat" was conducted by Washington is at least a gross exaggeration. But it is Orme's influence that is most worrisome. This influence is perhaps even more evident in Peyton's "Journal," the account he sent his mother from Monakatooka Camp. The journal immediately precedes Peyton's letter of July 13 in the appendix to *The Adventures of My Grandfather*. There is not one verifiable point made in that journal that is not made by Orme in his standard account of the expedition. But we are not dealing here with a normal case of self-corroboration, that is, one in which one reporter provides information for another. If the letter is authentic, Captain Peyton was in at least as good a position to view the battle as was Orme. He would, in fact, have accompanied Burton's detachment on its fateful mission, while Orme remained behind with Braddock.

It is not therefore Captain Peyton's credibility that is in question. It is *John Lewis* Peyton we are primarily concerned with. Assuming that there was a letter at all, how much did the historian alter or interpolate? A great deal, I would suggest. I do not claim that the evidence adduced is overwhelming, but I do consider it to be substantial enough to justify my decision not to cite Peyton's letter in the text, with the other eyewitness accounts. I have not reached my decision lightly. If genuine, Peyton's report ranks with those of British A, Cholmley's Batman, Gordon, and Orme as one of our five most useful. It is obviously quotable, and the allusions to Washington, who was indeed Peyton's friend, are of great interest. Peyton provides us with a full account by a member of the main body, particularly welcome in view of the fact that aside from Orme that segment of the army is not known to have produced a reporter who excelled in detail. Most important of all, we have here an eyewitness with no apparent ax to grind. He is writing not to a superior, in the hope that he may glorify himself or place blame on others. Rather, he addresses his mother. But we cannot accept an account simply because it would be desirable to do so. The letter in question may never have existed at all. Even if it did, we may not assume that any given statement printed in *The Adventures of My Grandfather* is authentic. Unless the original letter comes to light, it seems quite unwise to put any stock in Captain Peyton's "account."

Sir John St. Clair

[My source for the following report is Pargellis's *Military Affairs,* pp. 102–03. St. Clair's letter, addressed to Napier, is dated Wills Creek, July 22, 1755.]

I wrote to you a letter on the 12th of June, which I hope you have received by this time, that letter gave you an Account of the obstructions we was like to meet with on our march on account of Carridges: a few days after writeing that letter, General Braddock with the Army arrived at the little meadows; about the 17th of June General Braddock sent for me and told me, he laid down a Scheme of his own for marching on, which before that time, had been given to the Brigade Major in orders. The Scheme was, that a detachment should be form'd of those of the British Battalions, which Came from Ireland and that those should march with the artillery together with three Companys of the Virginia forces, under the Command of General Braddock, the remaining part of the Army under the Command of Colonel Dunbar, was to follow with the Great Convoy, this Step I look'd upon to be a prelude to marching in divisions, which was the only way we Could have brought up our Convoy.

This strong detachment march'd on and arrived at the Strong Camp of the Great-Lick which is Twenty one miles on the other side of Yanehagane and Eighty miles from this fort. The Great advantages of this strong Ground made me propose to the General, to halt with his detachment to bring up Colonel Dunbar with his Convoy; this proposal, was rejected with great indignation; we march'd on 'till the seventh of July Twenty three miles further, I then objected to our marching any longer in that order of march with a Convoy, and proposed, since this small body must march to the french fort, that we should march part of our small numbers and take post before the Fort leaving our Convoy to Come up I urged strongly that no General had hitherto march'd up at midday to the Gates of the Town he was to beseige leading his Convoy and if Genl. Braddock attempted it, he must look to the Consequences.

Tewsday the 8th we march'd to a riseing ground within three quarters of a mile of the Monongahela and Encamp'd there.

Wensday the 9th Colonel Gage with about 300 men march'd at daylight, past and repast the Monongahela where he took post, the Workmen and Cover'ers immediately follow'd and then the rest of the detachment—so that the whole had past by half an hour after Twelve o'Clock, being three miles; The reason of passing the Monongahela twice was to avoid the Narrows, which is a road on the bank of the River, Commanded by a high hill, which would have taken a days work to have made passable. After Colonel Gage and I had pass'd the river, we received orders from Cap: Morris Aid du Camp to March on; the underwood Continued very thick for about one quarter of a mile beyond the Monangahela then we Came into an open wood free from underwood with some gradual riseings, this wood was so open that Carridges Could have been drove in any part of it; about a mile on the other side of the last Crossing, we began to feel the Enemys fire and to hear their Shouts; those who were under my Command immediately form'd. On those in my front falling back upon me, I ran to the front to see what the matter was, when I received a Shot through the body. I then return'd to my own people, posted Cap: Polsons Company of Artificers and Cap: Periwees Company of Rangers to Cover my two Cannon. I then went up to General Braddock who was then at the head of his own Guns and beg'd of him for God-Sake to gain the riseing ground on our Right to prevent our being Totally Surrounded. I know no further of this unlucky affair to my knowledge being afterwards insensible. It will be needless for me to give you any account by hear-say. Our affairs here are as bad Can make them, with regard to my self in particular. I was fully resolved, if we had met with Success to desire leave to have been recalld, finding I could be of little use being never listen'd to: but as our affairs stand at present it is a thing I shall not think of and should be glad of haveing another opportunity of makeing use of the knowledge I have of the Country and its inhabitants; by the time I shall have your answer I hope to be in a Condition of doing my duty therefore should be glad you would point it out to me whether its to be here or in New England under General Shirrly.

Commentary

St. Clair's comments on the last stages of the march are highly interesting. On the battle itself he is, however, a minor source. We have seen in the text that his statements can be unreliable, and of course his claim that he was unconscious during most of the fighting limits his usefulness. On the last point, one should note Colonel Dunbar's remark (see Appendix E) that he had received an account of the battle from St. Clair, "who saw the whole." It is impossible to know whom to credit here. In any case, St. Clair's account, as reported to Napier, seems to dovetail perfectly with his self-interest. Sir John had written earlier of the important role he had played in masterminding and guiding the expedition. Now, in the wake of defeat, it is clearly wise for him to wash his hands of it. He does this by claiming that his advice had lately been consistently ignored. As for the defeat itself, the testimony he presents is entirely to his own benefit. How can he be blamed if, in the first place, his troops rallied round him while chaos spread elsewhere, and if, in the second, he was unconscious after the first few moments? I am not accusing him of misrepresenting the facts. We have seen that, at the very least, his advice was on several occasions rejected. And British B, for what it is worth, seems to confirm his point about being insensible throughout most of the battle. But we should be aware of the directions self-interest would lead him in his report. We have judged a parallel case in our discussion of Gage and have done the same, respecting Orme, in Appendix C.

Adam Stephen

[There are two versions of the following account, neither in print. One is among the Newcastle correspondence in the British Museum, Add. 32,857, fol. 216. This copy of Stephen's letter is dated Fort Cumberland, July 18, 1755, and is addressed to John Hunter. It is referred to by Evan Charteris, in *William Augustus Duke of Cumberland and the Seven Years' War* (London: Hutchinson & Co., 1925), p. 166. The one I have transcribed, however, is neither addressed nor dated. It is to be found in the Hardwicke Papers, Add. 35,593, fol. 234, and is referred to briefly by Pargellis in "Braddock's Defeat."]

July the 9th: about two o'clock in the Afternoon. The first Division of our forces consisting of about 1300 effective chosen Men & Officers under the immediate Command of General Braddock was attacked by a Party of French and Indians near to the River Monongahela about 8 Miles from Fort Du Quesne.

The Private Men of the two Regiments were entirely at a loss in the Woods. The Savages and Canadians kept on their Bellies in the Bushes and behind the Trees, and took particular Aim at Our Men, and Officers especially, most of whom are killed or wounded: The British Troops were thunderstruck to feel the Effect of a heavy Fire, & see no Enemy; they threw away their Fire in a most indiscreet Manner, and shamefully turned their Backs on a few Savages and Canadeans. General Braddock strove most incessantly to rally them, and make the proper Dispositions, but all was in vain. They kept in a mere huddle in spite of the most ardent Endeavours of many brave officers, and tho' our Numbers were sufficient to have surrounded them, fought them in their own way, and pursued our March. Shame unto the infamous Dogs! Their Numbers only served to increase the Number of the killed. They were infatuated to such a pitch, that they would obey no Orders, killed one another & deserted their Colours; and after about 3½ hours—(Shame! That it should be ever heard of) run from a small number of French and Savages, leaving them an easy Prey of a most valuable Train, a Stock of Ammunition, Provisions and Baggage. In short the Enemy obtained an easy and compleat Victory. The few independents and Virginians that were engaged behaved better and suffered much. There were but few of them engaged, as General Braddock had unhappily placed his confidence and whole Dependence on the Regiments. But his Excellency found to his woeful Experience, what had been frequently told him, that formal attacks & Platoon-firing never would answer against the Savages and Canadeans. It ought to be laid down as a Maxim to attack them first, to fight them in their own way, and go against them light & naked, as they come against Us, creeping near and hunting Us as they would do a Herd of Buffaloes or Deer; whereas you might as well send a Cow in pursuit of a Hare as an English Soldier loaded in their way with a Coat, Jacket, &c. &c. &c., after Canadeans in their Shirts, who can shoot and run well, or Naked Indians accustomed to the Woods. I escorted a Convoy of 100 Bullocks, and 100 Horse Load of Flour from Col. Dunbar's Camp to the General's which was 50 Miles. I had only 100 Men, and was dogged night and day by the Indians; but by Vigilance, which is the only thing can secure one against such an Enemy, joined the General four Days before the Engagement without the loss of a Man or Bullock. We beat them out of ther Ambushes, & always had the first Fire on them. The British Gentlemen were confident they never would be attacked, and would have laid any Odds, that they never should, until they came before the Fort, yea, some went further, and were of opinion, that We should hear the Explosion of the French Fort blown up and deserted, before We approached it. These Notions which were very ill-grounded, served to lull them into a fatal Security which contributed not a little to the fatal Event which has lately happened.

I always declared openly & at the time was not the better thought of for it, that they would be attacked before they arrived at the Fort. My Reasons were, that the French must lose the Use of their Indians, if they did not. They had collected a Body of them, and they would not be cooped up in the Fort; and the character of the People We had to deal with would not permit Us to think but the French would take all Advantages. I had the Honour to receive the General's Thanks for my Services in the Field; and if he had lived a Week, I should have been provided for. Twelve Virginia Officers were engaged, six of whom were killed. I have two Bullet Holes in my Body at this instant. Lieut. [Walter] Stewart is wounded. Sr. Peter Halket fell in the beginning of the Day. Secretary Shirley & thirteen Officers of the Regiment are killed. Almost all wounded.

Commentary

An interesting account that would be much more important if it could be shown that Stephen himself participated in the central engagement. Stephen is more generally critical than any of our other eyewitnesses. Obviously, he is harsh in assessing the behavior of the troops, particularly the regulars. But he criticizes the officers as well, including Braddock, and one may conjecture that he would denounce the general even more boldly if he were not claiming his posthumous favor. Stephen is our prime exponent of Indian-style tactics. During the battle, he probably led his own rangers in an attack of this sort. However, because he was in the rear guard and absorbed in fighting in his own style, it appears unlikely that he saw much of what was going on up ahead. Undoubtedly, toward the close of the battle, when he helped to cover the retreat, he saw the panic he describes here, but he does not appear to have been on the scene when the troops in front first succumbed to terror. For this reason I used Washington, rather than Stephen, as my primary witness to the panic. Stephen's account of the battle also suffers from a lack of precision. But although his perspective and thoroughness may be questioned, his integrity ranks high, and in fact he does not make a single statement that can be successfully challenged on the strength of other evidence. For this reason, his claim that many officers during the march predicted an easy victory gains considerable credence. Although not without his weaknesses, Stephen generally deserves the benefit of the doubt.

Robert Stewart

[Stewart's account appears to be unknown to historians. It is in print in only one source, the *South Carolina Gazette*, no. 1104 (August 14–21, 1755), p. 2, col. 3. However, it is referred to briefly in several other newspapers of the time, including the *Pennsylvania Gazette*, no. 1391 (August 21, 1755), from which Sargent draws a reference (*History of an Expedition*, p. 363 n.).

Of all the letters concerning the battle that were printed by contemporary newspapers, this is the only one whose author is identified by name. The version in the *South Carolina Gazette* is headed "Copy of Capt. Robert Stewart's Letter to his Friend at Williamsburg" and is dated Wills Creek, July 19.]

As I did not till this Moment know of this Opportunity, have scarce Time to inform you, of my having escaped safe from the dreadful Havock we had on the 9th Instant, within *Six* Miles of the *French* Fort,—where General *Braddock,* with 1300 chosen Men and Officers, were attacked by the *French* and *Indians,* and, after a sharp and bloody Engagement of 3 Hours and 35 Minutes, our Troops yielded Ground; chiefly owing to the Consternation the *Indian* Method of Fighting threw the *British* into, and for the Want of Officers, most of them being either killed or wounded by that Time: Very soon after our giving Way, the Pannic became so general and great, that they shamefully turned their Backs, and, in a great Measure, abandoned their General and the Colours—notwithstanding the utmost Efforts of the few remaining Officers to rally and return to the Charge, and tho' they had to retreat upwards of 60 Miles thro' a Wilderness, before they could join the other Division of the Army. As to Particulars, it's impossible yet to give them with any Certainty. We lost all our Artillery, Stores, Provisions, and Baggage of every Kind, by much the greater Number of our Officers, and most People think, at least Half of the Whole Number of Men we carried into the Field that Fatal Day. To give the finishing Stoke to our Misfortune, our great and brave (tho' unfortunate) General, died the 13th Instant. He was wounded in the Arm and Body, and I believe his Misfortune wounded his very Soul. I had the Honour of being close by his Side during the Action, and lost every Thing I had but my Blood, of which not a Drop was spilt, tho' I had two Horses shot under me, one Ball grazed my right Brow, another my Forehead, and a third shot away Sword and Scabbard from my Side. I had only a Detachment of my Troops with me of 29 Horses of which 25 were killed.

Commentary

Stewart was in a position to tell us a great deal about the battle. Unfortunately, he provides few details. Of course, he gives the impression that he was writing hurriedly, and presumably he was anxious to get letters off to his other friends and relatives. What he does provide is interesting enough. His reference to the chaotic nature of the retreat draws general support. On the other hand, his implication that the men did not panic prior to their retreat does not hold up. Perhaps his sense of time became distorted during the battle, a common problem among our eyewitnesses. In any case, his integrity is high, even if the same cannot always be said for his accuracy. The fact that he addressed his remarks to a friend favors his credibility, since he does not appear to have hoped for gain through his letter. As for his biases, none can clearly be established on the basis of this account. He implies that the panic was chiefly among the regulars, and he clearly condemns those who turned tail, but he does not claim that the Americans behaved particularly well. His sympathy toward Braddock is obvious, though this should not be taken to mean that he approved of his tactics.

George Washington

[Like Orme, Washington prepared several eyewitness accounts of the battle. His autobiographical notes, which were written years after the event, are discussed in Appendix E. The account I have generally relied on for his viewpoint, and the one reprinted here, represents virtually the whole of a letter he wrote to Dinwiddie, dated Fort Cumberland, July 18, 1755 (John C. Fitzpatrick, ed., *The Writings of George Washington* [Washington, D.C.: U.S. Printing Office, 1931], 1, pp. 148–50). It has been printed often in the past. Washington dispatched a series of letters on the battle (ibid., pp. 148–58), but unlike Orme he does not appear to have aimed at publication. Dinwiddie, however, publicized his account, possibly because he

was pleased that Washington had placed the Virginian troops
in a favorable light, or perhaps because it was the first one he
had received. On July 23, he sent copies to Robinson and Halifax. He then appears to have received Orme's somewhat fuller
account, and forwarded copies of it to several parties. On occasion he sent extracts from both, as he did to General Shirley on
July 29. Finally, in addressing the General Assembly, he laid
before the burgesses copies of both accounts (*The Official Records of Robert Dinwiddie*, ed. R. A. Brock, Virginia Historical
Society, *Collections*, n.s., 4 [1884], pp. 116–17, 130, 134). Perhaps it was as a result of this last act that fragments of the letter
began to appear in the provincial papers, for example, the
Pennsylvania Gazette, no. 1391 (August 21, 1755), p. 3, col. 1.
Washington's assertion that "the Virginian Companies behav'd
like Men and Died like Soldiers" soon became a catchphrase,
particularly in the colonies, and has remained so among historians to the present.]

As I am favour'd with an oppertunity, I shou'd think myself
excusable was I to omit giv'g you some acct. of our late En-
gagem't with the French on the Monongahela the 9th Inst.
We continued our March from Fort Cumberland to Frazier's
(which is within 7 Miles of Duquisne) with't meet'g with any
extraordinary event, hav'g only a stragler or two picked up by
the French Indians. When we came to this place, we were
attack'd (very unexpectedly I must own) by abt. 300 French
and Ind'ns; Our numbers consisted of abt. 1300 well arm'd
Men, chiefly Regular's, who were immediately struck with
such a deadly Panick, that nothing but confusion and disobedience of order's prevail'd amongst them: The Officer's in
gen'l behav'd with incomparable bravery, for which they
greatly suffer'd, there being near 60 kill'd and wound'd. A
large proportion, out of the number we had! The Virginian
Companies behav'd like Men and died like Soldiers; for I
believe out of the 3 Companys that were there that day, scarce
30 were left alive: Captn. Peyrouny and all of his Officer's,

down to a Corporal, were kill'd; Captn. Polson shar'd almost as hard a Fate, for only one of his Escap'd: In short the dastardly behaviour of the English Soldier's expos'd all those who were inclin'd to do their duty to almost certain Death; and at length, in despight of every effort to the contrary, broke and run as Sheep before the Hounds, leav'g the Artillery, Ammunition, Provisions, and, every individual thing we had with us a prey to the Enemy; and when we endeavour'd to rally them in hopes of regaining our invaluable loss, it was with as much success as if we had attempted to have stop'd the wild Bears of the Mountains. The Genl. was wounded behind in the shoulder, and into the Breast, of w'ch he died three days later; his two Aids de Camp were both wounded, but are in a fair way of Recovery; Colo. Burton and Sir Jno. St. Clair are also wounded, and I hope will get over it; Sir Peter Halket, with many other brave Officers were kill'd in the Field. I luckily escap'd with't a wound tho' I had four Bullets through my Coat and two Horses shot under me. It is suppose we left 300 or more dead in the Field; about that number we brought of wounded, and it is imagin'd (I believe with great justice too) that about two thirds of both [blank] received their shott from our own cowardly English Soldier's who gather'd themselves into a body contrary to orders 10 or 12 deep, wou'd then level, Fire and shoot down the Men before them.

I tremble at the consequences that this defeat may have upon our back settlers, who I suppose will all leave their habitations unless there are proper measures taken for their security.

Colo. Dunbar, who commands at present, intends so soon as his Men are recruited at this place, to continue his March to Phila. into Winter Quarters: So that there will be no Men left here unless it is the poor remains of the Virginia Troops, who survive and will be too small to guard our Frontiers. As Captn. Orme is writg. to your honour I doubt not but he will give you a circumstantial acct. of all things, which will make it needless for me to add more.

Commentary

Aside from his estimate of the size of the enemy force, a figure likely inherited from Gordon or Croghan, Washington apparently sticks to information drawn from what he himself had seen. Indeed, it is unfortunate that his report is not fuller, for he seems to have remained with Braddock throughout the fighting, and could have provided an unequaled account of the general's activities. Particularly welcome would be some sort of statement on how his commander reacted to the first firing, and what orders he gave to Burton and his detachment. Like Stewart, who was also in a good position to report, he lets us down here, possibly because he felt that Orme would provide the necessary details.

On the whole, Washington generalizes about the battle. It would be impossible to provide a sequential account from his testimony. However, much of what he says is extremely important. As we have seen, he is probably our most disinterested reporter on the behavior of the regulars. Indeed, his greatest contribution to an analysis of the battle lies in his criticism of the British soldiers. Since he plays a key role on a key question, it is particularly important to fix his reliability rating. In support of his personal integrity we have not only legend but the historical consensus. Even ignoring the point of whom we are dealing with, we see here an account which only on the question of enemy numbers fails to bear the weight of evidence. And as just noted, Washington was in a fine position to report on the battle, so his testimony cannot be disparaged on the grounds of faulty perspective. Integrity, accuracy—if not always detail—and physical proximity to the action he describes help to make Washington's account exceptionally reliable.

Other British Accounts

Note

I AM INCLUDING here three types of reports. First, there are
the genuine eyewitness accounts that were prepared too long
after the event to be rated as good risks on the question of
reliability. Second, there are the accounts written soon after the
battle by those who remained behind with Colonel Dunbar, or
at Fort Cumberland. Finally, there is one composite newspaper
account. Since these versions are not on the whole as important
as are those included in Appendix D, I am only describing and
commenting on them, rather than actually reprinting them.
There are, beyond these, countless second-, third-, and fourth-
hand accounts, some of which are interesting and incisive. I am
not including these here, but have made reference to the most
important of them elsewhere in this monograph.

British E

[This writer's account is included in a letter to an unnamed
addressee, dated Wills Creek, July 25, 1755. The entire letter is
printed in Pargellis, *Military Affairs,* pp. 112–24.]

Although not nearly so famous as the "Seaman's Journal,"
British E's account of the campaign and battle is in some ways
more interesting. First, it provides insight into the feuds that
divided the officers throughout the march. Second, Pargellis,
while referring to it as a "violent letter," made considerable use
of it in preparing his influential article on Braddock's Defeat.
The letter rambles somewhat, largely because the writer, who
was probably a British officer addressing a superior, seeks to

make two basic points. First, he wants to analyze the campaign, second, to single out various officers for praise or censure. He constantly shifts back and forth in mood between dispassion and anger; in topic, between march and battle.

He starts his account by casting blame. Braddock, he suggests, was a good and brave man, but lazy and sadly misled by his favorites, particularly Orme. British E moves next to the battle, but his narrative of the action here is rather weak. Going on the testimony he had heard from eyewitnesses, he asserts that the enemy force numbered no more than three hundred, and perhaps only one hundred. The attack itself he depicts as truly an ambush, initiated by a sudden volley fired on the British by the enemy stationed on the rising ground.

Aspects of his account seem to suggest particular sources. He appears to have adopted from St. Clair the conviction that the woods surrounding the battlefield were light. Our anonymous critic seems in any case to have been close to Sir John. Other comments by him suggest the influence of Croghan and possibly Gordon. But his discussion of Braddock's behavior during the battle most closely resembles that of British B, whose biases he shares. Their accounts differ in that he does concede that the vanguard retreated, but he repeats British B's claim that the main body was not put in any order before it marched to the front. Furthermore, like British A and Furnis, he states that it was Braddock himself who led the confused advance. However, while criticizing the general here, he, unlike British B, gives him credit for his attempts to rally the troops after their collision had brought chaos. But he feels that they should have been in better order to begin with, and that for this reason the disintegration of the army was only partly their fault. This is perhaps the core of his analysis: "The General would have Changed his disposition (or more properly made one) but the Men were then turn'd stupid and insensible and would not obey their officers in makeing the intended movements which were unhappily too late attempted. The officers behaved extremely well as possibly Could be."

While praising the officers for their courage, he criticize those in command for having blundered into an ambush. On the other hand, he singles out Gage and Halket for commenda tion. In his praise of Halket, we see clear evidence that the writer is no critic of Continental tactics, particularly since he lauds the colonel for having prepared his troops to fire by platoons. British E's criticism of Braddock is implicitly based on his conviction that the general failed to apply standard proce dure correctly, by not having his troops ordered, and by allow ing the main body to march in such a way that the troops were always separated from their respective officers by the wagon train, thus making ordering difficult. Having given his account of the battle, the anonymous officer bemoans the destruction of the ammunition, and the retreat. Then he suddenly backtracks to denounce Orme for his arrogance. Casting the captain as villain, he describes the confrontation between Orme and Colo- nel Dunbar, the same one British B is recounting at the start of his truncated letter. And again putting Halket, his hero, in a favorable light, he notes with clear approval Sir Peter's at- tempts to limit Orme's influence. The long letter ends on an anticlimactic note, as its author suggests that a major lesson to be drawn from the Braddock expedition is that in the future no army of similar size should be burdened with so many wagons. On the whole British E's report is honest and percep- tive, but his discussion of the battle itself is marred by his apparent tendency to rely on the testimony of his friends, most of whom were anti-Braddock and anti-Orme. The result is an exceptionally partisan account, which on several important points does not hold water.

Billy Brown

[A summary of this account appears in John Fanning Wat- son's *Annals of Philadelphia, and Pennsylvania, in the Olden Time* (Philadelphia, 1887), 2, p. 141. I have made my own transcrip- tion of the notes Watson made during an interview with

Brown, the original being in the Manuscript Department of the
Historical Society of Pennsylvania, Historical Collections, Am.
3013.]

According to Watson, Brown had been born free in Africa,
but had been captured at an early age and had come to Amer-
ca as the slave of Colonel Brown. After Braddock's Defeat, he
had become Washington's slave. When Watson interviewed him
in 1826, he described him as being "in the ninety-third year of
his age—possessed of an observing mind and good memory . . . incapable of fraud, and . . . a religious man, of the
Methodist profession." Although, as I have suggested, Watson
lacked a strong critical sense, he did not blindly accept all of
Brown's testimony. However, he probably would have done
well to accept far less.

Before starting to analyze the account in question, we
should note that no Colonel Brown fought under Braddock,
nor any commissioned officer with that surname. But perhaps
Watson himself was confused by the testimony, so let us assume that Billy Brown was at the battle, in the service of some
British officer. Brown's memory appears to have been erratic.
Some of his statements are accurate, and he furthermore re-
fuses to answer questions when he is uncertain, a tribute to his
honesty. His claim that after Braddock was buried wagons
were driven over his grave—in order to conceal its location
from the Indians—is true enough, and is supported by other
sources. However, the bulk of Brown's testimony is totally inaccurate. His assertion that Washington was captured during
the battle, only to escape, is so far-fetched that not even Watson accepts it. Similarly far from the truth is his recollection
that the engagement continued for two days. Throughout his
testimony, Brown is highly critical of Braddock and of the
British officers in general. His unkindest cut is the claim that
those in command were so incompetent that the enemy did
not attempt to kill them.

Despite their inaccuracy, his assertions provide some tenuous insight into the mood of the troops after the debacle. A case in point is his statement that "Braddock all the time wore a white handkerchief loosely tied over his hat & the men after the disaster said it was a sign he had betrayed his trust & meant them to have been taken!" There could well have been a rumor of betrayal. And certainly Brown echoed a popular tale when he said that the general was shot by one of his own men named Pritchett. As noted in Appendix A, Watson identifies Pritchett with Faucett. Brown, who "reports" various statements supposedly made by Braddock during and after the battle, also makes an exceptionally quotable source, as numerous historians, most recently McCardell, have discovered. On balance, however, his account is worth little, being primarily the stuff of legend, prepared in an age that tended to remember only the worst of Braddock. The fact that it is honest only serves as a reminder that ninety-three-year-old men, recalling events that had occurred more than seventy years in the past, do not make very reliable sources.

William Butler

[I am working from the summary of Watson's interview with Butler, included in the historian's *Annals of Philadelphia*, 2, pp. 139–41.]

There is even less chance that Butler would be reliable. This hardy Pennsylvanian was no less than 104 when Watson interviewed him in 1833. As with Brown, we immediately run into the problem of identifying those officers who he claimed were on the fateful expedition. For example, he states that at the start of action "he saw Generals Braddock, Forbes and Grant talking." By Forbes, he probably means the eventual conqueror of Fort Duquesne. His "General Grant" may well have been Colonel James Grant, who failed in his attempt. These two did not accompany Braddock. If my assumptions as to their identity are correct, this suggests only what we would expect in a man of Butler's age, the tendency to telescope events. Butler, like Brown, sees Braddock as the villain of the piece, and Washington as the hero. He, too, claims that the general was shot by a soldier in his own army, singling out Faucett as the culprit. Butler seems to have had less than Brown to say about the battle itself, or at least Watson reports less. Furthermore, he is even less reliable—if "reliability" is the term to use when referring to its nearly total absence.

Thomas Dunbar

[There are several sources for Dunbar's testimony. Easily the best is his letter to Napier, July 24, 1755, printed in Pargellis, *Military Affairs,* pp. 109–11. See also my reference to Burd's letter on p. 79.]

Dunbar's report to Napier is for the most part the apology of a modest man, who may well have had cause for modesty. First and foremost, the colonel presents testimony on the question of why at the time of battle his troops were so far behind Braddock. Such emphasis may suggest that he expected criticism on this point. By contrast, he spends little time defending his retreat, perhaps indicating that he considered his reasons self-evident. He concludes on an almost pathetic note: "This Climate by no means Agrees with My time of Life and bad Constitution, I was willing to try and hoped I should be Able to go through all that came in My Way, but find it otherwise, therefore beg Your Interest to gett Me leave to go home."

Regarding the battle itself, Dunbar has little to say, despite the certainty that he had a great deal of material to work with. He notes that he has already forwarded Orme's account of the action and implies that he considers it reliable. However, he also includes some comments probably drawn from St. Clair, who he states had witnessed the entire battle. For example, he claims that there had been a suggestion made, and rejected, that Braddock bring up his detachment before moving against

the fort. This certainly sounds like Sir John's testimony. Dun
bar also notes Gage's assertion that he had not seen even one o
the enemy. But perhaps the colonel's most interesting commen
relative to the battle represents his synthesis of various reports
"The Officers by All Accounts behaved As Well as Men coul
and the Soldiers dont seem to think they deserve all that i
Said. That they fought an invisible Enemy is by All Account
Certain." Dunbar may not have been inspirational, but he wa
more understanding than most.

Tom Faucett

[Andrew Stewart reported Faucett's account in "Was Gen
Braddock Shot Down by One of His Own Army?", *New York
Times,* October 19, 1913, sec. 5, p. 5.]

Faucett's reported testimony revolves entirely around his reasons for, as he claims, having shot Braddock. This point, and
hence the key to assessing his reliability, has been discussed in
Appendix A. Here we may note two other factors which should
aid in determining value. First, Stewart is himself recalling the
testimony of his grandfather, a friend of Faucett's. Second,
Faucett was ninety-nine when he allegedly in 1812 helped a
road crew to unearth Braddock's remains, and then delivered
the singular graveside oration quoted in Appendix A. Three
memories are therefore at work here, any of which may have
failed. It is only because of Faucett's key place in the realm of
Braddock legends that Stewart's version of his testimony is
worth noting.

William Johnston

[J. Cook Wilson provides us with this account, under the title
"The Campaign of General Braddock," *English Historical Review,* 1 (1886), pp. 149–52. The letter containing Johnston's
report is dated Philadelphia, September 23, 1755. It is addressed only to "Frank," probably a close friend or relative.]

The writer, an Englishman, provides us with yet more testimony favorable to Orme, for he notes that he is "under great obligations" to the captain. However, his account does not bear Orme's imprint, and he seems to have relied on several other witnesses. The point is not really very important, for this report contains nothing new, and nothing that could be considered controversial. Johnston had been left behind with Dunbar's detachment in order to guard the military chest, and one might hope for worthwhile information on that section of the army. Again, however, there is nothing new, though Johnston does corroborate the testimony of Dunbar and others that the slow progress of the detachment was primarily due to the weakness of the horses. Even the account of Dunbar's retreat is standard. Johnston's report is reliable enough, but particularly in regard to the battle he has nothing to say that merits our attention.

Maryland Gazette

[This report was printed in no. 533 (July 24, 1755), p. 3, col. 1.]

The problem here is that the *Gazette* prints an amalgam, based on the testimony contained in a letter from "an Officer in the Army"—undoubtedly Orme—and on an interview with "two young Gentleman Volunteers, who went from this Province, and who were in the late Action," Joseph Hopkins and James Calder. Although there is no proof that Hopkins and Calder actually served in battle, neither is there reason to doubt it. The real issue is the extent to which their testimony shapes the *Gazette* report. To judge, it is necessary to assume that Orme submitted his standard account. Given this, we note that the *Gazette* does not mention the telescoping and implies instead that it was the intensity of the enemy fire that caused panic. Nor is the description of the onset of battle Orme's. I know of no case where he attempts to discuss the first firing up front, yet here we read that as the British "were about to ascend a Hill, they were fired upon, from the Top of the Hill by a great Number of *French* and *Indians*." This could suggest an attempt to occupy the rising ground, but more probably involves only the fact that the army was apparently marching up a slope—"upon the ascent," according to William Dunbar—when attacked. In any case, this description of the early fighting suggests that the informant or informants had a poor perspective and did not realize that Gage had advance notice of the enemy's presence. One last line is of some interest: "The Officers, with some of the Men, fought gallantly for about 3 Hours." Orme tends not to note *any* case of heroism among the men. That this account does, suggests the influence of one or both of the Marylanders. But the claim that some of the troops behaved well is scarcely a revelation, and in fact the *Gazette* account as a whole merits only passing interest.

John Rutherford

[Captain Rutherford's letter to his wife, dated "camp on Laurel Hill," July 12, 1755, is printed entire in *Historical Magazine,* 6 (1862), p. 160. An extract of it is enclosed in a letter from Goldsbrow Banyar to Johnson in James Sullivan, ed., *The Papers of Sir William Johnson* (Albany: University of New York, 1921), 1, p. 712.]

This is the earliest known account of the battle, first- or secondhand. It appears for a brief time to have been the "standard" version, until replaced by the fuller reports of first Washington and then Orme. Rutherford's account is both brief and vague. Like so many, he expresses grief over the loss of Sir Peter Halket, whose death is "regretted by all Mankind." He also lists some of the other officers killed or wounded, with Braddock at the time falling into the latter category. Rutherford seems to be particularly upset by reports that the enemy force had been small: "The Slaughter on our side is surprising Considering General Braddock had 1500 and I dont believe the Indians had 300, but they chose a very advantageous

Ground." As for the commander who had left him and his New York independent company back with Dunbar, Rutherford has nothing but criticism: "The General told us he would never be 5 miles from us, so that the one Division might support the other whenever attacked, what made him change his resolution and order Colo Dunbar to keep us behind with Provisions and tired waggon Horses God knows, it seems Infatuation, he thought he had men enough and was vain of his Artillery." From his tone, it is possible that Rutherford was of the St. Clair-Halket faction, but there is no real evidence.

"Seaman's Journal"

[There are two basic versions of this account. The longer, sometimes known as the "Morris Journal" because it was at one time the property of Rev. Francis-Orpen Morris of Yorkshire, is printed in Sargent, *History of an Expedition,* pp. 366–89. Sargent also provides lengthy extracts from the other version in footnotes, and Archer Hulbert prints it entire in *Braddock's Road,* pp. 83–107. The full title of the former provides some insight into its contents: "A Journal of the proceedings of the Seamen (a detachment), ordered by Commodore Keppel to assist on a late expedition to the Ohio, from the 10th of April, 1755, when they received their first orders from the Army at Alexandria in Virginia, to the 18th day of August following, when the remaining part of the Detachment arrived on board His Majesty's ship 'Garland' at Hampton: with an impartial account of the action that happened on the banks of the Monongahela, and the defeat of Major General Braddock on the 9th of July, 1755." The latter version, in its title, proves useful in dealing with the question, "*Whose* 'impartial account'?" for here it is noted that the report of battle is that "related by some of the Principal Officers that day in the Field." The fact is that the midshipman who wrote the shorter version of the journal took ill before the march got underway and was hospitalized on June 10. This is why he relies on others to describe the battle, and why there are no entries in the journal between June 15 and July 9. Hulbert claims that the fuller version was the work of Gordon, who expanded upon the material in the original. Although he offers some evidence in support of his view (pp. 80–82), the respective accounts given in the two versions both differ markedly from Gordon's own, the engineer's version being unknown in Hulbert's day. I therefore agree with Pargellis's assertion that the fuller journal and the original "were pieced together from various accounts, including perhaps that of Gordon himself, after the army's return to Wills Creek" (*Military Affairs,* p. 104, n. 1).]

More than any other secondhand account, the "Seaman's Journal" has held the attention of historians. I not only think this reasonable, but have consistently looked to it as a corroborative source on various aspects of the battle. It is also useful in analyzing the campaign as a whole, but I intend to restrict my remarks to that portion of it which details Braddock's Defeat itself.

The account of the battle appears to be a smooth synthesis, rather than a mere conglomerate of opinions. This has its unfortunate aspect, in that it is generally impossible to tell which officer is making a given contribution. Since it has been suggested that Gordon wrote the expanded version, it is worth noting the reporter's remark that in regard to the enemy's numbers, "it was believed that they had at least man for man." On this point, at least, Gordon is definitely not the source. Neither is Croghan, nor Washington. The journal in no place bears the imprint of Orme, St. Clair, or Gage. If one were to suggest the eyewitness account that the seaman's report most nearly resembles, particularly in the original version, it would be that of British A, but even here there are significant differences. The fairest inference is that both versions are drawn from the testimony of at least a half-dozen officers, probably including several subalterns as well as "Principal Officers." It is quite possible that one or more of the informants did not himself leave an eyewitness account. But even if we assume this, it is nevertheless certain that more than one source of testimony is involved.

Be that as it may, the end product of the synthesis is controversial on only a few details. The broad sweep of the seaman's argument is that the battle was lost because the troops panicked; and certainly Orme, Gage, and most of our reporters would applaud this conclusion. For Braddock himself, the writer has nothing but praise, and in fact he provides material on the general's activities during the battle that is not to be found elsewhere. The commander's death, he claims, was "greatly lamented by the whole Army." The American troops receive no individual mention here, which is not surprising, since the author himself was British. In terms of bias, as well as content, the two versions of the "Seaman's Journal" do not differ markedly, and they may be the work of the same author. But even if not, their common significance is that they are both syntheses drawn from a considerable number of firsthand reports, some of which appear not to have come down to us, and may never have been recorded by the eyewitnesses themselves. That the seaman's account is a synthesis adds to its impact on the key question of the troops' behavior, where it strongly corroborates the testimony of Orme, among others.

Thomas Walker

[Walker's account is included in a letter from Jasper Yeates to an unknown addressee, dated Philadelphia, August 21, 1776. The letter is printed entire in *Hazard's Register*, 6, pp. 104–05, and by Charles I. Landis, in "Jasper Yeates and His Times," *Pennsylvania Magazine of History and Biography*, 46 (1922), pp. 212–14. On Walker, who was commissary general of the Virginian forces on Braddock's expedition, see Kenneth H. Tuggle, "Dr. Thomas Walker Bicentennial Celebration," Filson Club, *History Quarterly*, 24 (1950), pp. 276–79.]

Yeates's letter again presents us with the problem of who is giving what testimony. Not one, but two, eyewitnesses are involved, though Walker seems to have been the more important contributor. Yeates explains that recently he and a party of friends had visited Braddock's Field. Such a visit had naturally encouraged reminiscence: "The observations I heard Sir Francis Halket make of the disasters of that bloody day, and his filial expressions of affection to the memory of his worthy father, Sir Peter Halket, rushed to my recollection." The former commissary general was a member of Yeates's party, and spoke his piece: "My feelings were heightened by the warm and glowing narration of that day's events by Dr. Walker, who was an eye witness. He pointed out the ford where the army crossed the Monongahela (below Turtle creek 800 yds.)." This is the first and last reference by Yeates to Walker, though it appears that other aspects of the brief account are drawn from the latter's testimony, including the description of Braddock's troops splashing happily across the Monongahela on the morning of the fatal day. But the overall appraisal of the battle appears to have been Yeates's, though Walker may have shared or even encouraged it.

Yeates is hard on Braddock, more so than any eyewitness noted in the last appendix, with the possible exception of British B: "My indignation was greatly excited against the commander of the British army, in suffering so many brave men to perish from an obstinate adherence to European rules of war. . . . The Savages and French had hardly an idea of victory when they made the attack. Braddock appeared almost to have courted defeat. Against every remonstrance of Sir Peter Halket, Major Washington, and others of his officers, he refused to let a man leave his rank; they fired in platoons against no object—how very dispiriting to a gallant soldier; they were shot down in whole ranks. The enemy observing the *infatuation* of the General, felt assured of victory, redoubled their exertions, and fired with such fatal precision as to cause our men to throw away their guns and run off in the greatest disorder. The

officers in vain attempted to arrest their course—they were
compelled to follow their example."

Here we have a conclusion not differing greatly from that of
British E; that is, that while the men may have panicked, others
were to blame for mishandling the situation in such a way as to
encourage hysteria. The differences are that Yeates singles out
Braddock as the culprit, with no mention of Orme, and that,
more important, he argues that the general should have used
irregular tactics. His harsh criticism of Braddock, not only as
an individual, but as a proponent of what he takes to be an
outmoded and excessively regimented style of warfare, is rep-
resentative of the sort that was rife throughout the late eighteenth and nineteenth centuries. Needless to say, the fact that
he wrote during the Revolution did nothing to improve the
attitude of the patriotic Yeates toward a British general who
had led many Americans to their death.

George Washington

[The autobiographical notes discussed here were prepared in
1783 for the use of David Humphreys. The notes are printed
entire in Fitzpatrick, *Writings of Washington,* 29, pp. 36–50, the
portion on Braddock's expedition being on pp. 41–44.]

One point that can be made with certainty in comparing this
account with that included in Washington's letter to Dinwiddie
is that the writer had become much more critical of Braddock
over the years. On the surface, the two versions are similar. In
both, Washington claims that the main cause of defeat was that
the troops panicked. However, virtually every detail he includes in his memoir that is not in the letter tends toward
Braddock's detriment. First, he states that during the march he
often attempted to persuade the general and his subordinates—
including, presumably, Orme, whom he mentions only in passing—that they should prepare the men to fight Indian style,
but that because of their overreliance on discipline they had

rejected his advice. He also asserts that during the battle he had asked permission, probably Braddock's, "to head the Provincials and engage the enemy in their own way; but the propriety of it was not seen until it was too late for execution." Like his earlier letter, Washington's memoir is vague on the precise flow of events. This makes it difficult to check his accuracy on details, some of which are included in his notes and nowhere else. However, it does appear that time had by 1783 clouded his memory to a noticeable degree. For example, his claim that the enemy attacked at 10:00 A.M., while the rear guard was still crossing the river, is clearly incorrect.

On the whole, Washington held out admirably against the consensus of his countrymen that Braddock displayed criminal negligence and incompetence during the battle. But as time wore on and the tide of hatred did not abate, it is possible that he weakened and remembered his late commander in a more critical light than he had at first. Furthermore, he may have gotten caught up in his own legend, which suggested that he would have led the provincials to victory over the enemy, had he not been thwarted by Braddock himself. The account of 1783 is much more in step with the Washington saga than is that of 1755. The difference does not involve contradiction so much as elaboration. For this reason, it is difficult to judge the merits of the later version.

APPENDIX F

French Accounts

Contrecoeur

[CONTRECOEUR'S ACCOUNT is included in a letter to Duquesne's successor, the marquis de Vaudreuil, dated Fort Duquesne, July 14, 1755. Only an extract remains. It is printed entire in Pargellis, *Military Affairs*, pp. 129–32. Francis Parkman, in *Montcalm and Wolfe* (Boston, 1884), 2, p. 424, quotes a portion of the extract and apparently adds punctuation to it. My translation includes portions of the letter that appear only in Pargellis, but I am not giving the whole nor the accompanying lists of French casualties and of supplies taken from the English.]

Since the start of this month, I had been sending Frenchmen and Indians to harass the British, whose forces I knew to number about three thousand. While still thirty or forty leagues from the fort they prepared to besiege it; their troops marched constantly on guard, always in a line of battle, so that all of the efforts of the detachments were to no avail.

Finally, hearing always that the troops were coming closer, I sent le sieur La Parade, an officer, with some Frenchmen and Indians, in order to learn precisely where they were. The next day, the 8th, he told me that the English were about eight leagues from the fort.

I immediately sent another detachment, which the same day reported to me that they were not more than six leagues away, and that they marched in three columns.

That day still I organized a party to engage them, including in it all those whom I could spare from the fort. It was com-

249

posed of 250 Frenchmen and 650 Indians, totaling nine hundred men. M. de Beaujeu, a captain, commanded them. There were also two other captains, MM. Dumas and Lignerie, as well as several subalterns.

This party marched the 9th at 8:00 in the morning, and at 12:30 found itself in the presence of the English, about three leagues from the fort. Firing commenced on both sides. Twice the fire of the enemy artillery caused our party to fall back a little. M. de Beaujeu was killed by the third volley. M. Dumas took command, and served with excellence. Our Frenchmen, sustained by the Indians, despite the enemy artillery, fired at the English, who were fighting boldly in a line of battle, and drove them back in their turn. Furthermore, seeing the ardor of our people, who fought with infinite vigor, they collapsed entirely, after four hours of intense firing. MM. Dumas and Lignery, who had only a score of Frenchmen with them, did not pursue. They returned to the fort, because a large party of Canadians had unfortunately behaved like children and had fled at the first fire. . . . If the enemy had returned with the thousand fresh troops that they had in reserve some distance to the rear—we do not know how far—they could have greatly embarrassed us. . . .

All of the Indians from Detroit and Michillimakinak left the day after the action, despite my attempts to stop them. These Indians, like those who are domiciliated and those of the Belle Riviere, have done very well. It is necessary to recompense them.

Commentary

As I have suggested in the text, Contrecoeur's account, like several others, appears to draw heavily on Dumas. It is most useful on the background to the battle and serves as strong evidence that Contrecoeur knew very little about the English force, even as it neared the fort. His reference to several bands of Indians leaving is confirmed by Roucher.

Dumas

[On July 24, 1756, Dumas, who had been in command at
Fort Duquesne since September 1755, wrote to Machault, the
minister of the marine. His very lengthy letter was explicitly
written in order to defend himself against his critics and to win
recognition for his achievements. He discussed his administration of the fort, particularly his success in winning over the
Indians. But the longest single section he dedicated to detailing
his role in Braddock's Defeat. The bulk of this portion is
printed in Parkman, *Montcalm and Wolfe*, 2, p. 425, while the
whole letter is included by F.-J. Audet, *Jean Daniel Dumas: Le
Héros de la Monongahéla* (Montreal: G. Ducharme, 1920), pp.
22–34. The following is my translation.]

When we learned that the enemy was marching toward us
with a force very much superior to ours, and with a train of
artillery that was quite formidable for a place like this, it was
my remonstrance alone that urged M. de Contrecoeur to send
us to fight them on the road. M. de Courtmanche, who was
present with many others, supported my plea. . . .

M. de Beaujeu consequently marched, and under his orders
M. Desligneris and I. He attacked the enemy with much daring,
but with his troops in total disorder. We fired our first volley
while they were out of range. The enemy waited until they were
nearer before firing. And in the first moment of combat, one
hundred militiamen—one-half of our French forces—shamefully turned tail, shouting "Every man for himself!" . . .

This retreat encouraged the enemy to resound with cries of
"Long live the King!," and they advanced quickly toward us.
Their artillery, having been prepared during this time, commenced firing. This terrified the Indians, who fled. On the
enemy's third discharge of musketry, M. de Beaujeu was
killed. . . .

It was then, Monseigneur, that by word and gesture I sought
to rally the few soldiers who remained. I advanced, with an
assurance born of despair. My platoon gave forth with a

withering fire that astonished the enemy. It grew imperceptibly, and the Indians, seeing that my attack had caused the
enemy to stop shouting, returned to me. Now I sent M. le
chevalier le Borgne and M. de Rocheblave to tell the officers in
charge of the Indians to seize the enemy's flanks. The cannon,
being in front, encouraged this order. The enemy was attacked
on all sides, but fought with an unyielding stubbornness. Entire
ranks fell; all the officers perished. And eventually disorder
spreading from within put the whole to flight.

The pillage was horrible, on the part of both the French and
the Indians. The wounded officers, all of whom had received
their wounds at the outset, remained without aid. I sent MM.
de Normanville and Saint-Simon to gather the soldiers; all
returned. MM. de Carqueville, Leperade, le Borgne, Mommidy, and Hertel were carried off, the first two dying on their
arrival at the fort. It meant a great deal to me to find the body
of M. de Beaujeu. I found it hidden in a gully near the road.

Commentary

In the text, I suggested on several occasions that Dumas was
a basic source for some and perhaps most of our French reporters. We can see this in various details echoed by one or
more of them: that Beaujeu was killed by the third volley; that
the British, as they advanced, shouted "Long live the King!";
that the French and Indians broke, only to be rallied by Dumas. Note also that, like him, they leave out details of the
battle, except for the first few minutes of fighting. He may have
felt that, despite the enemy's "unyielding stubbornness," the
outcome was settled early on, and those who relied on him may
have accepted this opinion. But Godefroy's account, which does
not bear traces of Dumas's version, also lacks details of the
action, and one would do better to look for positive signs of the
captain's influence than negative ones. Going beyond this
point, it must be admitted that we cannot *always* detect
influence. Even French reporters who relied heavily on Dumas
may have gleaned material from other sources as well. There is

yet another problem. Returning from the battle, Dumas may have passed along information that he forgot in the interval before he wrote to Machault, or that he did not include in his letter. It can be shown beyond a reasonable doubt that certain reporters borrowed certain points from Dumas. But their accounts may still be useful, as we have already seen in the case of Contrecoeur. Such usefulness is, however, largely limited to the respective reports on French preparations.

French A

[Sargent prints this account, *History of an Expedition,* pp. 409–10. So does J. D. G. Shea, in *Relations diverses sur la bataille de Malangueulé* (New York, 1860), pp. 26–29. It is translated by E. B. O'Callaghan in *Documents Relative to the Colonial History of the State of New York* (Albany, 1855–1858), 10, pp. 303–04, but the translation that follows is my own. There is no indication when this report was written, or by whom. However, it was probably contained in a letter to Machault and seems to have been prepared shortly after the battle.]

M. de Contrecoeur, captain of infantry, commandant of Fort Duquesne of the Belle Riviere, having been informed that the English were arming in Virginia in order to come and attack him, was told soon afterwards that they were on the march. He dispatched scouts into the countryside, who advised him faithfully of their route. The 7th of this month he was told that their army was composed of three thousand English troops and was six leagues from the fort. He used the next day to make arrangements, and on the 9th he detailed M. de Beaujeu, seconded by MM. Dumas and de Lignery, all three captains, with four lieutenants, six ensigns, twenty cadets, one hundred soldiers, one hundred Canadians, and six hundred Indians, with orders to lie in ambush in a favorable spot which had been reconnoitered the night before. Before it had reached this station, the detachment came into contact with the enemy, some three miles from the fort. M. de Beaujeu, seeing that his ambush had failed, decided to attack. This he did with so much vigor that, although the enemy awaited us in the best possible order, it was stunned. But when their artillery fired a round, our company was shaken in its turn. The Indians also, terrified by the noise of the cannon rather than by the harm it had done, began to give ground. When M. de Beaujeu was killed, M. Dumas at once applied himself to reanimating his detachment. He ordered the officers in command of the Indians to lead them in attacking the enemy's flanks, while he, M. de Lignery, and the other officers who led the French, attacked the front. This order was executed so promptly that the enemy, which had been shouting "Long live the King," now were occupied with defending themselves. The battle was unyielding on both sides, and success was long in doubt, but at last the enemy collapsed. Vainly were commands given in an attempt to make the retreat an orderly one. The war cries of the Indians, echoing through the forest, struck terror in the heart of the enemy. The rout was complete. . . . Such a success, which no one had expected, is the fruit of M. Dumas's experience, and of the activity and valor of those officers under his command.

Commentary

Although this anonymous reporter occasionally writes in the first-person plural when referring to Beaujeu's detachment, this does not indicate that he actually participated in the battle. I tend to doubt that he did. His account is less individualized than most. One can graft Contrecoeur's discussion of the background to the battle onto Dumas's account of the battle itself and have very nearly the entire basis for French A's report. He does add a few details, for example, giving a more thorough breakdown of the French troops than does Contrecoeur. There are also minor contradictions: Activities that Contrecoeur claims took place on July 8, French A places a day earlier. In a portion of this account that I have omitted, French A notes intelligence reports relative to Dunbar's retreat. This additional news may indicate that the writer was in the garrison, but may mean only that Contrecoeur or some other officer in a responsible position had kept him abreast of events. Again, it is possible that French A was an eyewitness to the battle, but his lack of originality militates against it.

French B

[This account, the most famous of all, is printed in the original French by both Sargent (*History of an Expedition*, pp. 411–12), and Shea (*Relations diverses*, pp. 17–20). It is entitled "Relation depuis le départ des trouppes de Quebec, jusqu'au 30 du mois de Septembre, 1755." The account presented here may leave some doubt as to whether the anonymous writer actually participated in the battle. However, the fuller version, printed and translated in O'Callaghan, *Documents*, 10, pp. 337–38, reveals that neither he nor his force was at Fort Duquesne any time during July 1755. The translation that follows is my own.]

The enemy had three army corps, one of which was destined for the Three Rivers where it was defeated. This corps was three thousand strong and was commanded by General *Braudolk*. It intended to besiege Fort Duquesne. The troops were equipped with a great deal of artillery—much more than is necessary to besiege forts in this region. Most of it was not needed, although it had cost the King [of England] a great deal. M de Beaujeu, who was in command of the fort, had been informed of the march, and although he had very few men, he had become anxious to prevent the siege; he had therefore determined to attack the enemy. This he proposed to the Indians who were with him, but they at first rejected his opinion and said to him: "Father, you want to die and sacrifice us. The English are more than four thousand, and we are only eight hundred, yet you wish to attack them. Certainly you must see that you are making no sense. We ask of you until tomorrow to make up our minds." They then consulted among themselves, as they always do before marching. The next morning M. de Beaujeu left his fort with the few troops he had and asked the Indians for the result of their deliberations. They answered that they could not march. M. de Beaujeu, who was kind, affable, and sensible, said to them: "I am determined to confront the enemy. What—would you let your father go alone? I am certain to defeat them!" With this, they decided to follow him. The detachment then was composed of 72 regulars, 146 Canadians, and 637 Indians. The engagement took place four leagues from the fort, the 9th of July, at 1:00 P.M. M. de Beaujeu was killed during the first volley. The Indians, who loved him greatly, avenged his death with all the bravery imaginable. They forced the enemy to take flight after a considerable defeat. This is not extraordinary. Their mode of fighting is quite different from that of the Europeans, which is worthless in this region. The enemy formed a line of battle, and made a front, which allowed those behind the trees to knock over one or two with each shot. . . . One can number the enemy casualties at 1,500 men. M. de *Braudolk*, their general, was killed, as were many officers. . . . We have lost three officers, among them M. de Beaujeu, and twenty-five soldiers, Canadians, and Indians, with about as many wounded.

Commentary

Ever since Sparks first used this account as the basis for his rendering of Beaujeu's dramatic speech, it has been a favorite among historians. Besides its quotability, various qualities enhance its usefulness. It is, first of all, original. There is no trace of Dumas's influence here—the captain is not even mentioned. The statistical breakdown of the forces given by French B parallels Roucher's, but this does not mean that the anonymous reporter borrowed from him. It is entirely possible that they had a common source, or that this account, like the "Seaman's Journal," is a smooth synthesis of several reports. In any case, the analysis by the writer seems to come from within, rather than from his sources. He is clearly a proponent of irregular tactics. Moreover, unlike Dumas, who sees Indians as a necessary evil at best, French B openly admires them. Nor are they only fighting machines to him. They are human beings, capable of affection and loyalty.

French C

[The French original, designated "Relation officielle, imprimée au Louvre," is printed in Shea, *Relations diverses,* pp. 30–32. As a portion of a much longer document, it appears in translation in O'Callaghan, *Documents,* 10, pp. 381–82. The following translation is mine.]

The army that had been assembled for action by the Belle Riviere was composed of regiments of regular troops, which had been sent from England to Virginia, and of regiments of militia, which had been formed in that and adjoining colonies. It totaled three thousand men, at the time when General Braddock took command, and marched against Fort du Quesne. The sieur de Contrecoeur, captain in the Canadian troops and commandant of the fort, had been informed of the preparations being made in Virginia, but he did not expect to be attacked by such a large force. Having sent different detachments to points along the English route, he learned on July 8 that [they were only six leagues from the fort and that (O'Callaghan version only)] they marched in three columns. He immediately formed a detachment of all he could spare from the fort, in order to engage them. This detachment was composed of 250 Frenchmen and 650 Indians. Sieur de Beaujeu, who commanded it, had with him the sieurs Dumas and Ligneris, and in addition several subalterns. He marched at 8:00 A.M., and by 12:30 he found himself in the presence of the English, about three leagues from the fort. He attacked them immediately, with great spirit. The first two volleys from the enemy artillery caused his small force to fall back a little. On the third volley, he had the misfortune to be killed, but the sieur Dumas, who took command, as well as the sieur de Ligneris and the other officers—followed by the French and Indians—fell on the English with such vigor that they forced them to fall back in their turn. The latter continued to fight boldly for some time, but finally after four hours of fierce firing they collapsed, and the rout was general. Our forces pursued them for some time, but sieur Dumas, having learned that General Braddock had left some leagues to the rear a corps of seven hundred men under the orders of Colonel Dunbar, ordered a halt. The English have lost nearly 1,700 men. Almost all of their officers are dead, including General Braddock, who died a few days after, from his wounds.

Commentary

It is obvious that this is primarily a rehash of Contrecoeur's account, with perhaps some minor embellishments from other sources. There are occasional discrepancies, most notably involving the numbers of British dead—Contrecoeur presents the slightly inflated, but much more reasonable, figure of six hundred. Of course, there is always the possibility that his report was misread, or that there was some clerical error in the preparation of the "official account." Although it could be that Vaudreuil himself is "French C," this is unlikely, since he is mentioned at several points in the fuller account, always in the third person. It is entirely possible, however, that the document in question is a slightly altered version of his report.

Godefroy

[I know of this account only through Shea, who prints it under the title of "Relation sur l'action . . . par Mr. de Godefroy, officer en garnison au dit fort" (*Relations diverses,* pp. 9–16). Godefroy includes lengthy lists of casualties and of the British losses in men and materiel. These should be compared to Contrecoeur's, which differ slightly. The portion of Godefroy's account that I am translating here involves the battle and its immediate background (pp. 10–12).]

The 6th [of July], we learned from an Indian of the Five Nations that the English were on the bank of the Monongahela River. The chevalier de La Perade was detached to reconnoiter.

The 7th, he reported that the enemy was near. That same day, a detachment was prepared to engage.

The 8th, the Indians wished to delay. But the prudent Normanville brothers persuaded them to reconnoiter, and they found the enemy at six leagues distance.

The 9th, the day of the action, M. de Beaujeu left with about 150 Frenchmen, as many officers as cadets, and in addition regulars, militiamen, and five hundred Indians. He marched at 8:00 A.M. Three hundred of the Indians took a route different from that of their commander. They crossed the Monongahela River, so that as it approached the enemy the detachment was very weak, but as it prepared to strike the three hundred Indians rejoined the party, and all advanced together on the attack, which took place at a point about three and one-half leagues from Fort Duquesne, where the enemy had stopped to eat. The enemy troops cried out and struck back from high ground, which was very disadvantageous to us, but although on three occasions we retreated slightly, it was not more than ten paces. They had their cannon charged with grapeshot. M. de Beaujeu was killed on the third volley, and M. Dumas took command. The Canadians held firm to the front of the enemy troops, facing their cannon, while the Indians fired on the opposing army from both flanks. They both did their duty so well that although the battle lasted until 4:00 P.M. they did not fall back, and they forced the enemy to abandon their principal pieces of cannon, which fired more than eighty rounds. The English numbered two thousand men. They were always in column, unfortunately for them, for that made them easy to kill. But when they left the field, they did so in such good order that they did not seem to retreat, that instead by half-ranks they wheeled right and left, and regrouped to charge from the rear.

Commentary

Dumas's influence here is very limited, though perhaps it is manifested in the claim that Beaujeu was killed on the third volley. Judging from the fact that Godefroy singles out the Canadians for praise, he may himself have been a native of New France, or else have been relying primarily on the testimony of Canadian officers and militiamen. This account contains interesting details not found elsewhere—the role of the Normanvilles in rallying the Indians, the temporary division of Beaujeu's forces—but the errors contained in it, particularly that the British were attacked while dining, suggest that one should not rely on Godefroy too heavily.

Lotbinière

[Lotbinière's report appears in a letter to the minister of war, the Count d'Argenson, dated "Au camp de Carillon," October 24, 1755. Those portions relevant to the battle are printed in French by Sargent, *History of an Expedition,* pp. 412–13, and by Shea, *Relations diverses,* pp. 40–44. The entire letter is translated in O'Callaghan, *Documents,* 10, pp. 365–68. The following is my translation.]

Last autumn, as I had the honor of informing you, the English began to construct a fort at the foot of the Aliganai mountains, and named it Fort Cumberland. The fort is 110 miles from ours on the Belle Riviere, according to their estimation. Last winter, two regiments of regular troops, numbering five hundred men apiece, departed from Europe under the command of General Braddock, and they arrived at Alexandria in Virginia on February 24. The king had given him the commission of general of all the forces in North America, and it was he who was to carry out operations planned at the court in London, invading this country even as it diverted the attention of the French court with a thousand propositions of peace. As soon as he arrived in Virginia, General Braddock began to prepare his campaign, with the intention of marching in early April. He reserved for himself the reduction of the fort on the Ohio, and took all precautions to assure success. However, since he had not been provided for according to his wishes by the provinces of New England [that is, the colonies in general] and since he had to wait a long time for the wagons and other things he lacked to be supplied by them, he was not able to leave Fort Cumberland until the first days of June. Our Indians had reported to us during the winter that the English were making great preparations, but M. Duquesne, to whom the news was brought, treated it as a boast and said that it was a flash in the pan. Consequently, he did not take any of the precautions necessary against such a general movement. M. de Vaudreuil arrived in the month of June, and was told that the government was in a marvelous state. M. Duquesne, who had known that his fort was menaced, had sent help there, neglecting totally the other areas. Aid arrived at the place named, and Contrecoeur, knowing that the enemy was only three leagues from Fort Duquesne, sent 891 men, including 250 Frenchmen, the rest Indians, under the command of M. de Beaujeu, the captain of our troops. At 11:00 A.M., Beaujeu found himself face to face with the enemy. He attacked with great vigor, and after five hours of fighting our detachment succeeded in putting totally to rout a vanguard of 1,300-odd men, not including wagoners. General Braddock was among them. His rear guard was about eight leagues distant and was not attacked.

Commentary

Although Lotbinière's comments on the battle are too brief to be of use, his account is important for two reasons. First, it epitomizes the anti-Duquesne propaganda that various officials put out in the wake of the governor general's departure from New France. Since it was Vaudreuil who spearheaded the campaign, it is possible that he inspired Lotbinière's attack on Duquesne. Second, Lotbinière in his account reveals the extent to which the captured British documents enabled the French to piece together a history of Braddock's expedition.

Pouchot

[The portion of Pouchot's memoirs that relates to Braddock's Defeat is reprinted in the original French by Shea, *Relations diverses*, pp. 21–25. However, the version I am producing is taken from Franklin B. Hough's translation, in *Memoir Upon the Late War in North America, Between the French and English, 1755–60* (Roxbury, Mass., 1860), 1, pp. 39–43.]

We will give here an account, as received from some Canadian officers who were present, of the order of battle in which the English were found.

M. de Contre-coeur being apprised by the Indians, of the march of a large body of English from Fort Cumberland, who were opening the road from day to day as they advanced;— sent a detachment of two hundred Canadians and colonial troops, under Captains Beaujeu and Dumas, with several other officers, having under them Indians of the upper country, and our domiciliated Indians, to the number of five hundred. This detachment expected to meet the English at some distance, and hoped by some surprise or check, to retard their march, rather than to prevent them from reaching Fort Du Quesne, as the officers were told that the enemy was in greatly superior force.

But the latter, confident in their numbers, proposed to come and form an establishment, feeling assured that it would cost them little beyond the trouble of showing themselves, and convinced that they could take the fort in a day. They, however, marched with great caution, and upon arriving within three leagues of Fort Du Quesne, they halted after crossing a little stream near the house of a blacksmith named Frazer, a German who had settled there to begin his trade with the Indians, but had left when the French began to occupy upon the Ohio.

About eleven o'clock in the morning, the English began to defile over a hill forming a little mountain, with twenty cavalrymen at the head, ten carpenters, two companies of Halke[t]'s grenadiers, the seven companies of that regiment, six recent companies of Virginia troops, three on the right and three on the left, while the regiment of Dunbar, and its grenadiers formed the rear guard. Then followed the laborers and twenty horsemen, forming the column under the orders of General Braddock. The artillery was in the centre, and the regimental baggage munitions and provisions were in the rear. All these equipages were well protected by troops who were ranged by companies in alternate order.

The cavalry upon reaching the hill top, having discovered the French who were marching down a hill, fell back upon the advance guard, who were distant from them a full musket shot.

The French, on their part, upon seeing the English, threw themselves behind trees and began to fire, while the Indians passed to the right and left of the hill. They were thus exposed to a fire of musquetry and artillery from the column, and were not accustomed to hear such loud discharges, but seeing the French remain firm, and noticing that the fire was not very destructive, they with their accustomed cries, resumed each a place behind every tree.

The English were not expecting this attack, yet they held a firm aspect, facing to the front and flanks, but seeing that they covered too much ground, they made a movement to advance, and returned a very sharp fire, their officers on horseback, sword in hand, animating their men. After the death of M. de Beaujeu, who was killed on the first fire, M. Dumas took command of the French, or rather, they continued each one to do his best in the place they were in.

Soon afterward, the English abandoned two pieces of artillery, and fell back toward the rear of their column, which still pressed towards the front, to attack, but they lost their cannon one by one, and were thinned out by the musketry during a space of five hours. The Indians taking this movement of the column from the front towards the rear, as a tendency to retreat, rushed upon them with their tomahawks, as did the French also, when they disbanded, and a great massacre followed.

They pursued the English, who threw themselves into the stream to swim, and many were killed in crossing. They did not, however, pursue far, because the Indians could not wait to plunder and drink. . . . The total loss was estimated at 1,270. They abandoned their wounded, who mostly perished in the forest. Of one hundred and sixty officers, only six escaped. . . .

This action, the most important and glorious that the Indians had ever witnessed, and which was partly won by the accuracy of their own fire, only cost them eleven killed, and twenty-nine wounded.

If on a battle field, with no natural advantage, this event should happen to brave and well disciplined troops, from not knowing how to fire steadily, and not being acquainted with the kind of enemy they had to deal with, it is an impressive lesson upon these two points. This victory, which was received on the 9th of July, put the whole country in good spirits.

Commentary

The Canadian officers who reported to Pouchot appear not to have been anxious to share their triumph with Beaujeu or Dumas. Add to this Pouchot's own apparent dislike of Dumas (see Sargent, *History of an Expedition,* p.224 n.), and we get an account that glorifies the French troops and the Indians, rather than their commanders. Pouchot does not seem to have been very interested in the preparations for the battle, and perhaps his informants, anxious to describe their own hour of glory, had little to say on this score. The writer's account of the disposition of Braddock's forces is likewise not particularly useful. As regards the battle itself, Pouchot provides the most detailed report known from the French side. One might wish, however, that he had more to say about their own disposition. His remarks about the British behavior are interesting, not because he includes any material that is both new and reliable, but because he provides insight into what the French and Indians may have believed they were seeing. His reference to a British advance seems to involve Burton's detachment. On the other hand, his comment that one section of the army left two pieces of artillery and retreated, only to be met by the rear, "which still pressed towards the front," is an apparent reference to the telescoping of forces, and may suggest that Burton was advancing before the combined vanguard began its retreat, though this is a tenuous inference. As for the "very sharp fire" that came from Braddock's troops, we can be quite certain that the men did fire a great deal, but not for the most part in an orderly way, and not very effectively. Pouchot's statement that the British had suffered "from not knowing how to fire steadily" may in fact be his way of saying that, from what he had heard, Braddock's men fired wildly.

Roucher

[The following is my transcript of a translation of Roucher's account. The translation is among the Chatham Papers at the Public Record Office, P.R.O.30/8/98, pt. 1, fols. 1–2. It is in a polished hand, but some portions are badly worn, and a number of words are torn off at the margin. I have therefore supplemented the manuscript with a French draft which appears in *Rapport de l'archiviste de la province de Quebec*, 1932–1933, pp. 307–10. I also used the French version to correct the more important errors in the English translation, particularly where names are involved. All material incorporated into the latter is bracketed. The English manuscript also serves to embellish the *RAPQ* text, suggesting that there was originally at least one other copy in existence. The editor of the French version credits it to the chevalier de La Pause, but although he may have had a copy of it among his personal papers, it is doubtful that he was the author. The P.R.O. document is accompanied by the translation of a letter from Louis Perrault to M. Pascaud, the French treasurer, undated, but on the basis of internal evidence written at Fort Duquesne a few days after Braddock's Defeat. Perrault opens by writing that "this is to accompany a Journal which Mr. Roucher gave me to send to you, at the same time he desired me to make his most sincere Compliments & let you know he has a larger Present to make you—a Copy of a Journal he has and will keep of all that has past or shall happen with our enemy." Perrault's letter suggests Roucher as our most likely author. It is likely that the P.R.O. version, all of which is printed below, is an extract from Roucher's first journal. The document reproduced in the *RAPQ* is considerably longer and includes material not related to Braddock's Defeat.]

Fort Duquesne July 6th 1755

The Hurons who had been out on the discovery, brought Advice that the English were within 8 leagues marching briskly with their Artillery.

The Chevalier de la Parade an officer; was sent with some french and Indians to be certain of the discovery the Hurons had made; but his Guide (who was an Iroquois of the five Nations settled on the River Ohio) [not wishing] to conduct him above 3 or 4 leagues, he was obliged to return

The [Ottawas] and Missillimakinaks, from the falls, who should have gone in a party that day against the English; were detained by [the] other Nations to hold a Conference with Monr: Contrecoeur; at which it was [held] that all the Indians Nations should march together; and the Expedition was defered till next day.

Messr: de Contrecoeur & Beaujeu sent Monsr: De la Parade & Mr: Bailleul with a party of french and Indians on the discovery by two different Routes.

We understood at the Return of these Gentlemen, and that of Mr: Rigoville (out ever since the 28th: of last month with 120 Indians; Hurons and of the Nations from the falls [Detroit], & 10 french men; in a party against the english) that they were but 8 Leagues distant that they marched in [a] body of 3000 Men with a strong train of Artillery.

Mr. Roctoyade, who had been out with a party of Indians & french on the same design, informed us that his party had fixed on the Enemy and had kill'd some of them; but the ndians (according to their cruel Custom) had not been able to calp them; the English always keeping in good order.

After all these discoveries which confirm'd one another, together with the Certainty Mr: Contrecoeur had of the Approach of the English with a train of Artillery which seemed considerable, it was resolv'd we should the next day march out to meet them with all the Indians, only reserving some french for the Defence of the Fort.

8th. All the Indian Nations were called together, & invited to joyne & assist the french to repulse the English who came to drive them out of that land they were then in possession of.

Mr. Beaujeu began the Warsong & all the Indian Nations Immediately joined him except the Poutiawatamis of the Narrows [Detroit], who were silent. Which occasioned all the other Nations to desire not to march till next day.

The Chawanons & Iroquois of the five Nations, who [are] all near Fort Duquesne came to wait on Mr: Contrecoeur & told him that being informed he was determined to oppose the English who was very near, they came to joyne him and assist to repulse them.

They were genteelly entertained in order to engage the other Nations, and not to spin out time, all their demands were granted; & in consequence thereof were arm'd & equipt the same day.

9th. Mr. Beaujeu proposed to march at daybreak, but the Indians not being quite ready retarded him. He was oblig'd in order to hurry them to advance with the detachment of french two Musket Shot from the Fort; from whence he could not march till 8 o'Clock, the Indians not having joyned him sooner. The Poutiawatamis march'd with the rest.

Detachment of French & Indians that marcht against the English

3 Captains Vizt. Messrs. Beaujeu, Dumas & Deligney

4 Lieutenants, Messrs. Courtmanch, La Bourque, Mommidy & Carqueville

6 Ensigns. Messrs. Longueville, La Parade, Bailleul, Corbreare, Bleury; & the Chevr. de [Celeron]

23 Cadets. Messrs. Pecudy, Courtmanch, Beaulac, St. Cherre
    Hartell, Cabanac, [Demuy,] Rocheblas, Saquepec, So
    anna, St. Simon, Labourque, Linctot, the Elder, [and the
    younger], Daillebout, La Framboise, Normanville, Rocto
    rade, Calaron, Blanville, Monsr. St. Ours & Morandiere
112 [72] Regular Troops
146 Militia
<u>637</u> Indians
891 Men in all

At one in the Afternoon we heard from Fort Duquesne [the
blast of great guns & Musquetry which made us apprehend our
detachment had joined in with the English Army nearer than
they imagined, & that they were ingaged.

Our Scouts had indeed about that time discovered the English Army [had called] the Halt (who probably had receiv'd
intelligence of us) & immediately acquainted Monsr. Beaujeu
who was at No very great distance. That Commander directly
advanced with his detachment & was soon engaged with the
English Army; the Indians instantly set up the Warr Cry as is
their Custom, our detachment was posted in the woods, it was
very clear. The English Army which form'd a Coloum of about
15 men in front made a brisk fire from both Artillery and
Musquetry with all the order imaginable, & was answer'd with
the same Vivacity by our detachment who having advanced
under cover of the Woods and the Indians being posted behind
the Trees, attack'd the column of English in front, of whom
they made a great Slaughter.

The English seeing that the fire of their Musquetry made no
impression on our Detachment, their Artillery was of no more
service, & that our fire did not Slacken; broke their Ranks, which
gave fresh Courage to our detachment, they retreated in good
order, but we did not fail to pursue them for 4 or 5 hours: The
Indians seeing us Masters of the Field of Battle & Artillery
stoped to Scalp, we french then halted by parts return'd to carry
of the wounded, the remainder with some Indians pursued the
English as far as the River Monongahela 3/4 of a League from

the Field of Battle, which they had forded that Morning, but now repast in disorder.

Messrs. Dumas & Lignery when they march'd home left Messrs. Courtmanch, Montigny & Bleury to take care of the Artillery and sent to demand an hand to strengthen the guard whom Mr. Contrecoeur sent under the command of Monsr. Godfiore; and Indian frighten'd at the first discharge took flight and alarmed us in the fort about 4 of the Clock in the afternoon with an account that french and Indians were defeated.

But two hours after we learn'd the Victory which our detachment had gain'd over the English; however our joy was mingled with greif as we understood that Mr. De Beaujeu was kill'd the third discharge: Mr. Dumas having taken on him the Command, appeared at the head of the detachment with a real bravery and encouraged the troops all he could by his Countenance.

Monsr: Deligney was nothing behind him, several Officers & Cadets wounded likewise some soldiers & Militia; but could one gain so compleat a Victory without some loss; the Indians also have lost men and some wounded.

The Officers, Cadets, Soldiers, a great part of the Militia & almost all the Indians fought with an invincible Courage; we may judge it by the loss of the English which is very Considerable, in spite of their strength and Artillery whose number or Quantity we are as yet ignorant of. We reckon they were from 1500 to 2000 men, all regular Troops.

Mr. De la Bourque, Lieutt. Mr. Bailleul Ensign, Messrs. Normanville, Hartell & St. Cerre, Cadets, all wounded march'd on foot to the fort, Messrs. Carqueville & Laparade were carried, but Monsr. Carqueville died on his Arrival.

Mr. Rocheblas Cadet brought in the same evening on horseback two [iron] Cohorn morters.

10th. Monsr. de Courtmanche, who had remain'd all Night to guard the Artillery sent to desire Canoes in order to carry them off having heard nothing of Mr. Godfiore who having wandered in the woods during the Night had not then joyn'd him.

Monsr. Contrecoeur immediately dispatched 12 Canoes with

six men each Commanded by Mr. de Coleron the elder. Mr. Laparade died and was buried with Monsr. Carqueville deceased the Night before.

The greatest part of the Indians who had remained behind to scalp and plunder arrived with many horses loaded with spoils of the English consisting of furniture Cloaths, Utensils, Gold, Silver &c. they brought in but 20 prisoners whereof Seven Women or Girls where of the Number, but they brought an infinite Number of Scalps.

Some Indians afraid that the French would wrong them of their plunder Spread the Report that the English had rallied & were on the March to recover their Cannon, Orders were immediately sent to Mr. De Celeron to halt and send out parties on the Discovery.

After a long deliberation, it was determined, that as the Artillery was the principal subject to hinder the English from attempting a second Attack this Year, it was absolutely necessary to be Masters of it.

Captain Dumas offered to conduct that Expedition Mr. de Lerie (whom Mr. Contrecoeur had prevented going to the Engagement the day before, by command [that he oversee] the Artillery & Works,) was given him for a Second with a detachment of 100 french & some Indians to go on the look out.

Mr. Dumas having rejoyn'd Mr. De Celeron sent some french & Indians in the Discovery, who reported that the English were retired having seen nothing but dead bodies for more than six Leagues from the field of Battle; this news made our detachment pass the night a great deal more at their ease.

The Utowawas, Misillimakinaks & Poutiawatamis at the Narrows demanded leave of Mr. Contrecoeur to return home to their Wives and Children, having drove the English back a great way.

Mr. Contrecoeur, replyed, that they were not so far off, perhaps, as they Imagined, & that they ought to defer their departure: but notwithstanding all the Arguments he made use of, they departed the next day with their horses & a great booty.

July 11th: At 4 of the Clock this morning a Piece of brass Cannon of 12 lb. bore was brought here which Messrs. De Lerie & Dumas had put on board a canoe the preceding Evening. At 3 in the afternoon those Gentlemen return'd, & brought with them

3 Peices of Brass Cannon of the same bore.

2 Peices of Brass Cannon 6 lb. bore

4 Mortars brass of 7½ Inches diameter

the same evening this artillery was brought into the Fort, there was likewise brought in about 80 head of horned Cattle with which the Indians made as great Slaughter as they had done with the English.

They return'd without the Body of Mr: Beaujeu which they could not find altho strongly recommended to them.

Messrs: de Montigny et Corbrere were sent with Canoes & a detachment to bring in the Bomb shells, Balls, Granedoes & powder, & to destroy what they could not bring away.

Monssr: de Montisembert was also sent with some french & Indians [to] observe the Retreat of the English.

A Party of the Missisaque Indians came in this Evening [with a] Scalp, which they told us was of an Officer belonging to the English army, [whom] they had found in the morning six leagues or thereabouts from the field of [battle] And told us that the Enemy no Longer march'd in Order.

Messrs. de Montigny & Corbrere returned from the field of Battle & brought in their Canoes the Body of Monsr. de Beaujeu in a Coffin sent on purpose: He was buried with all the marks of Honour due to his Bravery.

These Gentlemen brought with them in their Canoes

19740 Musquet Cartridges fill'd

   17 Barrels of Powder, each 100 lb:

  192 Bombshells of 43 lb. Weight

   55 Grenadoes of 6½ lb.

  175 Twelve pound Balls

   57 Six pound Balls. Shovels &c.

The French & Indians at the time of Battle have kill'd a Quantity of Horses, they have kill'd a great many more since,

broke all the Carts & destroyed every thing they possibly cou'd
Powder & Flower are scatter'd over the Field of Battle the
Indians have brought off a great deal of the last.

The Bodies of a great number of men kill'd & those of eight
Women or Girls entirely strip'd, lie promiscuously with dead
horses for more than half a League.

It is assured that the General of the English Army, whom
they called Mr: Braddock is kill'd with the Officers of Artillery
and Engineers; there is all the just appearance that, that army
will not rally again, as the Principal Officers are left on the field
of Battle.

That Army march'd not to attack a wooden Fort, but the
Strongest fortified in Canada. Without saying too much of it,
one cannot say enough.

Commentary

In the wake of Braddock's Defeat, both sides sought out
enemy accounts of the battle. One British report used by the
French, translated by them and then put back into English by
Albert J. Edmunds, is in print: "Unpublished Contemporary
Account of Braddock's Defeat," *Pennsylvania Magazine of History
and Biography,* 20 (1896–1897), pp. 409–11. It is thirdhand,
however, and is not particularly interesting. Certainly the
French cannot have discovered a more important source of
information than the British did in Roucher's account. This is
not only the longest and fullest French narrative of events
pertinent to the battle—it is also in many ways the best. We
have here the most thorough account of French preparations
for the engagement, as well as an excellent discussion of the
salvage operation that took place in its wake. I have printed this
document entire, including the lists of materiel. Similar lists in
Contrecoeur and Godefroy have not been given, since they are
available in print. In any case, the differences among the three
are not dramatic.

The care for detail that Roucher reveals in his account of the
salvaging is typical of him. He is, in fact, a welcome change

from the other French reporters, who tend to be vague. As I have noted in the text, he is more specific in discussing the Indian forces than is any other contemporary source. Likewise, he alone identifies the French officers who participated in the action. His account of the battle, apparently drawn from several eyewitness reports, including Dumas's, ranks only behind Pouchot's in detail. Like all French versions of the affair—and most of the British ones, for that matter—Roucher's concentrates on the first few minutes of fighting, an emphasis that may cause some confusion. When Roucher refers to "the English Army" firing "with all the order imaginable," he really means the advance party, prior to its retreat. This is made clear in the next paragraph. The French and Indians did not pursue the retreating army "for 4 or 5 hours." After all, Roucher later mentions that the chase ended at the Monongahela, which is correct. What he means in suggesting a lengthy pursuit is that during the battle, which lasted for "4 to 5 hours"—in reality, slightly less—the French and Indians kept up the pressure on the British, who first collapsed into a dense mass and later retreated.

Although in his account of the battle, which is, after all, secondhand, Roucher needs interpretation, he generally stands as a very reliable source. His reference to certain Indian tribes having been present stands corroboration, as we have seen. A point he makes in passing, that the parties of Roctoyade and Rigoville did not return from their respective missions until July 7, reconciles perfectly the otherwise incongruous data that, on the one hand, British sources confirm that Braddock's army was constantly harassed by parties of French Indians, and that, on the other, Contrecoeur knew very little about his enemy until just a few days before the battle. In view of his reliability and taste for detail, it is highly unfortunate that Roucher was not himself an eyewitness to the battle.

Notes

The following abbreviations are used throughout the notes:

AHR	*American Historical Review*
AM	*Archives of Maryland,* ed. William H. Browne
BD	*Braddock's Defeat,* ed. Charles Hamilton
CR	*Minutes of the Provincial Council of Pennsylvania* (standard abbreviation for "Colonial Records")
MA	*Military Affairs in North America 1748–1765,* ed. Stanley Pargellis
NYCD	*Documents Relative to the Colonial History of the State of New York,* ed. E. B. O'Callaghan
NYHSColls	New-York Historical Society, *Collections*
PA	*Pennsylvania Archives,* ed. Samuel Hazard
PH	*Pennsylvania History*
PMHB	*Pennsylvania Magazine of History and Biography*
Shirley Corr.	*Correspondence of William Shirley,* ed. Charles H. Lincoln
Walpole's Corr.	*Horace Walpole's Correspondence,* ed. W.S. Lewis
WHSColls	Wisconsin State Historical Society, *Collections*
WPHM	*Western Pennsylvania Historical Magazine*

Preface

1. "Braddock's Defeat," *AHR,* 41 (January 1936), p. 253.

Chapter 1. March to the Monongahela

1. Regarding the number of troops in Braddock's army and the relative strength of Britons and Americans, see chap. 3., n. 4. Their uniforms are described in detail by Franklin T. Nichols, "The Organization of Braddock's Army," *William and Mary Quarterly,* 3d ser., 4 (1947), pp. 126–27, 133. See Nichols also for further references on equipment.

2. The mood of the troops toward the close of their march is entirely the subject of speculation. On June 30, an officer wrote a letter from camp that was excerpted in the *New York Mercury,* no. 154 (July 21, 1755), p. 3, col. 1. In part, he claimed that "our Men are all in high Spirits, and have Plenty of Provisions."

At least the second point is doubtful and is, in fact, contradicted by two letters appearing in the following number of the *Mercury,* p. 3, col. 1; see also p. 72.

3. All three basic journals of the expedition give several instances of Indians attacking those who became separated from the main body. Since only those sections of the journals dealing with the battle itself are appended to the present work, I shall here note page references. On the various Indian attacks prior to July 6, see "The Journal of Captain Robert Cholmley's Batman" and "The Journal of a British Officer," both in *Braddock's Defeat,* ed. Charles Hamilton (Norman: University of Oklahoma Press, 1959), pp. 21, 23, 44–45, hereafter cited as *BD.* See also "Captain Orme's Journal," appended by Winthrop Sargent to *The History of an Expedition Against Fort Du Quesne in 1755: Under Major-General Edward Braddock,* Pennsylvania Historical Society, *Memoirs,* 5 (Philadelphia, 1856), p. 341. The author of the letter in the *Mercury* of July 21 also states that "the Indian Scouts have killed three Batmen, a Waggoner, and one Horse."

4. *BD,* p. 44. This reporter is hereafter called "British A."

5. Although the journals in note 3, as well as the "Seaman's Journal" (see Appendix E), provide some insight into the activities of the working party, they include very little material on road-building during the last three weeks of the campaign. Some information on the type of work needed to cut a path through the forest may be found in the brief notes by Mackellar, which he appended to his map of the route. This map and the notes are reproduced in a plate facing p. 94 of *Military Affairs in North America 1748–1765,* ed. Stanley Pargellis (New York: D. Appleton-Century, 1936), hereafter cited as *MA.* Pargellis does not identify the author here, but he does so in his article, "Braddock's Defeat," p. 259, n. 16.

6. This is a composite account. The authors of all three journals mentioned in note 3 give considerable space to the incident, including the funeral; and while they include different details, they do not contradict each other on any point. See *BD,* pp. 25–26, 47–48, and Sargent, *History of an Expedition,* p. 350. British A and Orme both claim that the Indians were mollified by the presents they received, and indeed Monakatooka himself may have been less concerned by the death of his son than by the fact that the brave had been shot by an ally (*BD,* 48; [William Smith,] *A Brief View of the Conduct of Pennsylvania, for the Year 1755* [London, 1756], p. 47 n.). On Monakatooka, who was also known as Scarrooyady and Half-King, see Sargent, *History of an Expedition,* p. 173, n. 2, and Wilbur R. Jacobs, *Diplomacy and Indian Gifts: Anglo-French Rivalry Along the Ohio and Northwest Frontiers, 1747–1763,* Stanford University Publications in History, Economics, and Political Science, 6 (Stanford: Stanford University Press, 1950), p. 90, n. 4. The seven Indians who fought for Braddock, all of whom survived the battle, are identified by Robert Morris in a speech he addressed to them and their fellows on August 15, 1755 (*CR,* 6, p. 524).

7. On Braddock's intentions, see Sargent, *History of an Expedition,* p. 302, n.

1, and Benjamin Franklin, *Autobiography*, ed. John Bigelow (New York: G. P. Putnam's Sons, 1927), p. 271. On June 23, Governor Horatio Sharpe informed the Maryland Assembly that Braddock had told him that after capturing Fort Duquesne he would make any repairs necessary and garrison it with provincial troops, before pushing on with his regulars. *South Carolina Gazette*, no. 1104 (August 14–21, 1755), p. 1, col. 1.

8. For the troops' crossing, see Cholmley's Batman's account; *BD*, pp. 7–8. On initial delays, Sargent, *History of an Expedition*, pp. 137–39, provides good coverage.

9. On Braddock's past life and career, see Lee McCardell, *Ill-Starred General: Braddock of the Coldstream Guards* (Pittsburgh: University of Pittsburgh Press, 1958); see also Appendix A.

10. Very little has been written on why Cumberland chose Braddock. McCardell suggests possible motives (*Ill-Starred General*, p. 124). John Entick, in his *General History of the Late War* (London, 1763), implies that the officer was selected because his "courage and military discipline had recommended him, as of ability for so great a trust" (1, p. 114). Cumberland had begun his military career in the Coldstreams and had been acquainted with Braddock for some time. I feel that the duke chose him because he believed that Braddock, being both a disciplinarian and an administrator of ability, was capable of organizing an offensive in America quickly and efficiently. The commander-in-chief had to do more than simply direct a campaign; he was generally responsible for placing the colonies on war footing. See Harry M. Ward, *"Unite or Die": Intercolony Relations 1690–1763* (Port Washington, N.Y.: Kennikat, 1971), pp. 39–41, 94–95. In addition, he had to whip a rather motley assortment of troops into an efficient fighting machine.

11. Braddock's instructions are printed in Sargent, *History of an Expedition*, pp. 393–97, and in *Documents Relative to the Colonial History of the State of New York*, ed. E. B. O'Callaghan (Albany, 1855–1858), 6, pp. 920–22, hereafter cited as *NYCD*. On the origins of this document and on the planning of the campaign generally, see T. W. Riker, "The Politics Behind Braddock's Expedition," *AHR*, 13 (1908), pp. 742–52; L. H. Gipson, *The Great War for Empire: The Years of Defeat, 1754–1757, The British Empire Before the American Revolution*, 6 (New York: Knopf, 1946), pp. 54–58; and McCardell, *Ill-Starred General*, pp. 123–30, 132–33. Shirley's proposed strategy for the campaign was similar to Halifax's (McCardell, p. 127). For Braddock's reaction to the suggestion by Shirley, see Douglas E. Leach, *Arms for Empire: A Military History of the British Colonies in North America, 1607–1763* (New York: Macmillan, 1973), pp. 355–56.

12. It is impossible to know how much money Braddock actually had to work with, or even how much was allocated by the colonies. Apparently Virginia provided £36,000 for the expedition itself, Pennsylvania £5,000, North Carolina £8,000, and South Carolina £6,000, while the Maryland legislature refused to contribute anything (Hayes Baker-Crothers, *Virginia and the French and*

Indian War [Chicago: University of Chicago Press, 1928], p. 78). However, funds were sometimes granted under different guises; for example, the assembly in Pennsylvania gave £15,000 "for the king's use" in the campaign (Ward, *"Unite or Die,"* p. 94). The collection of funds was much hampered by political in-fighting between the governors and their legislatures, and sometimes between the two houses of bicameral assemblies; note, for example, Arthur M. Schlesinger, "Maryland's Share in the Last Colonial War," *Maryland Historical magazine,* 7 (1912), pp. 147–48, 248. On the origins of the scheme to provide a common fund for financing the war, Braddock's advocacy of this plan, and its failure, see Ward, *"Unite or Die,"* pp. 93–94. Concerning British allocations for the campaign and army finances in general, see McCardell, *Ill-Starred General,* p. 130; Dora M. Clark, "The British Treasury and the Administration of Military Affairs in America, 1754–1774," *PH,* 2 (1935), pp. 197–204; and Stanley Pargellis, *Lord Loudoun in North America* (New Haven: Yale University Press, 1933), chap. 11, esp. pp. 279–92. The most famous incident revealing negligence on the part of Braddock's contractors involves Thomas and Michael Cresap, father and son (McCardell, *Ill-Starred General,* p. 200).

13. Braddock to Newcastle, March 20, 1755 (*MA,* p. 80)

14. Braddock's desperation and anger may be seen in his letter to Sir Thomas Robinson, dated June 5, 1755. A condensed version of the letter is among the Hardwicke Papers, no. 136, ms. 17; Manuscripts and Archives Division, New York Public Library, Astor, Lennox and Tilden Foundations: "Govr. of Virginia [Robert Dinwiddie] upon the credit of £2000 Currency Voted by the assembly made a Contract for 1100 Beeves to be delivered in July & Augst. Convoys regulated accordingly—Contractor informed the Genl. that the assembly had refused to fulfill the Governors Engagement & the contract was Void[.] The Genl. offered to Advance the Money . . . But the Contractor rejected this unless the Genl. paid him one third more and postpone the Delivery. . . . This Behaviour of the people does not only provide infinite difficulty but also greatly Encreases the Expences[.] The Charge thereby . . . is many times more than double the Original Cost."

15. Mrs. Conway R. Howard, ed., "Extracts from the Diary of Daniel Fisher, 1755," *PMHB,* 17 (1893), p. 272.

16. McCardell gives good coverage to the foraging (*Ill-Starred General,* pp. 200–03). Orme provides a very detailed account of the beginning of the march (Sargent, *History of an Expedition,* pp. 326–33).

17. *BD,* p. 48. On the road, see Appendix A.

18. D. S. Freeman, *George Washington: A Biography* (New York: Scribner's, 1948), 2, p. 52; McCardell, *Ill-Starred General,* pp. 222–23. Reports that enemy reinforcements were on their way to Fort Duquesne were common and, of course, true. On July 1, an anonymous correspondent wrote a letter in which he reported that: " 'Tis said, this morning the general has had advice, that 500 regulars are in full march to the fort, which is the reason he is determined to

be there before him [sic]" (*South Carolina Gazette,* no. 1106 [August 28–September 4, 1755], p. 2, col. 3).

19. Easily the most detailed account of the composition of Braddock's army after the division is given by Orme (Sargent, *History of an Expedition,* p. 336). British A, British B, Duncan Cameron, Thomas Gage, and Harry Gordon (the most complete, aside from Orme) also provide details; see Appendix D.

20. On St. Clair's activities relative to Braddock's campaign, see Charles R. Hildeburn, "Sir John St. Clair, Baronet, Quarter-Master General in America, 1755 to 1767," *PMHB,* 9 (1885–1886), pp. 2–7. Hildeburn is something of an apologist for St. Clair and, I think, not a convincing one. At the very least, he cannot clear Sir John of the charge of shooting from the hip.

21. This incident is detailed by Sargent, *History of an Expedition,* pp. 158–60. He quotes from the letter containing those portions printed above; the entire text is in *CR,* 6, pp. 368–69. Sargent also prints Franklin's famous advertisement for wagons, in which the latter makes reference to "Sir John St. Clair, the Hussar" (pp. 164–66).

22. However, Braddock did chastise St. Clair for his tirade of April 12 and relayed Sir John's apologies to Morris (William Shirley [the younger] to Morris, May 21, 1755, *PA,* 2, p. 317; and Braddock to Morris, May 24, 1755, *CR,* 6, p. 400). Still, such a dressing-down was clearly called for and does not suggest either that the general was growing cool toward St. Clair or that their eventual split in any way stems from the latter's outburst.

23. St. Clair claims that his proposal was rejected "with great indignation"; see Appendix D. Orme's account of what happened (Sargent, *History of an Expedition,* pp. 346–48) is much more plausible, as far as I am concerned. For further discussion, see pp. 106–07.

24. More biographical details on Orme and Washington appear in chapter 3. On Burton's relationship with Braddock, see McCardell, *Ill-Starred General,* p. 159. Daniel Dulany, a violent critic of Orme's (see Appendix C), claims that from the moment Braddock arrived in America, "I heard of young men being favorites, and of other, whose rank and age and character entitled them to respect, being in disgrace, and kept at a distance" ("Military and Political Affairs in the Middle Colonies in 1755," ed. John H. B. Latrobe, *PMHB,* 3 [1879], p. 13). He is obviously implying that Orme was one of the "young men," and in fact the captain would have been close, but St. Clair, at least in his own mind, held great influence over Braddock prior to the march from Wills Creek.

25. St. Clair's version is in Appendix D; for Orme's, see Sargent, *History of an Expedition,* p. 352.

26. The quotation is from Gordon's journal; see Appendix D.

27. Edward P. Hamilton breaks down the forces into percentages of composition, which I have approximated here (*The French and Indian Wars* [Garden City, N.Y.: Doubleday, 1962], p. 158). However, he makes the mistake of assuming that the men who actually fought under Braddock were divided along

the same lines. The make-up of the army that saw action is discussed in chap. 3, n. 4.

28. The recruitment of Braddock's forces on both sides of the Atlantic is best handled by Nichols, "Organization of Braddock's Army," pp. 127–32, 136–39. See also J. Allen Rogers, "Impressment in Western Pennsylvania, 1755–1759," *WPHM*, 52 (1969), pp. 255–62. A good idea of when and where the American troops enlisted may be gained from the list of deserters published in the wake of the battle (*Pennsylvania Gazette*, no. 1394 [September 11, 1755], p. 1, cols. 1–3). One should avoid the tendency to speak of Braddock's provincial troops simply as "Virginians," even though the general himself did so on occasion.

29. On Braddock's early career, see McCardell, *Ill-Starred General*. There is some possibility that he had seen action; Sargent believes this (*History of an Expedition*, pp. 126–27). However, there is no real evidence to back up such an assertion, and the material accumulated by McCardell suggests that whenever British armies were engaged in a major battle, Braddock was elsewhere.

30. The first two quotations are from letters to Robert Napier, June 8 and April 19, 1755, respectively (*MA*, pp. 83, 84). Cameron's entire statement is included in Appendix C. For the order of June 17, see "Halkett's Orderly Book," *BD*, p. 109. Braddock was certainly not alone in his attitude toward provincial troops; see Peter Wraxall to Henry Fox, September 27, 1755 (*MA*, p. 141). In his letter to Napier, dated February 9, 1755, St. Clair provides a fairly balanced review of the independent companies (*MA*, p. 62).

31. Freeman gives the best description of The Narrows, as well as a fine discussion of the difficulties involved had the army attempted to pass through it and to cross Turtle Creek (*George Washington*, pp. 62–63). According to Orme, St. Clair, on returning from reconnaissance, had suggested an alternative route; it had been found impracticable, but only after St. Clair's efforts (presumably, the attempts by his working party to make the route passable) had caused a halt in the march (Sargent, *History of an Expedition*, pp. 351–52). However, it appears from other journals that any delay involved was insignificant, and British A asserts that the march was held up only because the guides lost their way (*BD*, p. 48).

32. The accounts of this consultation are similar, except that Orme alone claims that the guides told Braddock the two fords "were very shallow, and the banks not steep" (Sargent, *History of an Expedition*, p. 352). See also St. Clair and Gordon, in Appendix D.

33. Letter to his brother, John Augustine Washington, June 28, 1755, in John C. Fitzpatrick, ed., *The Writings of George Washington* (Washington, D.C.: U.S. Government Printing Office, 1931), 1, p. 143. St. Clair claims (Appendix D) that Braddock told him that the plan to divide the forces was his own. British E discusses the Braddock-Halket feud (*MA*, pp. 121–22).

34. The importance of winning over, or winning back, neutral Indians and "bridling" those tribes loyal to the French is noted several times in Braddock's

"secret instructions." On the possibility that he hoped his Indians would fight as well as scout, see p. 98.

35. Gist served as the general's guide and on July 4–6 undertook an important and dangerous reconnaissance mission. On the whole, little is known of his activities during the march and battle; he does not appear to have left behind an account of his experiences. On Croghan, see chap. 3.

36. Gage himself says this. Cholmley's Batman and Gordon both claim that he marched at 2:00; see Appendix D. The point is scarcely crucial. It may well be that while he was supposed to march at 2:00 (Halket's Orderly Book; *BD*, p. 120), he was delayed.

37. Quotation drawn from Dr. Thomas Walker's account; see Appendix E. See also Peyton and British A in Appendix D.

38. Gordon's quotation; see Appendix D.

Chapter 2. The French Prepare

1. Shirley (the younger) to Morris, June 7, 1755 (*PA*, 2, p. 347).

2. There are two excellent and full accounts of Fort Duquesne, both accompanied by good sets of references: William A. Hunter, *Forts on the Pennsylvania Frontier, 1753–1758* (Harrisburg: Pennsylvania Historical and Museum Commission, 1960), pp. 106–12; and A. P. James and C. M. Stotz, *Drums in the Forest* (Pittsburgh: Historical Society of Western Pennsylvania, 1958), pp. 128–37. Although it was the largest in the area, Fort Duquesne was only a fraction of the size of its successor, Fort Pitt; see Stotz's sketch comparing the two, p. 163.

3. [John Mitchell,] *The Contest in America Between Britain and France* (London, 1757), pp. 182–83, 188. As a botanist who spent more than twenty years in North America, Mitchell presumably had visited the Ohio Valley. Moreover, he was in contact with many Americans who were interested in the area. See Lyman Carrier, "Dr. John Mitchell, Naturalist, Cartographer, and Historian," in American Historical Association, *Annual Report* (1918), pt. 1, pp. 199–219.

4. Translated and quoted by Hunter, *Forts on the Frontier*, p. 113.

5. There are numerous studies of the French move into the Ohio Valley and of Washington's Fort Necessity campaign. One lesser-known piece I recommend, for bibliography as well as content, is Ronald D. Martin, "Confrontation at the Monongahela: Climax of the French Drive Into the Upper Ohio Region," *PH*, 37 (1970), pp. 130–50. On Contrecoeur and Ward, see Hunter, *Forts on the Frontier*, pp. 102–04. There is a good biographical sketch of the French captain by Reuben G. Thwaites, "The French Regime in Wisconsin—1743–1760," Wisconsin Historical Society, *Collections*, 18 (1908), p. 49, n. 82. A volume of his correspondence has appeared, edited by Fernand Grenier (*Papiers Contrecoeur et autres documents concernant le conflit anglo-français sur l'Ohio de 1745 à 1756* [Quebec: Presses Universitaires Laval, 1952]. Hunter, in particular makes good use of it. It

provides some insight into preparations to meet Braddock, but nothing new on the battle itself.

6. Translated and quoted by Hunter, *Forts on the Frontier*, pp. 103–04.

7. Walter O'Meara, *Guns at the Forks* (Englewood Cliffs, N.J.: Prentice-Hall, 1965), p. 135; Hunter, *Forts on the Frontier*, p. 115.

8. Duquesne to the Marquis de Vaudreuil, July 6, 1755 (*NYCD*, 10, p. 300).

9. See Martin, "Confrontation," pp. 147–48. Duquesne's role in reinforcing the fort helps to defend him against the charge of negligence that was leveled at him by his incompetent successor, Vaudreuil; see Charles W. Dahlinger, "The Marquis Duquesne, Sieur de Menneville, Founder of the City of Pittsburgh," *WPHM*, 15 (1932), pp. 251–54. It is not known exactly how many French and Canadian troops occupied the fort on July 9, 1755, but we can deduce an approximate figure. Between July 30 and August 3, three detachments, totaling 321 men, departed from the fort. Captain François-Marie le Marchand, sieur de Ligneris, left on July 22, but we do not know how large a company went with him. These departures left a garrison of 260 (Hunter, *Forts on the Frontier*, p. 116). Since it does not appear that any large body of reinforcements arrived after July 9, one may infer that the total on that date stood between six and seven hundred men and officers, depending on the size of Ligneris's party.

10. For the accounts by French B, Contrecoeur, and Dumas, see Appendix F. Burgoyne in 1777 credited Langlade with having planned the ambush (Joseph Tasse, "Memoir of Charles de Langlade," in *WHSColls*, 7, p. 133). Several writers, most notably John D. G. Shea ("Daniel Hyacinth Mary Lienard de Beaujeu," *PMHB*, 8 [1884], p. 124, n. 1), have claimed that Beaujeu had already succeeded Contrecoeur by July 9. This point has been ably refuted by Francis-J. Audet, *Jean Daniel Dumas: Le Héros de la Monongahéla* (Montreal: G. Ducharme, 1920), pp. 65–75. The accounts printed in Appendix F tend to support him. On Beaujeu, see also the article in the *Dictionary of Canadian Biography*, 3 (1741–1770) (Toronto: University of Toronto Press, 1974).

11. The faultiness of French and Indian reconnaissance is recognized implicitly in several of the accounts in Appendix F; see Contrecoeur, Roucher, and French A, B, and C. There is some danger of self-corroboration here, but it is insufficient to discredit the conclusion, especially since Contrecoeur himself obviously wrote on the basis of "inside information."

12. See Jacobs, *Diplomacy and Indian Gifts*, esp. pp. 90, 116–17, 130. Although on the whole this is a fine work, the author in my opinion exaggerates the role the French tactics of violence played in winning over the Indians.

13. One can only estimate the number of Indians present at Fort Duquesne on July 9, 1755. Our only source is Augustin Grignon, Langlade's grandson, who relates that "how large a band my grandfather led from the North-West [I do not know]; but I remember his saying, that when they assembled at Fort Du Quesne, the total number of French and their Indian allies amounted to not

far from fifteen hundred; and my strong impression is, that nearly all the Indian force was composed of the bands led forth by my grandfather" (Lyman C. Draper, ed., "Seventy-Two Years' Recollections of Wisonsin," *WHSColls,* 3 [1857], p. 213). The total of about 1,500 jibes well with the general body of data, balancing as it does the suggested total of 600 to 700 Frenchmen and Canadians with the fact that a reported 637 Indians actually fought. Adding those warriors who remained at the fort for any of various reasons, a total of 800 seems reasonable. In 1748, Indian agent Conrad Weiser estimated that there were 789 warriors in the Ohio Valley, the Delawares, Senecas, and Shawnees being most numerous (Hunter, *Forts on the Frontier,* p. 9).

14. Draper, "Seventy-Two Years' Reflections," pp. 212–13. Grignon also provides an account of the battle (pp. 213–15), but in view of the fact that he related it more than a century after the event I have decided not to append it. As one might expect, it is grossly inaccurate on some points, but interestingly it contains a tale also told by Godefroy (see Appendix F): that Braddock's forces were attacked while they were eating dinner. Perhaps Langlade was a common source.

15. Roucher's account is printed in Appendix F. On the Shawnee role, see Vaudreuil to Machault, August 8, 1756 (*NYCD,* 10, p. 437). In early 1763, the Indian trader James Kenny overheard one Delaware tell another that "at Braddock's Defeat there was not One of the Delawares & only four Mingoes & three Shawanas, all the rest Northrn Indians" (John W. Jordan, ed., "Journal of James Kenny, 1761–1763," *PMHB,* 37 [1913], p. 183). Grignon's statement that almost all of the Indians at Fort Duquesne at the time of the battle were those who had accompanied Langlade (n. 13) may be somewhat exaggerated, and in fact Roucher refers to two substantial war parties composed of Indians who had apparently long been present; but it tends to bear out the point that "Northrn Indians" were a preponderant majority. Some Delawares, however, do seem to have fought against Braddock; see chap. 6. Croghan (see Appendix D), working from rumor, conjectures on the composition of the Indian contingent, but the numbers he suggests are vastly inflated. His opinions are interesting nevertheless, for he had access to exceptionally capable informants.

16. Jacobs, *Diplomacy and Indian Gifts,* p. 27.

17. Shea, "Beaujeu," p. 123. The commands he had earlier held, at Niagara and, apparently, at Detroit, both called for officers experienced at Indian diplomacy. That he received the Cross of St. Louis while at Niagara, as well as his later assignment to replace Contrecoeur, indicates that he was considered capable.

18. Godefroy claims that three hundred Indians became separated from the rest and crossed the river before rejoining the main force. Such an odd twist, if it actually happened, might well have delayed Beaujeu, although Godefroy does not claim that it did. In any case, I consider the episode suspect. Godefroy is not a particularly accurate source (see commentary in Appendix F) and is not

corroborated on the point in question. That, for whatever reason, Beaujeu's troops had not reached the site chosen for ambush at the time they confronted the English is supported by the fact that they were rushing and out of order when contact was made (see chap. 4). Historians have generally assumed that Beaujeu planned to ambush the enemy at the river (Francis Parkman, *Montcalm and Wolfe* [Boston, 1884], 1, p. 220; Shea, "Beaujeu," p. 124). I tend to agree, but in fact the evidence is spotty. Grignon (Draper, "Seventy-Two Years' Recollections," p. 213) asserts that this was indeed the French design, and British B (see Appendix D) cites a rumor to the same effect.

19. French B; entire text in Appendix F.

20. On Beaujeu's receiving communion, see Shea, "Beaujeu," pp. 125, 127. In a letter to Sir Thomas Robinson, dated November 5, 1755, Shirley noted this testimony: "The Baron de Dieskau (the French General who was taken Prisoner at Lake George) in speaking of General Braddock's defeat, said that none of their (the French) Officers were in the least Surprised at it, as it was a Maxim with them never to Expose Regulars in the Woods, without a sufficient Number of Indians and Irregulars for any Attack that might be Expected" (Charles H. Lincoln, ed., *Correspondence of William Shirley* [New York: Macmillan, 1912], 2, pp. 319–20, hereafter cited as *Shirley Corr.*). According to Pouchot, the French did not hope to defeat the British through ambush, but only "to retard their march."

21. Historians have generally assumed that Contrecoeur was about to surrender the fort when Beaujeu persuaded him to make at least one stand, in the form of an ambush; see, for example, Sargent, *History of an Expedition*, p. 221. However, Roucher asserts that Contrecoeur retained some of his troops "for the Defence of the Fort" when he sent out the detachment under Beaujeu. Indeed, he probably would not have held back such a large contingent had he not intended to defend the fort. The chances for a successful defense were, however, reduced by structural defects in the fort; see Hunter, *Forts on the Frontier*, pp. 109, 112–13; James and Stotz, *Drums in the Forest*, pp. 128–37.

22. The account of the division of weaponry and gunpowder comes from Colonel James Smith, who was a prisoner at Fort Duquesne at the time of the battle (Samuel G. Drake, ed., *Tragedies of the Wilderness* [Boston, 1846], p. 183). Smith recorded his testimony forty-four years after the event, but the scene as he describes it suggests a vividness that time would not likely dull.

23. French B. He may not have included officers. See Roucher, Appendix F.

Chapter 3. The Pen and the Sword

1. Cholmley's Batman claims that the advance party crossed in line of battle, apparently at Gage's orders. Peyton, on the other hand, suggests that the men were drawn into battle line only after they had crossed; and by stating that this order involved the whole army, he implies that it came from Braddock. British

B, a violent critic of the general's, writes that Halket and St. Clair persuaded Braddock to order the army into a line of battle, apparently after the second crossing, but that he soon took it upon himself to order the men back into a line of march. Hereafter, unless otherwise noted, the reader may assume that all material from British accounts is printed in Appendix D, from French accounts, in Appendix F.

2. McCardell, *Ill-Starred General*, p. 246.

3. Gage himself states this.

4. The number of men who accompanied Braddock to the Monongahela has been the subject of much speculation. Pargellis ("Braddock's Defeat," p. 257, n. 14) deduces that there were 1,319 rank and file, including, by inference, about 250 provincials. Including the officers probably present would bring the total to about 1,410. Gipson, citing an official list, sets the number present at the battle at 1,459, including 86 officers (*Great War for Empire*, p. 96). Both of these figures may be a bit high. Not a single eyewitness suggests there were more than 1,300 officers and men, and only Washington, Stewart, and Stephen note that high a total. British A, British B, Cameron, Furnis, Gage, and Orme (in his letter to Napier, July 18, 1755, *MA*, p. 98) all speak of 1,200 men, while Campbell suggests 1,150, and Dunbar and Gordon 1,100. In some cases, the lower figures do not include officers. The consensus seems to be 1,200, and several who use it were certainly in a position to know. If we add in the officers and allow for some leeway, we reach a total of 1,300. In the wake of the Defeat, the numbers in Braddock's army were exaggerated by some sources, such as the *Boston Evening Post*, which claimed that the total number of troops who had faced the enemy was 1,689, including 217 Americans, "besides Pioneers, Waggoners, Suttlers and Gentlemen's Servants, about 250 killed and wounded; and out of 54 Women only 4 returned" (no. 1042 [August 18, 1755], p. 2, col. 1). To our basic figure of 1,300 we may add perhaps 200 who would likewise have been armed and capable of fighting, chiefly batmen and volunteers, and perhaps also pioneers and seamen, as well as smaller groups like Indians. Some wagoners may have been armed, but as a group they fled during the battle. Braddock probably had more Americans under his command than is generally assumed. Despite his order of June 17, his detachments of regulars could not have been drawn entirely from those who had accompanied him from Ireland. An epidemic of "bloody flux" (dysentery) had dogged the march from the beginning, and undoubtedly illness caused many regulars to remain behind with Dunbar. Cameron's assertion that he was one of "800 old Regulars pick'd out" for the final march seems reasonable. The shortage of regulars would have been counterbalanced by the use of American recruits.

5. Orme, in Sargent, *History of an Expedition*, p. 350. See also Larry G. Bowman, "Virginia's Use of Blacks in the French and Indian War," *WPHM*, 53 (1970), pp. 57–63. Bowman argues convincingly that batmen, including blacks, fought and died in Braddock's Defeat (p. 59).

6. Croghan himself claims that "he had a free sight of the Enemy as they approached." This suggests that he was up front with the guides, and in any case, that would have been his natural position. There are several biographies of Croghan, the finest of which is Albert T. Volwiler's *George Croghan and the Western Movement 1741–1782* (Cleveland: Arthur H. Clark Co., 1926). The pages on Croghan's activities during Braddock's expedition contain some errors; for one thing, Volwiler makes the common mistake of assuming that Monakatooka and Scarrooyady were two different men. As a check, see Jacobs, *Diplomacy and Indian Gifts,* pp. 140–44.

7. In my analysis of the line of march, I am relying primarily on the two maps by Mackellar reprinted in Appendix D. A detailed plan of the advance party, ascribed to Orme but probably also by Mackellar (see Appendix D), is printed in Sargent, *History of an Expedition,* facing p. 352, and is the source of some of my comments on that detachment and on the flanking parties.

8. There are surprisingly few biographies of Gage. The best is John R. Alden's *General Gage in America* (Baton Rouge: Louisiana State University Press, 1948); pp. 21–31 are relevant to Braddock's expedition. Although generally his work is excellent, Alden is somewhat too critical of Orme; see Appendix C. He also tends to take Dulany's favorable remarks on Gage at face value. They may be sincere, but Dulany was highly antagonistic toward Orme and would have favored those who criticized the captain in print, as did Gage, at least by implication, after the battle (see p. 65).

9. Dunbar died as a major while serving in Canada (*Gentleman's Magazine,* 58 [1788], p. 1125). Charles Lee attests to his heroic behavior. See his two letters to his sister, Miss Sidney Lee, December 7, [1758], and July 30, [1759], *Lee Papers,* New York Historical Society, *Collections,* 4 (1871), pp. 18–19.

10. Duncan Cameron, *The Life, Adventures and Surprising Deliverances of Duncan Cameron, Private Soldier in the Regiment of Foot, late Sir Peter Halkett's,* 3d ed. (Philadelphia, 1756).

11. On Cholmley's Batman, see Hamilton's introductory comments, *BD,* pp. 5–7. His linking of the young servant to Cholmley represents a good job of editing. I derive my statement that the batman was courageous from his unpretentious remarks about his own activities during and immediately after the battle.

12. Sources relative to Gates's career prior to 1760 are scanty. Samuel W. Patterson, his major biographer, satisfactorily recounts his involvement in the expedition (*Horatio Gates: Defender of American Liberties* [New York: Columbia University Press, 1941], 12–16). Although there is no reason to doubt its veracity, we should note that the story of Gates's meeting with Newcastle comes only from Walpole.

13. The quotation is drawn from St. Clair's eyewitness account. Hildeburn's account, "Sir John St. Clair," is the fullest. See also Pargellis's sketch in *MA,* p. 58, n. 1; this volume, incidentally, contains the bulk of St. Clair's printed correspondence.

14. The best account of Gordon and Mackellar, as well as of their role in Braddock's army, is George T. Ness, Jr., "The Braddock Expedition, 1755," *Military Engineer*, nos. 339–41 (1959), pp. 20–21, 211–13. That Mackellar was in the rear of the working party is revealed by Shirley in his letter to Robinson, *Shirley Corr.*, 2, pp. 320–21. Mackellar's writings are largely in print, including a journal and several letters by him printed in *MA*, and his journal of the capture of Quebec, used as a common source of reference by A. Doughty and G. W. Parmelee, *The Siege of Quebec and the Battle of the Plains of Abraham* (Quebec: Dussault and Proulx, 1901). Loudoun valued his services; note the earl's two letters to Cumberland, November 22, 1756, and October 17, 1757 (*MA*, pp. 278, 407). Pargellis includes not only much of their correspondence, but fine biographical sketches of Gordon and Mackellar (*MA*, pp. 104, n.1, 187, n.1).

15. On Furnis, see Edward G. Williams, "Treasure Hunt in the Forest," *WPHM*, 44 (1961), pp. 386–88, and William S. Ewing, ed., "An Eyewitness Account by James Furnis of the Surrender of Fort William Henry, August 1757," *New York History*, 42 (1961), p. 307. Furnis likely rode with Thomas Ord, who was in command of the wagon train, as reported by Governor James De Lancey in a letter to Morris, June 5, 1755 (*PA*, 2, p. 346).

16. There is a fine sketch of Stewart by William C. Stewart, "A Study of Some Stewart and Allied Families," Kentucky Historical Society, *Register*, 61 (1963), pp. 80–83.

17. On the seamen and pioneers, see Sargent, *History of an Expedition*, pp. 195–96, British D, and analysis of the "Seaman's Journal" in Appendix E.

18. The best accounts of Orme are by Sargent (*History of an Expedition*, p. 283, n. 1) and Pargellis (*MA*, p. 98, n. 1). See also Appendix C.

19. Needless to say, every cradle-to-grave biography of Washington includes a discussion of his role in Braddock's expedition. Freeman gives easily the fullest and best account (*George Washington*, 2, pp. 1–102). Washington's comment about the whistling of bullets is included in his letter to John Augustine Washington, May 31, 1754, in John C. Fitzpatrick, ed., *The Writings of George Washington*, 1, p. 70. In attending Braddock, Washington was breaking (or perhaps forgetting) a promise he had made to the French when surrendering Fort Necessity not to reenter the Ohio Valley for at least one year.

20. In this discussion of Peyton, I am working on the basis of his purported account and related correspondence, printed by John Lewis Peyton, in *The Adventures of My Grandfather* (London, 1867). Regarding the trustworthiness of this material, see Appendix C.

21. The chaplain's account of the battle is anonymous. See Appendix C on the probability that Hughes was the author. It is not certain that he was with the main body, but the detachments were specialized, and he would have had no place among them.

22. On the whole, my sketch is derived from Mary V. Mish, "General Adam Stephen, Founder Martinsburg, West Virginia," *West Virginia History*, 22 (1961),

pp. 63–75. The quotations come from his autobiographical notes, "The Ohio Expedition of 1754," ed. Bunford Samuel, *PMHB*, 18 (1894–1895), p. 44. Pargellis ("Braddock's Defeat," p. 256) states that Stephen was in the rear guard but offers no proof, and there seems to be none. However, the rangers he captained appear to have been in the rear guard, those of Captains Peyronie and Waggoner having joined St. Clair in the working party. On the latter point, note the order of June 27, *BD*, p. 114. If Stephen's company did indeed serve in the rear—not certain, but probable—it is fair to assume that he was likewise there.

23. Leslie's rank is a matter of some dispute. Sargent designates him a lieutenant in the Forty-Fourth (*History of an Expedition*, p. 360, n. 1); Pargellis, in the index to *MA*, lists him as one in the Forty-Eighth (p. 501). Samuel Hazard refers to him as "Major Leslie" (*Register of Pennsylvania*, 5, p. 191). A letter written by the officer himself is endorsed "Capn Leslie" (*PA*, 2, p. 356), although Sargent says he was not promoted to a captaincy until 1760. Something of his activities during the Braddock expedition may be gleaned from the letter noted earlier, which he directed to Morris, as well as from one by the latter to the Committee of the Assembly of Pennsylvania, May 19, 1755 (ibid., p. 316). He later served Wolfe in a similar capacity and also reconnoitered for him (Doughty and Parmelee, *Siege of Quebec*, 2, pp. 10, 153). On St. Clair's attitude toward Leslie, note Loudoun to Cumberland, October 2, 1756, *MA*, p. 234. As for Campbell, the note that introduces his account refers to him as "one of General Braddock's Messengers" (*CR*, 6, p. 481).

24. My reasons for having positioned British A and C as I have are discussed in Appendix D. So are my suspicions that British B and C may not actually have witnessed the battle. My concern is not as great in their cases as in Peyton's.

25. Only Stewart and Washington definitely escaped unscathed. On the other hand, British D, Cameron, Dunbar, Gage, Gates, Gordon, Hughes, Leslie, Mackellar, Orme, St. Clair, and Stephen are known to have been wounded, though some just slightly. This information is drawn from their respective accounts and, where applicable, from the various lists of officers who saw action. The best of these lists is the one appended to British A's narrative, *BD*, pp. 54–58. Hamilton provides cross-references to two other lists.

26. As regards Furnis, see his second letter to the Board of Ordnance, October 7, 1755, in Williams, "Treasure Hunt," pp. 390–95. Gates is also critical of Braddock, but there is no way to prove that he was biased previously. Washington, like Gage, Gordon, and Stephen, claimed that Braddock had promised him preferment, but the Virginian did so some months after the battle, by which time he had already decided on a military career (letter to Loudoun, January 1757, in Fitzpatrick, *Writings*, 2, p. 18).

27. Generally, see introductory remarks in Appendix D. Although in the cases of British A, Dunbar, and Gordon the addressee is not known, they

almost certainly realized that their accounts would be forwarded to superiors. The last even asks that his letter be passed along, while it is probably not coincidental that the reports of the first two are to be found among the Hardwicke Papers. The same may be said of Mackellar and Stephen. Both knew their accounts would be forwarded, and in fact this helps to explain the polemical style of the latter.

28. See citation of Dumas's account in Appendix F. Only the portion of his letter relevant to the battle is appended. On Dumas personally, see Sargent, *History of an Expedition,* p. 224, n. 1. It is probable that he, as well as Contrecoeur and other French principals in Braddock's Defeat, will receive articles in the forthcoming volume 4 of the *Dictionary of Canadian Biography.* Meanwhile, there is the French biography by Audet.

Chapter 4. *"The Indiens Was Upon Us!"*

1. Peyton suggests the same: "Our treacherous foe could not be seen through the trees and thick undergrowth." Mackellar, however, backs St. Clair in his notes accompanying a rough sketch of the area: "The Woods are pretty open upon the Field of Battle." Freeman reproduces the sketch (*George Washington,* 2, between pp. 67 and 68).

2. On Beaujeu's dress, or lack of it, see "Seaman's Journal" (Sargent, *History of an Expedition,* p. 387).

3. The distance of the battlefield from the river is mooted among the eyewitnesses. Gage gives the extremely low figure of a quarter-mile, British A, British B, Dunbar, and Gordon all opt for a half-mile or 800 yards; Cameron and St. Clair say one mile, and Cholmley's Batman, a mile and a half. By this they mean the distance marched by the vanguard after completing the second ford. On the basis of Mackellar, as well as the probable location of the hillock by which the battle was fought, I feel that the higher figure of one mile is most reasonable. The line of march itself was clearly more than a half-mile in length, even if Mackellar is not entirely accurate.

4. The quotation is from Cholmley's Batman. He would have been on the scene and appears not to have been biased against Gage. Note that he also mentions prudent actions Gage had taken earlier in the day, such as drawing out the cannon for possible use. Dunbar, who was also in the advance party, confirms that it had left camp that morning with two six-pounders, while Mackellar's first sketch reveals that, at the onset of battle, the cannon were being pulled along by the working party. The position of the troops relative to the rising ground is clearly shown by Mackellar, and he is by inference supported by the mass of evidence. British B refers to a rise on the left as well, and may possibly be correct, but even if the second rise did exist, it appears not to have played an important role in the battle.

5. One o'clock is a compromise figure. It is the one given by Cholmley's

Batman and Dunbar. Campbell says noon; British A, between 12:00 and 1:00; Furnis, 1:30; Stephen and Orme, 2:00.

6. The same sequence is suggested in the "Seaman's Journal" (Sargent, *History of an Expedition*, p. 387); however, the author may simply be relating Gordon's or Croghan's testimony. There is a possibility that the Indians acted on their own.

7. Jared Sparks, who himself covered every inch of the battlefield, popularized the idea that Braddock's enemies fired from natural trenches. On this legend and generally for descriptions of the terrain, see Herbert B. Adams, ed., *The Life and Writings of Jared Sparks Comprising Selections from His Journals and Correspondence* (Boston, 1893), 1, pp. 551–52; Hazard, *Register of Pennsylvania*, 16 (1835), pp. 97–99; and Sargent, *History of an Expedition*, pp. 218–20. The use to which the legend has been put by Braddock's critics is dealt with in Appendix B. There seems to be some confusion on the question of whether any of the trenches ran parallel to the road, but the consensus seems to be that most, if not all, of them cut across it. Mackellar's sketches reveal "a Hollow Way" which from its location is apparently to be identified with the "remarkable ravine" described by Sparks. However, Sparks claims that the ravine was six to ten feet deep. Perhaps erosion had deepened it by his day, but it could not have been so in 1755, or else the vanguard would never have been able to get past. Indeed, one apparent reason the legend was so enduring is that Sparks and most of his contemporaries seem not to have known that the vanguard had already passed the hill, and hence the defile, before encountering the enemy. Potter was apparently referring to a different trench (Hermanus Alricks to Morris, July 22, 1755, *PA*, 2, p. 383). Note also Morris's letter of July 1755, quoted in Appendix C.

8. Peyton backs this testimony almost exactly, but the similarity here is actually one of my main reasons for questioning the authenticity of his account.

9. Nos. 1388 (July 31), p. 3, col. 1, and 1393 (September 4, 1755), p. 4, col. 3. Dulany also identifies Gage as the author of the advertisement ("Military and Political Affairs," p. 17).

10. I have some reservations in treating British B as an eyewitness. See Appendix D.

11. This is quoted from Washington's letter to Dinwiddie, which I have appended. However, note that he gives almost the same account to his mother, Mary Washington (July 18, 1755, in Fitzpatrick, *Writings*, 1, p. 151). Incidentally, some may wonder why I am bothering to "prove" that the men panicked, when the point is generally conceded. First, not all consensuses are reliable, although I agree with this one. Second, as we have seen, not every reporter suggests that there was panic, though most do. Third, I intend to lean heavily on the issue of panic in the next chapter and therefore need a firm foundation.

12. *Shirley Corr.*, 2, p. 312.

13. British B supports Cholmley's Batman: "The men on that day the battle

was fought, [had eaten] little or nothing for two days, and drank only water, under an excessive hot sun." The weight of evidence, in fact, supports the argument that the men were short on rations. However, it should be noted that, according to Halket's Orderly Book, on the evening of July 8 the troops were supposed to be supplied with provisions, including meat and flour, which were to sustain them until the 10th (*BD*, p. 120).

14. Shirley raises a similar objection during the course of his analysis of the testimony (Shirley to Robinson, November 5, 1755, *Shirley Corr.*, 2, p. 317).

15. In his letter to Albemarle, Gage comments that "I can't ascribe their behaviour to any other cause than the talk of the country people, ever since our arrival in America—the woodsmen and Indian traders, who were continually telling the soldiers, that if they attempted to fight Indians in a regular manner, they would certainly be defeated." However, Gage may have written the "court findings" himself, so one must beware of self-corroboration in this case; see Appendix D.

16. Describing the Battle of Niagara (1759), the editor of the *Annual Register* (8th ed., 1810) writes that "the engagement began by a violent and horrid scream of the enemy's savages, according to their barbarous custom. It was this scream, perhaps the most horrid sound that can be imagined, which is said to have struck a panic into the troops of General Braddock, and was one of the principal causes of that defeat" (p. 34). Note the parallel impact of the Scottish war cries (see p. 120).

17. British A claims that these Americans accompanied Braddock. I have already suggested that the general himself did not at first ride up, and that in any case it appears unlikely that the Americans would have been associated with him, since they were but a small part of the main body. British A may have seen members of the working party, which was largely composed of provincials, and mistaken them for troops from the main body. It may be said with greater certainty that he was confused about time regarding the early stages of the battle.

18. The view expressed in this paragraph is substantially that of Pargellis, "Braddock's Defeat," p. 261. I agree that the disordering of the ranks played some part in causing the panic but feel that he overestimates its impact.

19. Colonel Dunbar unwittingly contradicts him. Note Appendices D and E.

20. The scene was not entirely one of chaos and cowardice. We have already noted the evidence provided by Cholmley's Batman and Leslie to the effect that some of the men were actually heroic. British D, a writer not often given to praise, also suggests that at least some of the regulars behaved well. But they appear to have been exceptional.

21. On the massing, see Mackellar, Dunbar, Orme, Gage, Gordon, and Stephen.

22. Although the implicit dispute is not of earthshaking importance, one may note that five horses is the apparent consensus and is also the number given by Cholmley's Batman, who provided several of the mounts for Braddock.

23. Peyton also singles out Burton.

24. Shirley, in enclosing the two maps in his letter to Robinson, comments that they were "approv'd of by the principal Officers in the action" (*Shirley Corr.,* 2, p. 321). This suggests that they represent a consensus, thus adding to their value. British E (see Appendix E) asserts that Halket ordered his men to fire by platoon. Mackellar's second map suggests that, in accordance with Braddock's orders, the rear guard was attempting to guard the baggage.

25. *CR,* 6, p. 501. This account meshes well with that of Tom Faucett; see Appendices A and E. Regarding the Americans' behavior, it appears that the rangers companies at the front generally stuck together. Those secreting themselves were largely or primarily recruits. Although there is no firm proof, all evidence tends to lead to the conclusion that even before the troops were divided there had been bad blood between Braddock and Dunbar. Washington stated this for a fact, but many years after the event (*Niles' Register,* 14 [1818], p. 179; see also Orme's letter of August 25, Appendix C).

26. Orme claims that the troops were confined to the road, which was only twelve feet wide. Mackellar's second sketch, however, appears to support Furnis's assertion that the battlefield was a clearing.

27. Judging from Mackellar's second map, the British retained control of at least three of their six field pieces, and according to Godefroy they made much use of them, though this apparently had little effect. A sixth piece was apparently surrounded by the Indians (Mackellar's second map), but they would not have used it.

28. See p. 84 on Burton's attack. Gage may exaggerate the enemy's tendency to retreat, and the consensus on both sides supports British A's claim that the Indians "never gave ground." But see chap. 5, n. 40. Whatever British counterthrusts there were may have been enough to convince Dumas that he faced a stubborn foe.

29. [William Smith,] *An Historical Account of the Expedition Against the Ohio Indians* (London, 1765), p. 45. Colonel James Smith later recalled a message received at Fort Duquesne during the battle: "Braddock would certainly be defeated; . . . the Indians and French had surrounded him, . . . and if they did not take the river, which was the only gap, and make their escape, there would not be one man left alive before sundown" (Drake, *Tragedies of the Wilderness,* p. 184). It is noteworthy that the British seem to have retreated only after the artillery was taken. Perhaps this enemy success convinced them that the day was indeed lost.

30. Faucett's account supports this, in the case of Braddock himself. See also p. 97.

31. Although there is a possibility that British B was not an eyewitness (Appendix D), in this case the question is unimportant, for he would nonetheless have heard the surgeons' reports only in Dunbar's camp.

32. British A, Cholmley's Batman, and Furnis all claim that the retreat began

between 4:00 and 5:00. Campbell is probably somewhat off, fixing on 3:00, while Dunbar and Stephen opt for 5:00 and 5:30, respectively.

33. Gage and British A both imply that the wagoners, who included in their number a young Daniel Boone, fled only toward the close of battle, but circumstantial evidence indicates that a sizable proportion had left earlier. The list of casualties in the *Boston Gazette*, no. 23 (September 1, 1755), p. 2, col. 3, includes this appended comment: "What seems most remarkable is, that all the Waggoners . . . have returned safe but two." It *is* remarkable, and I would suggest that, even though the enemy was undoubtedly centering its fire up ahead, such a low figure indicates a rapid retreat on the part of many, if not most, wagoners. Furnis implies an early flight. See also Orme, Peyton.

34. Most eyewitnesses make no mention of an order being given to retreat, and several, notably British A, strongly imply that the men simply quit the field.

35. Croghan himself confirms the story of the pistols. However, neither he nor any other eyewitness provides insight into which individuals were responsible for rescuing Braddock. I would judge that Croghan was probably one, since he cared enough for the general to stop and attend him. Apparently only legend credits Stewart (Sargent. *History of an Expedition*, p. 232; William H. Lowdermilk, *History of Cumberland, . . . with a History of Braddock's Expedition* [Washington, D.C., 1878], p. 162). Washington, in his autobiographical account, gives himself the credit for having saved his commander (Fitzpatrick, *Writings*, 29, p. 43). The rumor about Orme, which he himself apparently started, is related by Walpole in a letter to Sir Horace Mann, August 28, 1755 (W. S. Lewis, ed., *Horace Walpole's Correspondence* [New Haven: Yale University Press, 1960], 20, p. 495). The various accounts are not contradictory, and all are plausible. Regarding Braddock's sash, in which he was carried from the field, see Appendix A.

36. Ord and Furnis detail the ordnance lost during the battle, and also that destroyed by Dunbar prior to his retreat (*MA*, pp. 96–97). Three French accounts provide further information. That by Roucher is appended, but not those by Contrecoeur and Godefroy. Roucher also provides details on Dumas's salvage operations. The captain does likewise and discusses his fears that the British might counterattack, but this is in portions of his letter that are not appended. Lotbinière includes in his account information gleaned from Braddock's papers. On the French use of the papers for propaganda, see Guy Frégault, *Canada: The War of the Conquest*, trans. Margaret M. Cameron (Toronto: Oxford University Press, 1969), p. 97. Regarding the general's war chest, I agree with Williams's assertion that most sources tend to exaggerate the amount of cash lost ("Treasure Hunt," pp. 395–96).

37. The accounts of casualties vary considerably; note British A, Dunbar, and Mackellar. Gipson, citing an official list, states that "of 1,373 non-commissioned officers and privates, but 459 were neither killed nor wounded; of 86 officers,

but 23" (*Great War for Empire,* p. 96). The *Pennsylvania Gazette* provides totals of 456 killed, 421 wounded, and 583 safe (Sargent, *History of an Expedition,* p. 238), while the *Boston Evening Post,* which I have already suggested exaggerates in its listing, prints figures of 308, 474, and 707, respectively. The *South Carolina Gazette,* no. 1104 (August 14–21, 1755) prints the account of one of Braddock's subordinates (p. 2, col. 3; after Stewart's letter). He claims that of 350 wounded, three-quarters were expected to die. Although such a view may have been pessimistic, in view of the poor hygiene of the day many undoubtedly died from even minor wounds.

38. Washington's memoir, in Fitzpatrick, *Writings,* 29, p. 44.

39. Roucher claims that they took "20 prisoners whereof Seven Women or Girls where of the Number."

40. Drake, *Tragedies of the Wilderness,* p. 184.

41. Peter D. Keyser, ed., "Memorials of Colonel Jehu Eyre," *PMHB,* 3 (1879), p. 303. After having taken Fort Duquesne, Forbes ordered a detail to bury the remains of Braddock's men, but perhaps rain had exposed the skeletons.

Chapter 5. Retrospect

1. Letter to Orme; in Fitzpatrick, *Writings,* 1, p. 154.

2. On the privates' charges (and Gage's), see chap. 4. Gage had other criticisms as well. More than two decades after the event, he told an interviewer that "the cause of General Braddock's disaster, is to be attributed, first, to the Province's disappointing him in the carriages and provisions, they engaged to furnish by a stated time; by which he was detained several weeks, when otherwise ready to proceed; and the plan he had concerted with the Governors, to march with expedition to Fort Duquesne, before the enemies' reinforcements could arrive, was, by that means, prevented" ("Queries of George Chalmers, with the Answers of General Gage, in relation to Braddock's Expedition—The Stamp Act—and Gage's Administration of the Government of Massachusetts Bay," Massachusetts Historical Society, *Collections,* ser. 4, vol. 4 [1858], p. 368). At the same time, Gage acknowledged that inexperience in wilderness warfare had been costly to Braddock's army.

3. Cumberland was seldom criticized openly, in deference to his rank. However, the strategy he laid down for the Braddock expedition often was, particularly his decision, originally Newcastle's, to launch the attack from Virginia instead of Pennyslvania. See Entick, *History of the Late War,* 1, p. 141; *Gentleman's Magazine,* 25 (1755), p. 389.

4. Dunbar's retreat has received too little attention, in view of its impact and the various controversies that surrounded it at the time. See Freeman, *George Washington,* pp. 104–06, particularly on Dinwiddie's criticism. The fullest and most able defense of the colonel's conduct is contained in an anonymous letter written by one of his subordinates. It appeared in the *New York Mercury,* no.

160 (September 1), p. 2, col. 2; the *Boston Gazette*, no. 23 (September 8), p. 2, col. 3; and the *Virginia Gazette*, no. 247 (October 3, 1755), p. 1, col. 1. The writer blames the general situation on Braddock.

5. Not all historians have been antagonistic. See Appendix B.

6. Shirley's comments are in *CR*, 6, p. 407. On the anonymous critic, see Appendix E (quotation from *MA*, p. 119); and Franklin's *Autobiography*, p. 271.

7. Lee's comments are included in a letter to his sister, June 18, [1756], *NYHSColls*, 4 (1871), p. 5. Findley recalls Washington's statement in a letter to *Niles' Register*, 14 (1818), p. 180. As Findley suggests, the "one person" who objected to Braddock's tactics may well have been Washington himself.

8. The break between traditional and modern accounts is discussed further in Appendix B.

9. "Major-General Edward Braddock's Orderly Books," p. xxxiv. This transcript was published separately in 1880 but was first appended to Lowdermilk's *History of Cumberland*. The pagination is identical. It should be noted that the orderly book does not cover the greater part of the march, and that Halket's, which does, fails to give much insight into camp discipline. We therefore do not know whether Braddock became stricter as the march progressed. Among those accusing him of brutality is Evan Charteris (*William Augustus Duke of Cumberland and the Seven Years' War* [London: Hutchinson and Co., 1925], p. 130). Charteris claims that the general's martinetism stamped him as a member of the "old school," rather than the new, "enlightened" generation exemplified by Wolfe. But the age factor does not seem to have had much bearing on this question. Most of the officers under Braddock were young, yet there is considerable evidence that they were far stricter than was the general himself. According to Cameron, on the retreat they constantly whipped the men and on the whole dealt with them so harshly that he wondered if they had become barbarized (*Life, Adventures*, p. 14).

10. The quotation is from an anonymous letter that first appeared in the *London Evening Post*, September 9–11, 1755, and was reprinted by N. D. Davis in "British Newspaper Accounts of Braddock's Defeat," *PMHB*, 23 (1899), p. 316. I have assessed British D's claim in chap. 4. On the question of whether Braddock was shot by one of his own men, see Appendix A.

11. *Autobiography*, p. 272. Braddock may have spoken in this manner, but we should note that Franklin is recalling a conversation which had taken place more than thirty years before. And note that Braddock had been able to fend off Indian attacks prior to the Defeat. Most modern historians, including Pargellis ("Braddock's Defeat," p. 269), concede that at least prior to July 9, Braddock took all precautions necessary.

12. Monakatooka made this statement at a council held by Morris on August 22, 1755 (*CR*, 6, p. 589).

13. Historical Society of Pennsylvania, Manuscript Department, Autograph Collection of Simon Gratz, case 4, box 6.

14. Braddock's letter to Morris is in *PA*, 2, p. 290. Croghan's letter, dated May 12 and also addressed to the governor, is printed in *CR*, 6, pp. 374–75. For Croghan's statement, see Sargent, *History of an Expedition*, p. 408. Peters made his comments during a council held in Philadelphia on June 2, 1755 (*CR*, 6, p. 397).

15. Shingas gave this account in an attempt to justify the Delawares' decision to side with the French. For the text, see Beverly W. Bond, Jr., ed., "The Captivity of Charles Stuart 1755–57," *Mississippi Valley Historical Review*, 13 (1926), p. 63. C. A. Weslager notes this version, as well as Croghan's, and chooses to believe Shingas (*The Delaware Indians* [New Brunswick, N.J.: Rutgers University Press, 1972], pp. 224–25). Readers may be interested in his reasoning. Croghan's comments are printed in Sargent, *History of an Expedition*, pp. 407–08.

16. Orme's statement is contained in his journal (Sargent, *History of an Expedition*, p. 336). On the Iroquois' "ownership" of the Ohio, see Jacobs, *Diplomacy and Indian Gifts*, p. 89, and Hunter, *Forts on the Frontier*, pp. 15–16. It is quite possible that, as Croghan suggests, the Delaware chieftains—or at least Shingas—were already leaning toward the French at the time of the conference and may even have been committed to them. Twice during the two years previous, Shingas had responded coldly to British blandishments (Hunter, pp. 27, 56).

17. On the Glen-Dinwiddie feud and its consequences, see John R. Alden, *John Stuart and the Southern Colonial Frontier* (New York: Gordian, 1966), pp. 42–47. There were indeed several reasons why the Iroquois failed to support Braddock. See Johnson to the Lords of Trade, July 21, 1755, *NYCD*, 6, p. 963, and Wraxall's "Thoughts upon the British Indian Interest," ibid., 7, pp. 22–23.

18. Quoted in Sargent, *History of an Expedition*, p. 54, n. 1. When contemporary writers speak of "Half-King," they usually mean this man, Tanacharisson, though occasionally the reference is to Monakatooka.

19. For his part, Braddock may have wished that the Indians would be more forthcoming with their advice. It is quite possible that they were reluctant to reconnoiter; see Orme's comments, ibid., pp. 348–49. Of course, such unwillingness may have stemmed from their dislike of Braddock.

20. Washington's statements are included in his memoir, Fitzpatrick, *Writings*, 29, pp. 41–43. In this chapter, I am attempting to handle only what seem to be the most basic examples of purported advice; other suggestions are mentioned in the appended eyewitness accounts.

21. Pargellis, relying on British E and Mackellar, claims ("Braddock's Defeat," pp. 260–63) that the companies were divided by the wagon train as they marched, though he at the same time concedes that the Orme map (map 2, Appendix D) shows proper platooning. His assertion has drawn able but excessively violent criticism from Robert L. Yaple in "Braddock's Defeat: The Theories and a Reconsideration," *Journal of the Society for Army Historical Research*, 46

(1968), pp. 199–200. According to Yaple, "Mackellar's map seems so ambiguous that it 'can be interpreted' in several fashions." In chapter 3 and elsewhere, I have usually relied on Mackellar, rather than Orme, though I have noted exceptions. My reasoning has been that the Mackellar maps proper seem to have been drawn to the specifications of various officers and therefore represent a consensus. But Yaple's point is well taken, and certainly any of our maps can be pushed too far. Whatever Braddock's marching formation, it does not seem to have pleased British B. Clearly it was not a "line of battle" as defined in the text, my own definition being drawn from the entry for "Line" in *A Military Dictionary*, 3d ed., rev. (London, 1708). However, to show just how loosely the term was used in Braddock's day, we may note Contrecoeur's comment that the British marched most of the way from Fort Cumberland "in a line of battle." What he means is that they were on guard, perhaps in the fashion Gordon describes for the march of July 8. What precautions Braddock took as he marched from the river we do not know; Gordon implies negligence, at least in part the general's. As for the action itself, French B notes, with implied criticism, that "the enemy formed a line of battle." Again, the usage is vague.

22. If St. Clair relayed the opinion of Monakatooka, this comment applies to the latter as well. But despite any reservations he may have had, it appears that the sachem fought with courage (Smith, *Brief View*, p. 47 n.).

23. On the council of war, see Sargent, *History of an Expedition*, pp. 346–48. Regarding the behavior of Dunbar's troops on July 10, see *CR*, 6, p. 482. The quotation is drawn from the testimony of Mathew Laird, a wagoner who had fled and had later been captured. His tale is corroborated by two other witnesses (ibid., pp. 482–84).

24. Statements such as Washington's were to contribute mightily to the belief that Braddock's Defeat demonstrated the superiority of both American tactics and soldiers.

25. George Washington Parke Custis, *Recollections and Private Memoirs of Washington* (New York, 1860), p. 375. The first quotation is drawn from a letter originally printed in the *Public Advertiser* (Davis, "British Newspaper Accounts," p. 318).

26. The tendency of the regulars to fire at anything that moved in the forest is discussed on pp. 82–83.

27. Concerning the function of the rear guard, see Humphrey Bland, *A Treatise of Military Discipline: In Which is Laid Down and Explained the Duty of the Officer and Soldier, Through the Several Branches of the Service*, 8th ed., rev. (London, 1759), p. 138. John Schlebecker discusses further the issue of desertion ("Braddock's Defeat," *The Ohio State Archaeological and Historical Quarterly*, 58 [1949], pp. 172, 180–81). Washington's statement is to be found in his memoir (Fitzpatrick, *Writings*, 29, p. 43). Since he is recalling an event that had taken place more than a generation before, one may question his mem-

ory. But in this particular case the incident he describes is vivid; the reference may be to maneuvers by Polson or Peyronie.

28. Bland makes numerous statements suggesting his desire that the commander be decisive and expect strict obedience. For his own part, he was extremely authoritarian (see McCardell, *Ill-Starred General,* p. 117).

29. Pargellis, "Braddock's Defeat," *passim.*

30. The figure of one-quarter mile is given by Furnis and by the author of the "Seaman's Journal" (Sargent, *History of an Expedition,* p. 385). Both, however, are rather vague in defining the points whose distance apart they approximate. Mackellar's first map, which I relied on primarily in determining distances in chapter 3, indicates that the light horse was about four hundred yards behind the rear of the working party (not the rear guard of the advance party), and that the general's guard was perhaps one hundred and fifty yards farther back. On Braddock's orders to Burton, see p. 63. My differences with Pargellis, which in no way lessen my respect for him, center on his rejection of Orme; on this point, see Appendix C. His work suffers also from the limited number of his sources (no fault of his) and from reliance on an anonymous secondhand reporter whose account is not generally plausible (see "British E," Appendix E). On Pargellis, see also Appendix B. It should be mentioned here that I am not dealing with all of his criticisms of Braddock, though I feel that the ones discussed are most central, and that material noted in various contexts throughout this work serves as a basis for answering some of his remaining charges.

31. Bland, *Treatise,* p. 154. Immediately before making this statement, Bland comments that "it is impossible to say in what manner he is to act when he meets with the enemy, without knowing their numbers, quality, and disposition." This suggests another reason why he emphasizes drill, rather than tactics, in his treatise: There are fewer variables.

32. On the tactics Bland proposes, see *Treatise,* pp. 97, 135–38. The eyewitnesses most critical of platoon firing are British A and Stephen. On the wagon train, see p. 39. Pargellis, on the basis of British E's secondhand account (see appendix E), asserts that the wagons hindered Braddock's formations ("Braddock's Defeat," pp. 261, 263) but no eyewitness supports this claim.

33. That Braddock should immediately have ordered an attack on the rising ground is Schlebecker's view ("Braddock's Defeat," p. 178). In fact, it appears that the general did so, on several occasions (see chap. 4). Sparks argues for bayonets (Adams, *Life and Writings,* 2, p. 553). It would be surprising indeed if Braddock did not order this. The officers of the advance party did so, according to Dunbar, but were stymied by the mass panic. Sargent discusses the feint, but concedes that it would have been a very difficult maneuver (*History of an Expedition,* pp. 255–56). He, like many others, is impressed by the success enjoyed by Bouquet in his famous victory at Bushy Run (August 1763). On that occasion, Bouquet, after having been surrounded by Indians, used a feint to

lure them from the trees, and then put them to rout. Pargellis ("Braddock's Defeat," p. 269) claims that such a tactic could evolve only after years of experience in wilderness warfare, and would have been impossible for Braddock. Perhaps more important, Bouquet's men were battle-hardened and kept their heads, making the feint possible. See O'Meara, *Guns at the Forks*, pp. 236–44, on Bushy Run.

34. O'Meara (*Guns at the Forks*, p. 145) criticizes Halket for having "managed to ram his baggage train against the rear of Burton's column." It is true that Mackellar's second map reveals that the baggage moved ahead at some point after the battle began, but it is unclear who, if anyone, was responsible for this. Howard H. Peckham is also critical of Halket, in this case for having, after the initial collision, "stupidly moved forward and wedged against the desperate troops" (*The Colonial Wars, 1689–1762* [Chicago: University of Chicago Press, 1964], p. 146). No eyewitness suggests this to have been the case, and Mackellar goes quite against it. Gipson (*Great War for Empire*, p. 94) criticizes St. Clair, as well as Gage, for having failed to occupy the hillock to the right as their respective detachments first marched past it. But such occupation was primarily the job of Gage.

35. *Niles' Register*, 14 (1818), pp. 179–80. William Findley, who recorded Washington's conversation, used the president's recollection as the basis for charging Gage with cowardice. Note that there are two memories at work here. For this reason, and since we have Washington's own memoir, Findley's account is not dealt with in Appendix E.

36. On Gage's failure to occupy the rising ground, or to take along the field pieces, see also pp. 50–51. Hamilton likewise criticizes Gage for leaving behind the cannon (*BD*, p. xix). Leach (*Arms for Empire*, p. 366) and Gipson (*Great War for Empire*, p. 94) feel as I do that his decision not to secure the hill constitutes gross negligence. This is, incidentally, one case where Braddock's weak reconnaissance undoubtedly hurt, though the battle would probably not have gone differently had Gage been forewarned to occupy the hill.

37. Bland's quotation is from *Treatise*, p. 138. The relevant criticism of Braddock by Pargellis is in "Braddock's Defeat," p. 264.

38. *The History of the Late War in North-America* (London, 1772), pp. 21, 26. Bancroft, inspired by Mante, writes that when he first encountered the enemy "Gage should, on the moment, and without waiting for orders, have sent support to his flanking parties. His indecision lost the day" (*History of the United States, from the Discovery of the American Continent* [Boston, 1852], 4, p. 188).

39. Taking causation back one step further, one can also criticize Cumberland and Newcastle for having directed that Braddock use the route through Virginia and Maryland, instead of one through Pennsylvania. This would have reduced somewhat the problems of road-building and supply. This error on their part was particularly unfortunate in view of the fact that the Pennsylvan-

ians appear to have been more cooperative than other provincials, though undoubtedly the seeming cooperativeness was to a large extent merely a reflection of Franklin's ingenuity. Some might also feel, as did Shirley, that the duke was unwise in concentrating on Fort Duquesne and should instead have ordered a concerted campaign against Fort Niagara. The danger in attacking Cumberland and Newcastle is that there is a tendency to go too far. Braddock's assignment was difficult, and his route ill chosen. But he could easily have succeeded, if not for the delays he encountered before departing from Wills Creek and the panic of his men on the battlefield. Indeed, only uncanny good luck permitted the French to carry the day.

40. Smith, *Historical Account*, p. 45. This tendency to retreat makes somewhat more plausible Gage's assertion that the enemy gave way whenever the troops advanced "even on the most faint attack." Croghan's claim that the attackers "intended to dispute every inch of Ground between the river and the Fort" is quite plausible, although the product of conjecture or rumor.

41. J. W. Fortescue notes the impact on the soldiers of the Scottish war cry and also of the belief that the Scots tortured their prisoners (*A History of the British Army* [London: Macmillan, 1910], 2, pp. 141–43).

42. Wolfe's comments, as well as others critical of officers, are included in a letter to his father, September 4, 1755 (Beckles Willson, *The Life and Letters of James Wolfe* (London: William Heinemann, 1909), p. 274. More fatalistic are Mante (*History of the Late War,* p. 20) and Bland (*Treatise,* pp. 168–69); the latter is, of course, not writing in terms of Braddock's Defeat.

Chapter 6. *"So What?"*

1. Several historians have touched briefly on the question of significance, but usually in respect to only one or two points. To my knowledge, only Ness ("Braddock Expedition," p. 117) tries a systematic approach, but in keeping with the limitations of an article even he provides only a brief list of reasons.

2. Of course, Braddock's forces had not really been ambushed, although the French had planned to use the strategy. Rather, both sides had been surprised by the suddenness of the confrontation. It should also be noted that, while Americans were by and large more familiar with such strategy than were the British, they did not necessarily approve of it. This was particularly true of the more refined easterners. Not all Britons were averse to ambush. Thomas Simes went so far as to include in his military treatise a section on how to prepare one and suggested, among other things, that ambushers bribe the enemy's guides to lure them into the trap (*The Military Guide for Young Officers* [Philadelphia, 1776], 1, pp. 61–72). However, Simes's amoral approach to ambush was far from typical, and furthermore he wrote fully two decades after Braddock's Defeat.

3. The New York Public Library, Em. 2320. One ballad, written by Stephen

Tilden, is reprinted in James L. Onderdonk, "Colonial Patriotism in Song," *American Historical Register,* 3 (1895–1896), p. 476. A poem honoring the general is in Sargent, *History of an Expedition,* p. 415.

4. Edward McCrady, *South Carolina Under the Royal Government* (New York: Macmillan, 1900), p. 312. On the Indian attacks and their impact on the American mentality, see Winfred T. Root, *The Relations of Pennsylvania with the British Government, 1696–1765* (New York: D. Appleton and Co., 1912), pp. 304–05; Roger Wolcott to Richard Partridge, January 28, 1756, Connecticut Historical Society, *Collections,* 17 (1918), p. 196; and the remarks by Hugh McAden in *The Colonial Records of North Carolina,* ed. William L. Saunders (Raleigh, 1887), 5, p. 1202. The French themselves were in some cases shocked by the barbarity. See the abstract of an anonymous dispatch (1756) and the letter from Rev. Claude Godfroy Cocquard to his brother (March [?] 1757), *NYCD,* 10, pp. 481, 528.

5. "Captivity of Charles Stuart," p. 64. This aspect of Shingas's testimony seems reasonable. The Delaware support for the French prior to Braddock's Defeat was indeed limited; see chap. 2, n. 16. Shingas and his followers, however, may have been leaning toward France (chap. 5, n. 18). On the heroic behavior of the British Indians at Lake George, see Jacobs, *Diplomacy and Indian Gifts,* pp. 158–59.

6. Washington's quotation comes from his memoir in Fitzpatrick, *Writings,* 29, p. 45. The remainder of this paragraph is drawn from Pargellis, *Lord Loudoun,* pp. 299–300. Pargellis's discussion of the evolution of tactics, though brief, is the best of its kind. It falls in an area that requires far greater study than it has so far received. In passing, it should be noted that in his work on Lord Loudoun, Pargellis provides easily the fullest and best portrait of the British Army in North America during the French and Indian War. Perhaps because the title suggests a mere biography, *Lord Loudoun* is too seldom consulted.

7. Forbes is quoted by Leach, *Arms for Empire,* p. 440. Also on the rangers, whose usefulness varied, see Pargellis, *Lord Loudoun,* pp. 300–05.

8. On the colonies' contributions to the war cause in the wake of Braddock's Defeat, see Ward, "Unite Or Die," pp. 95–96. Information on the various witch hunts may be found in Dinwiddie to Colonel Charles Carter, July 18, 1755, in *The Official Records of Robert Dinwiddie,* ed. R. A. Brock (Richmond, 1884), 2, p. 102; Justices to Governor Horatio Sharpe, two letters, one n.d., the other October 21, 1755, *AM,* 31, pp. 80–81; and Howard, "Diary of Daniel Fisher," p. 274. On the anti-Catholic activity in Maryland, see also John W. McGrain, Jr., "Priest Neale, His Mass House, and His Successors," *Maryland Historical Magazine,* 62 (1967), esp. pp. 268–73.

9. Regarding the fall of the Quakers, see Robert L. Davidson, *War Comes to Quaker Pennsylvania 1682–1756* (New York: Columbia University Press, 1957), pp. 158–65, 179–88; and Daniel J. Boorstin, *The Americans: The Colonial Experi-*

ence (New York: Random House, 1958), pp. 53–62. The quotations are drawn respectively from *CR*, 6, p. 734, and Davidson, p. 188. Some might suggest that Braddock's Defeat was only indirectly responsible for the Quaker abdication, and even then that its influence was limited. Of course, the fact of war endangered their position, as did pressure from the government on both sides of the Atlantic. But, as Davidson observes (p. 187), "Strong opposition had not unseated them before—nor had the threat of war." What tested them, and finally forced them out, was the Indian situation—not only the raids, but their own failures in Indian diplomacy. And it seems fair to say that the sad state of Indian affairs in Pennsylvania stemmed primarily from Braddock's Defeat. On another point, some would perhaps argue that Pitt's rise was related to the Battle of the Monongahela. Certainly the affair helped to discredit Cumberland and the Newcastle ministry, but they were weakened much more by events on the Continent.

10. Not all of the Washington legends associated with the battle are plausible. For example, he certainly did not conduct the retreat to Dunbar's camp, although he played an important role in it. Bancroft quotes Halifax (*History*, 4, p. 190). Washington's quotation is drawn from his letter of July 18, 1755 (Fitzpatrick, *Writings*, 1, p. 152). Craik had been present at the battle but seems not to have left behind any testimony beyond a tribute to Washington's heroism: "I expected every moment to see him fall. His duty and situation exposed him to every danger. Nothing but the superintending care of Providence could have saved him from the fate of all around him" (quoted, as is Davies, by J. F. Schroeder, *The Life and Times of Washington* [New York, 1857], 1, p. 96). On the chieftain's statement, see Custis, *Recollections*, pp. 300–05, 375.

11. On this particular legend, see p. 104. Brown and Butler both confirm it (John F. Watson, *Annals of Philadelphia, and Pennsylvania, in the Olden Time* [Philadelphia, 1887], 2, pp. 139–41). Braddock's Defeat raised the age-old question of the usefulness of a professional army as opposed to a militia. The debate extended to Britain itself, as might be expected. See letter quoted by Davis, "British Newspaper Accounts," pp. 327–28.

12. The letter quoted is from Henry Laurens to James Cowles, August 20, 1755, reprinted in Ward, *"Unite or Die,"* p. 159. The popularity of the provincial soldiers in London circles actually led to some exaggeration of their feats, according to Washington; see his letter to Stephen, November 18, 1755, in Fitzpatrick, *Writings*, 1, p.237. Nor were the Virginians alone praised. Indeed, as a result of their role in the capture of Fort Beausejour, the New England militiamen received equal acclaim. Note the excerpt taken from a letter written by an anonymous New Yorker and printed in the *Boston Weekly News-Letter*, no. 2771 (August 14, 1755), p. 3, col. 1, and [Charles Chauncy], *A Letter to a Friend, Giving a Concise, but Just, Account . . . of the Ohio Defeat* (Boston, 1755), pp. 11–12. Newcastle reacted to news of the defeat by exclaiming, "Now we must employ Americans to fight Americans." Ligonier

had been of this opinion for some time. See Rex Whitworth, *Field Marshal Lord Ligonier: A Story of the British Army 1702–1770* (Oxford: Oxford University Press, 1958), pp. 202–03.

13. Franklin's quotation (*Autobiography*, p. 274) refers to the retreat, as well as the battle. On the question of what role Braddock's Defeat played in increasing American self-reliance, see also Leach, *Arms for Empire*, pp. 407, n. 44, 506–07.

Appendix B. Bibliographical Survey

1. "Braddock's Defeat," p. 253.

2. Sparks's account contains offhand references to his sources (*Life of Washington*, pp. 62–66). On Watson, Butler, and Billy Brown, see Appendices A and E. On the question of trenches, see p. 58. Besides French B, the reporters whose accounts Sparks discovered were probably French A and Lotbinière, since it is they to whom Bancroft and Sargent refer. See also version of Braddock's Defeat by Sparks in *The Olden Time*, ed. Neville B. Craig (Cincinnati, 1876), 1, pp. 126–33.

3. Among Sparks's admirers were Sargent (*History of an Expedition*, p. 220, n. 1) and Craig (*Olden Time*, 1, p. 126).

4. Bancroft's account (*History*, 4, pp. 186–92). He drew his criticism of Gage from Mante; see chap. 5, n. 38.

5. The quotations are from *Montcalm and Wolfe*, 1, pp. 225 and 198, respectively. For his characterization of Orme, see p. 210.

6. Although none is of high quality, the accounts by Hadden and Lowdermilk, as well as "From Braddock to Bouquet," *Kittochtinny Magazine*, 1 (1905), pp. 24–35, 123–35, 229–40, are better than most of the material that came out during this period. They are otherwise characteristic of it, as is C. de B. Boone, "Braddock's Campaign and Its Lessons," *The United Service Magazine*, n.s., 39 (1909), pp. 88–93. Boone's work is interesting in that he was a soldier, and a Briton, who nonetheless felt that Braddock should have allowed at least his American troops to fight Indian style.

7. Besides his four "finds" noted above, Pargellis discovered the set of Mackellar maps at Windsor, Parkman having used that in the Public Record Office. Pargellis, incidentally, makes fuller use of maps than does any other writer on the battle. In his article, he also deals with the accounts by Orme, Washington, and Gage, and notes Leslie's (p. 254, n. 3), but dismisses it as too brief. These nine he describes as having been the only eyewitnesses known to have come from the British side. He appears not to have heard of Peyton, which may be just as well. However, he should have known of British D and Croghan—the latter particularly—both of whom had been referred to by Sargent. More unfortunate, in my opinion, is his decision to use, and rely on, an anonymous secondhand account written by British E, one of those in Dunbar's detachment; see Appendix E.

8. Although historians since Pargellis's day have tended to claim that Braddock was justified in prohibiting his provincial troops from using Indian-style tactics, they have done so on different bases. Pargellis himself argues that the general, in view of his background, cannot be expected to have been familiar with them, or to have recognized their potential. Gipson feels, as I do, that those Americans who fought from behind trees were endangered by the panicky regulars, while Schlebecker insists that forest fighting tactics were simply inferior. These views are not mutually exclusive.

9. Quotation, *Great War for Empire*, p. 84; narrative of battle and analysis, pp. 94-98. It is through Gipson's excellent bibliographical volume, printed in 1968, that I first learned of British B's account.

10. Although this appendix deals primarily with Braddock's Defeat, I might mention that Freeman is an excellent source on the entire campaign. His discussion of the topography of Braddock's Road (*George Washington*, pp. 46-47) is typical of his originality, scholarship, and devotion to detail.

11. The narrative approach is by no means dead, nor should it be. To my mind, the most impressive narration of the campaign and battle to have come out in recent years, strictly from the stylistic point of view, is that by Harrison Bird, *Battle for a Continent* (New York: Oxford University Press, 1965), pp. 45-57. O'Meara's account is also quite readable.

Appendix C. Orme's Reliability

1. The earliest—July 16—and also possibly the fullest, appeared in the *Public Advertiser*, September 20; it is reprinted in Davis, "British Newspaper Accounts," pp. 316-18. The remainder, some brief extracts, others full and including lists of casualties, were published in various American newspapers: *Boston Evening Post*, no. 1041 (August 11), p. 3, col. 1; *Boston Gazette*, no. 19 (August 11), p. 1, col. 3; p. 2, col. 2; *Boston Weekly News-Letter*, no. 2771 (August 14), p. 2, cols. 1-2; *New York Mercury*, no. 156 (August 4), p. 2, col. 3; p. 3, col. 1; *Pennsylvania Gazette*, no. 1388 (July 31), p. 3, col. 1; *Pennsylvania Journal and Weekly Advertiser*, no. 660 (July 31), p. 2, col. 3; p. 3, col. 1; *South Carolina Gazette*, no. 1106 (August 28–September 4), p. 3, col. 3. Although written anonymously, his letters are easy to recognize, even without the evidence provided by Gates. They are all very similar to that which Orme wrote to Morris on July 18 (*CR*, 6, pp. 487–92).

2. Besides the letter to Morris, note those to Shirley, *Shirley Corr.*, 2, pp. 207–09; to Sharpe, *AM*, 6, pp. 252–54; to Napier and to Henry Fox, *MA*, pp. 98–101; and to Keppel, "Illustrative Documents Descriptive of the Defeat of Major-General Edward Braddock," American Antiquarian Society, *Proceedings*, n.s., 19 (1908), pp. 295–96.

3. Orme's influence was manifest among writers of his own day as well, such as Chauncy and Entick.

4. *CR*, 6, p. 496; *PA*, 4, p. 400.

5. Dulany, "Military and Political Affairs," pp. 20–21. Nor did all Britons accept Orme's account. In a letter to her brother, dated August 23, 1755, Elizabeth Anson, wife of the admiral, summarizes the respective versions of Orme and Washington, both of which had just arrived with Keppel. She concludes, "I really hardly know what I write, I believe with as much confusion as our People in America are in, by an endeavour to melt the two accounts into one; but Washington's is much the plainest, some having guarded his, & made no distinction between the behaviour of English and Americans, & slurred the whole a little, not to offend" (British Museum, Add. 35,376, fol. 127). But she seems to have been exceptional, and was in any case writing before Orme returned to England bearing further information.

6. Orme's letter dated March 2, 1756; in *Letters to Washington and Accompanying Papers,* ed. Stanislaus M. Hamilton (Boston, 1898), 1, p. 199. On his marriage, note *Walpole's Corr.*, 20, p. 495, n. 5.

7. "Braddock's Defeat," p. 267.

8. *Letters to Washington,* 1, p. 83.

Bibliography

Archival References

British Museum, London
    Additional
Henry E. Huntington Library, San Marino, California
    Loudoun Papers
Historical Society of Pennsylvania, Philadelphia
    Autograph Collection of Simon Gratz
    Historical Collections
    Peters Papers
New York Public Library
    Emmet Collection
    Hardwicke Papers
Public Record Office, London
    Chatham Papers

Newspapers and Journals

Annual Register, 1759
Boston Evening Post, 1755
Boston Gazette, 1755
Boston Weekly News-Letter, 1755
Gentleman's Magazine, 1755, 1788
Historical Magazine, 1862, 1867
Maryland Gazette, 1755
New York Mercury, 1755
New York Times, 1913
Niles' Register, 1818
Pennsylvania Gazette, 1755
Philadelphia Evening Bulletin, 1849
South Carolina Gazette, 1755
Virginia Gazette, 1755

Other Printed Primary Sources

Adams, Herbert B., ed. *The Life and Writings of Jared Sparks Comprising Selections from His Journals and Correspondence.* Vol. 1. Boston, 1893.

Bates, Albert C., ed. *The Fitch Papers.* Connecticut Historical Society, *Collections,* 18. Hartford, 1918.

Bland, Humphrey. *A Treatise of Military Discipline: In Which is Laid Down and Explained the Duty of the Officer and Soldier, Through the Several Branches of the Service.* 8th ed., rev. London, 1759.

Bond, Beverly W., Jr., ed. "The Captivity of Charles Stuart 1755–57." *Mississippi Valley Historical Review,* 13 (1926), pp. 58–81.

Brock, R. A., ed. *The Official Records of Robert Dinwiddie.* Virginia Historical Society, *Collections,* n.s., 4. Richmond, 1884.

Browne, William H., ed. *Archives of Maryland.* Vol. 6. Baltimore, 1888.

Cameron, Duncan. *The Life, Adventures and Surprising Deliverances of Duncan Cameron, Private Soldier in the Regiment of Foot, late Sir Peter Halkett's.* 3d ed. Philadelphia, 1756.

[Chauncy, Charles.] *A Letter to a Friend, Giving a Concise, but Just, Account . . . of the Ohio Defeat.* Boston, 1755.

Craig, Neville B., ed. *The Olden Time.* Vol. 1. First published in 1846. Cincinnati, 1876.

Davis, N. Darnell, ed. "British Newspaper Accounts of Braddock's Defeat." *Pennsylvania Magazine of History and Biography,* 23 (1899), pp. 310–28.

Drake, Samuel G., ed. *Tragedies of the Wilderness.* Boston, 1846.

Draper, Lyman C., ed. "Seventy-Two Years' Recollections of Wisconsin." Wisconsin Historical Society, *Collections,* 3, pp. 197–295. Madison, 1857.

Dulany, Daniel. "Military and Political Affairs in the Middle Colonies in 1755." Edited by John H. B. Latrobe. *Pennsylvania Magazine of History and Biography,* 3 (1879), pp. 11–31.

Entick, John, et al. *The General History of the Late War.* Vol. 1. London, 1763.

Ewing, William S., ed. "An Eyewitness Account by James Furnis of the Surrender of Fort William Henry, August 1757." *New York History,* 42 (1961), pp. 307–16.

Fitzpatrick, John C., ed. *The Writings of George Washington.* Vols. 1, 2, 29. Washington, D.C.: U.S. Government Printing Office, 1931.

Franklin, Benjamin. *Autobiography.* Edited by John Bigelow. New York: G. P. Putnam's Sons, 1927.

Grenier, Fernand, ed. *Papiers Contrecoeur et autres documents concernant le conflit anglo-français sur l'Ohio de 1745 à 1756.* Quebec: Presses Universitaires Laval, 1952.

Hamilton, Charles, ed. *Braddock's Defeat*. Norman: University of Oklahoma Press, 1959.

Hamilton, Stanislaus M., ed. *Letters to Washington and Accompanying Papers*. Vol. 1. Boston, 1898.

Harrison, Fairfax, ed. "With Braddock's Army: Mrs. Browne's Diary in Virginia and Maryland." *Virginia Magazine of History and Biography*, 32 (1924), pp. 305–20.

Hazard, Samuel, ed. *Pennsylvania Archives*. Vol. 2. Philadelphia, 1853.

———, ed. *Register of Pennsylvania*. Vols. 5, 6, 16. Philadelphia, 1820–1835.

Howard, Mrs. Conway R., ed. "Extracts from the Diary of Daniel Fisher, 1755." *Pennsylvania Magazine of History and Biography*, 17 (1893), pp. 263–78.

"Illustrative Documents Descriptive of the Defeat of Major-General Edward Braddock." American Antiquarian Society, *Proceedings*, n.s., 19 (1908), pp. 293–301.

Jordan, John W., ed. "Journal of James Kenny, 1761–1763." *Pennsylvania Magazine of History and Biography*, 37 (1913), pp. 1–47, 152–201.

Keyser, Peter D., ed. "Memorials of Col. Jehu Eyre." *Pennsylvania Magazine of History and Biography*, 3 (1879), pp. 296–307, 412–25.

Lee Papers, The. New-York Historical Society, *Collections*, 4. New York, 1871.

Lewis, W. S., ed. *Horace Walpole's Correspondence*. Vol. 20. New Haven: Yale University Press, 1960.

Lincoln, Charles H., ed. *Correspondence of William Shirley*. Vol. 2. New York: Macmillan, 1912.

Mante, Thomas. *The History of the Late War in North-America*. London, 1772.

Maryland Historical Magazine, 5 (1910), pp. 73–74.

Military Dictionary, A. 3d ed., rev. London, 1708.

Minutes of the Provincial Council of Pennsylvania. Vol. 6. Harrisburg, 1851.

[Mitchell, John.] *The Contest in America Between Britain and France*. London, 1757.

O'Callaghan, E. B., ed. *Documents Relative to the Colonial History of the State of New York*. Vols. 6, 7, 10. Albany, 1855–1858.

Pargellis, Stanley, ed. *Military Affairs in North America 1748–1765*. New York: D. Appleton-Century Co., 1936.

Pouchot, François. *Memoir Upon the Late War in North America, Between the French and English, 1755–60*. Translated by Franklin B. Hough. Vol. 1. Roxbury, Mass., 1866.

"Queries of George Chalmers, with the Answers of General Gage, in Relation to Braddock's Expedition—The Stamp Act—And Gage's Administration of the Government of Massachusetts Bay." Massachusetts Historical Society, *Collections*, ser. 4, 4, pp. 367–72. Boston, 1858.

Rapport de l'archiviste de la province de Québec. Vol. for 1932–1933.

Samuel, Bunford, ed. "The Ohio Expedition of 1754." *Pennsylvania Magazine of History and Biography*, 18 (1894–1895), pp. 43–50.

Saunders, William L., ed. *The Colonial Records of North Carolina.* Vol. 5. Raleigh, 1887.

Schutz, John A., ed. "A Private Report of General Braddock's Defeat." *Pennsylvania Magazine of History and Biography,* 79 (1955), pp. 374–77.

Shea, John D. G., ed. *Relations diverses sur la bataille de Malangueulé.* New York, 1860.

Simes, Thomas. *The Military Guide for Young Officers.* Vol. 1. Philadelphia, 1776.

[Smith, William.] *A Brief View of the Conduct of Pennsylvania, for the Year 1755.* London, 1756.

[————.] *An Historical Account of the Expedition Against the Ohio Indians.* Philadelphia, 1765.

Stotz, Charles M., ed. "A Letter from Wills' Creek—Harry Gordon's Account of Braddock's Defeat." *Western Pennsylvania Historical Magazine,* 44 (1961), pp. 129–36.

Sullivan, James, ed. *The Papers of Sir William Johnson.* Vol. 1. Albany: University of the State of New York, 1921.

Thwaites, Reuben G., ed. "The French Regime in Wisconsin—1743–1760." Wisconsin Historical Society, *Collections,* 18, pp. 1–122. Madison, 1908.

Walsh, Richard, ed. "Braddock on July 9, 1755." *Maryland Historical Magazine,* 60 (1965), pp. 421–27.

Wilson, J. Cook, ed. "The Campaign of General Braddock." *English Historical Review,* 1 (1886), pp. 149–52.

Secondary Sources

Alden, John R. *General Gage in America.* Baton Rouge: Louisiana State University Press, 1948.

————. *John Stuart and the Southern Colonial Frontier.* First published in 1944. Reprint ed., New York: Gordian, 1966.

Audet, Francis-J. *Jean Daniel Dumas: Le Héros de la Monongahéla.* Montreal: G. Ducharme, 1920.

Baker-Crothers, Hayes. *Virginia and the French and Indian War.* Chicago: University of Chicago Press, 1928.

Bancroft, George. *History of the United States, from the Discovery of the American Continent.* Vol. 4. Boston, 1852.

Bird, Harrison. *Battle for a Continent.* New York: Oxford University Press, 1965.

Boone, C. de B. "Braddock's Campaign and Its Lessons." *The United Service Magazine,* n.s., 39 (1909), pp. 88–93.

Boorstin, Daniel J. *The Americans: The Colonial Experience.* New York: Random House, 1958.

Bowman, Larry G. "Virginia's Use of Blacks in the French and Indian War." *Western Pennsylvania Historical Magazine,* 53 (1970), pp. 57–63.

Carrier, Lyman. "Dr. John Mitchell, Naturalist, Cartographer, and Historian." American Historical Association, *Annual Report,* 1918, pt. 1, pp. 199–219.

Charteris, Evan. *William Augustus Duke of Cumberland and the Seven Years' War.* London: Hutchinson and Co., 1925.

Clark, Dora M. "The British Treasury and the Administration of Military Affairs in America, 1754–1774." *Pennsylvania History,* 2 (1935), pp. 197–204.

Custis, George Washington Parke. *Recollections and Private Memoirs of Washington.* New York, 1860.

Dahlinger, Charles W. "The Marquis Duquesne, Sieur de Menneville, Founder of the City of Pittsburgh." *Western Pennsylvania Historical Magazine,* 15 (1932), pp. 3–33, 121–51, 219–62.

Davidson, Robert L. D. *War Comes to Quaker Pennsylvania 1682–1756.* New York: Columbia University Press, 1957.

De Hass, Wills. *History of the Early Settlement and Indian Wars of Western Virginia.* Wheeling, 1851.

Dictionary of Canadian Biography. Vol. 3 (1741–1770). Toronto: University of Toronto Press, 1974.

Doughty, A., and Parmelee, G. W. *The Siege of Quebec and the Battle of the Plains of Abraham.* 6 vols. Quebec: Dussault and Proulx, 1901.

Fortescue, J. W. *A History of the British Army.* Vol. 2. London: Macmillan, 1910.

Freeman, Douglas S. *George Washington: A Biography.* Vol. 2. New York: Scribner's, 1948.

Frégault, Guy. *Canada: The War of the Conquest.* Translated by Margaret M. Cameron. Toronto: Oxford University Press, 1969.

"From Braddock to Bouquet." *Kittochtinny Magazine,* 1 (1905), pp. 24–36, 123–35, 229–40.

Gipson, Lawrence H. *The Great War for Empire: The Years of Defeat, 1754–1757. The British Empire Before the American Revolution,* vol. 6. New York: Knopf, 1946.

Hadden, James. *Washington's Expeditions (1753–1754) and Braddock's Expedition (1755).* Uniontown, Pa., 1910.

Hamilton, Edward P. *The French and Indian Wars.* Garden City, N.Y.: Doubleday, 1962.

Hildeburn, Charles R. "Sir John St. Clair, Baronet, Quarter-Master General in America, 1755 to 1767." *Pennsylvania Magazine of History and Biography,* 9 (1885–1886), pp. 1–14.

Hulbert, Archer B. *Braddock's Road and Three Relative Papers.* Historic Highways of America, vol. 4. Cleveland: A. H. Clark Co., 1903.

Hunter, William A. *Forts on the Pennsylvania Frontier, 1753–1758.* Harrisburg: Pennsylvania Historical and Museum Commission, 1960.

Jacobs, Wilbur R. *Diplomacy and Indian Gifts: Anglo-French Rivalry Along the Ohio and Northwestern Frontiers, 1747–1763.* Stanford University Publications in History, Economics, and Political Science, vol. 6. Stanford: Stanford University Press, 1950.

James, A. P., and Stotz, C. M. *Drums in the Forest.* Pittsburgh: Historical Society of Western Pennsylvania, 1958.

Keppel, Thomas. *The Life of Augustus Viscount Keppel.* London, 1842.

Koontz, Louis K. *Robert Dinwiddie: His Career in American Colonial Government and Westward Expansion.* Glendale, Calif.: A. H. Clark Co., 1941.

Lacock, John K. "Braddock Road." *Pennsylvania Magazine of History and Biography,* 38 (1914), pp. 1–37.

Landis, Charles I. "Jasper Yeates and His Times." *Pennsylvania Magazine of History and Biography,* 46 (1922), pp. 199–231.

Leach, Douglas E. *Arms for Empire: A Military History of the British Colonies in North America, 1607–1763.* New York: Macmillan, 1973.

Lowdermilk, William H. *History of Cumberland, . . . with a History of Braddock's Expedition.* Washington, D.C., 1878.

McCardell, Lee. *Ill-Starred General: Braddock of the Coldstream Guards.* Pittsburgh: University of Pittsburgh Press, 1958.

McCrady, Edward. *South Carolina Under the Royal Government.* New York: Macmillan, 1900.

McGrain, John W., Jr. "Priest Neale, His Mass House, and His Successors." *Maryland Historical Magazine,* 62 (1967), pp. 254–84.

Martin, Ronald D. "Confrontation at the Monongahela: Climax of the French Drive Into the Upper Ohio Region." *Pennsylvania History,* 37 (1970), pp. 133–50.

Mish, Mary V. "General Adam Stephen, Founder Martinsburg, West Virginia." *West Virginia History,* 22 (1961), pp. 63–75.

Ness, George T., Jr. "The Braddock Expedition, 1755." *Military Engineer,* nos. 339–41 (1959), pp. 14–23, 111–17, 211–13.

Nichols, Franklin T. "The Organization of Braddock's Army." *William and Mary Quarterly,* 3d ser., 4 (1947), pp. 125–47.

O'Meara, Walter. *Guns at the Forks.* Englewood Cliffs, N.J.: Prentice-Hall, 1965.

Onderdonk, James L. "Colonial Patriotism in Song." *American Historical Register,* 3 (1895–1896), pp. 471–80.

Pargellis, Stanley. "Braddock's Defeat." *American Historical Review,* 41 (1936), pp. 253–69.

———. *Lord Loudoun in North America.* New Haven: Yale University Press, 1933.

Parkman, Francis. *Montcalm and Wolfe.* 2 vols. Boston, 1884.

Patterson, Samuel W. *Horatio Gates: Defender of American Liberties.* New York: Columbia University Press, 1941.

Peckham, Howard H. *The Colonial Wars, 1689-1762*. Chicago: University of Chicago Press, 1964.

Peyton, John L. *The Adventures of My Grandfather*. London, 1867.

Riker, T. W. "The Politics Behind Braddock's Expedition." *American Historical Review*, 13 (1908), pp. 742-52.

Ritenour, John S. *Old Tom Fossit*. Pittsburgh: J. R. Weldin Co., 1926.

Rogers, J. Allen. "Impressment in Western Pennsylvania, 1755-1759." *Western Pennsylvania Historical Magazine*, 52 (1969), pp. 255-62.

Root, Winfred T. *The Relations of Pennsylvania with the British Government, 1696-1765*. New York: D. Appleton and Co., 1912.

Sargent, Winthrop. *The History of an Expedition Against Fort Du Quesne in 1755: Under Major-General Edward Braddock*. Pennsylvania Historical Society, Memoirs, 5. Philadelphia, 1855.

Schlebecker, John. "Braddock's Defeat." *The Ohio State Archaeological and Historical Quarterly*, 58 (1949), pp. 171-84.

Schlesinger, Arthur M. "Maryland's Share in the Last Colonial War." *Maryland Historical Magazine*, 7 (1912), pp. 119-49, 243-68.

Schroeder, John F. *The Life and Times of Washington*. Vol. 1. New York, 1857.

Shea, John D. G. "Daniel Hyacinth Mary Lienard de Beaujeu." *Pennsylvania Magazine of History and Biography*, 8 (1884), pp. 121-28.

Sparks, Jared. *The Life of George Washington*. First published in 1839. Boston, 1855.

Stewart, Andrew. "Was Gen. Braddock Shot Down by One of His Own Army?" *New York Times*, October 19, 1913, sec. 5, p. 5.

Stewart, William C. "A Study of Some Stewart and Allied Families." Kentucky Historical Society, *Register*, 61 (1963), pp. 78-103, 169-90.

Tasse, Joseph. "Memoir of Charles de Langlade." Wisconsin State Historical Society, *Collections*, 7 (1876), pp. 123-87.

Thackeray, William Makepeace. *The Virginians*. London: Harper and Bros., 1900.

Thane, Elswyth. *Mount Vernon: The Legacy*. Philadelphia: Lippincott, 1967.

Tuggle, Kenneth H. "Dr. Thomas Walker Bicentennial Celebration." Filson Club, *History Quarterly*, 24 (1950), pp. 21-30.

Volwiler, Albert T. *George Croghan and the Western Movement 1741-1782*. Cleveland: A. H. Clark Co., 1926.

Wallace, Paul A. W. " 'Blunder Camp': A Note on the Braddock Road." *Pennsylvania Magazine of History and Biography*, 87 (1963), pp. 21-30.

Ward, Harry M. *"Unite or Die": Intercolony Relations 1690-1763*. Port Washington, N.Y.: Kennikat, 1971.

Watson, John F. *Annals of Philadelphia, and Pennsylvania, in the Olden Time*. Vol. 1. First published in 1844. Philadelphia, 1887.

Weslager, C. A. *The Delaware Indians*. New Brunswick, N.J.: Rutgers University Press, 1972.

Whitworth, Rex. *Field Marshal Lord Ligonier: A Story of the British Army 1702–1770*. Oxford: Oxford University Press, 1958.

Williams, Edward G. "Treasure Hunt in the Forest." *Western Pennsylvania Historical Magazine*, 44 (1961), pp. 383–96.

Willson, Beckles. *The Life and Letters of James Wolfe*. London: William Heinemann, 1909.

Yaple, Robert L. "Braddock's Defeat: The Theories and a Reconsideration." *Journal of the Society for Army Historical Research*, 46 (1968), pp. 194–201.

Index

Note: The appendices are indexed only for names; portions of appended documents mentioned in the text are noted here only in terms of their textual reference.

Advance party: van of, 33; composition of, 33–37; rear guard of, 39; fires on French, 51–52; panic spreads in, 59–60; falls back, 60–61; collides with working party, 61; mentioned, 18, 31. *See also* Gage, Thomas

Allison, Robert, 138

Americans: apathetic to expedition, 8; Braddock's attitude toward, 8, 9; influence of Braddock's Defeat on, 123–24, 129–32, 302n12; monetary contributions of, to campaign, 277n12
—in Braddock's army: background of, 15, 78; resist discipline, 15, 96, 97; spread panic, 72–73; fight Indian style, 78; berated by Braddock, 78–79; success of, in battle, 107–08

Anson, Elizabeth, 305n5

Army, British: uniforms of, 3; morale of, 3, 6, 18, 72, 275–76n2; fear of Indians of, 3, 6, 72–73; composition of, 3, 14, 15, 31–32, 285n4; quality of recruits in, 14, 106–07, 120; order of march of, 31–46 *passim;* effects of discipline on, 96–98; finances of, 277n12
—in battle: attempts to advance, 80–81; wild barrage of, 82–83, 108–09; flees field, 84–87; material losses of, 90; casualties in, 91, 293n37. *See also* Panic; Tactics

Army, French: confident of victory, 29, 284n20; composition of, 30, 282n9
—in battle: momentary panic of, 52–57; fights from behind trees, 58–59; fails to pursue British, 87–89; casualties of, 88

Bailleul, François Pierrot de, 266, 267, 269

Batman, Cholmley's.-*See* Cholmley's Batman

Batmen, 32, 285n5

Beaujeu, Daniel-Hyacinthe-Marie Liénard de: to replace Contrecoeur, 22; as possible planner of ambush, 22, 24; attempts to persuade Indians, 27–29; expects victory, 29; races toward river, 50; reacts to appearance of British, 51–52; killed, 52; background of, 283n17; mentioned, 56, 142, 250–71 *passim*

Bellamy, George Anne, 135–36

Blacks, 127, 285n5

Bland, Humphrey: rationale of judging Braddock by, 111–12; quoted, 112, 115; implied criticism of Braddock by, 113

Bleury, Ensign, 267, 269

Bolling, John, 138

Boone, Daniel, 293n33

Bougainville, Louis-Antoine de, 21

Bouquet, Henry, 298n33

Braddock, Edward: as center of

237, 244, 246, 288*nn25,26*. *See also*
Dunbar, Thomas
—account of battle by: quoted, 70, 89,
107; assessed, 70–71, 107, 233;
printed, 231–32; mentioned, xx,
62–63, 83, 144, 228, 285*n4*. *See
also* Dinwiddie, Robert; Findley,
William
—autobiographical account: quoted,
91, 109; analyzed, 247–48; mentioned, xviii, 104

Weiser, Conrad, 283*n13*
Wills Creek, 8. *See also* Fort Cumber-
land
Wolfe, James, 120
Women: with Braddock's army, 31; in
wagons, 47; with Indians, 100;
character of, 137
Woodward, Luke, 96
Working party: 6, 37–39, 61, 276*n5*

Yeates, Jasper, 245–46